DEAR CUSTOMERE

THANK YOU

FOR YOU ORDER

WWW.REALLYGREATSITE.COM

Hi talents! It is so glad to see you here and I would like to extend the warmest welcome to all the readers of my book. Your presence and interest in my work bring me immense happiness. It is my utmost desire to share my knowledge and experiences with you, and I am grateful for the opportunity to do so.

Thank you for joining me, and I hope you find inspiration, joy, and valuable insights within the pages of this book.

In this comprehensive exam preparation practice test, I am delighted to provide you with the carefully curated mock exam questions. These questions have been meticulously crafted to offer you a valuable opportunity to familiarize yourself with the format, style, and level of difficulty that you can expect during the actual exam.

This practice test goes beyond mere simulation; ***it serves as a testament to your dedication in acquiring a widely recognized professional qualification, showcasing your competence and unwavering commitment to your profession and career. By choosing my book, I firmly believe that you are setting yourself apart from your peers, positioning yourself as a standout candidate throughout your lifelong career.***

Good Luck and All the Best

Walter

Important Message

WalterEducation.com

*Important Message From Walter *

I am certain that you will find great value in the complimentary practice tests that I have meticulously created for your benefit. These tests offer a comprehensive glimpse into the authentic exam formats and simulate real-life exam conditions. Countless hours have been dedicated to their development, reflecting my unwavering commitment to excellence.

I would like to express my heartfelt gratitude for your support in purchasing my **FULL version exam practice tests book**. As a gesture of appreciation, I am delighted to offer you:

1. **A FREE COUPON of the exam simulation engine of this practice test at Udemy (udemy.com)**; and
2. **A FREE COUPON of a randomly selected practice test held by Walter Education at Udemy**

Once again, I am truly grateful for your support, and I look forward to having you in my future books & courses. If you believe that my work is deserving, kindly consider leaving positive comments and feedback.

Thank you,

Walter

FREE GIFTS

BUY A BOOK

Buy any Walter Education's Exam Practice Test Book

(Visit **WalterEducation.com**)

RATE A BOOK

Rate Walter's Book at Amazon and consider leaving a Positive Rating

See " How to Give a Rate "

GET FREE GIFTS

Send **Email** to Walter - Walter@WalterEducation.com with the purchase and review records, get **2 Free Gifts**

Up to 2 free gifts!

FOLLOW

  WalterEducation.com

  Walter@WalterEducation.com

HELP US IMPROVE!

TELL US WHAT YOU THINK

Kindly Requesting Your Valued Book Reviews

First and foremost, I would like to express my gratitude for choosing my book and your support as a valued learner. I am reaching out to you as I also publish this practice test in paperback and Kindle eBook format, and I kindly seek your support in taking a few moments to share your honest review of my books via the direct review links at the next page for the practice test.

As an author, reviews play a crucial role in shaping the success and recognition of my work. Your honest feedback and reviews not only help me improve as an author but also contribute to the credibility and visibility of the book for potential readers. Here are two important reasons why reviews are of significance:

1. Impact on Author's Growth: Reviews provide valuable insights and feedback that enable me to enhance future editions or create new study materials. Your constructive criticism, suggestions, and personal experiences can help me refine my content and make it even more beneficial for future readers.

2. Assistance to Fellow Customers: Your reviews are incredibly beneficial to other customers who are considering purchasing the book. By sharing your thoughts, you can help potential readers make informed decisions and gain confidence in the quality and relevance of the content. Your honest evaluation can guide them towards choosing a resource that aligns with their needs and goals.

To show my sincere appreciation for your time and effort in writing a review, I would like to offer you a free gift as a token of gratitude. Once you have submitted your reviews on the paperback and/or Kindle eBook versions of the book, please simply send me an email at   walter@waltereducation.com   with your review confirmation, and I will be delighted to provide you with the details of the free gift.

Please note that leaving a review is entirely voluntary, and I value your honest opinion above all else. Your feedback is instrumental in shaping the future of my work, and I genuinely appreciate your support in this endeavor.

Thank you once again for choosing my book and considering my request. If you have any questions or require further assistance, please feel free to reach out to me. I look forward to your valuable reviews.

Warm regards,

Walter

Direct URLs to visit all Walter's Practice Tests at Amazon

Visit Walter's author page:
http://WalterEducation.com

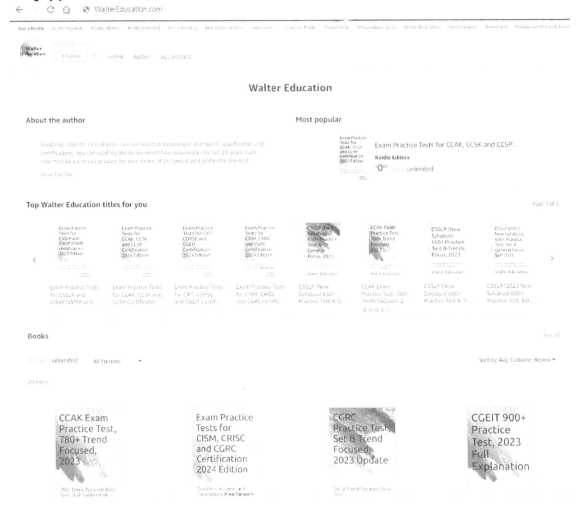

Or the **Links at Amazon Book Store:**

Or the **Links at Amazon Book Store:**

CRISC 1200+ Practice Test, 2023 (Exam Simulation and Core & Advanced Knowledge)	
Paperback Review URL:	- https://www.amazon.com/review/create-review?&asin=B0CJ43R78T
Kindle eBook Review URL:	- https://www.amazon.com/review/create-review?&asin=B0CJ72JJLY

How to give a Review and Rating:

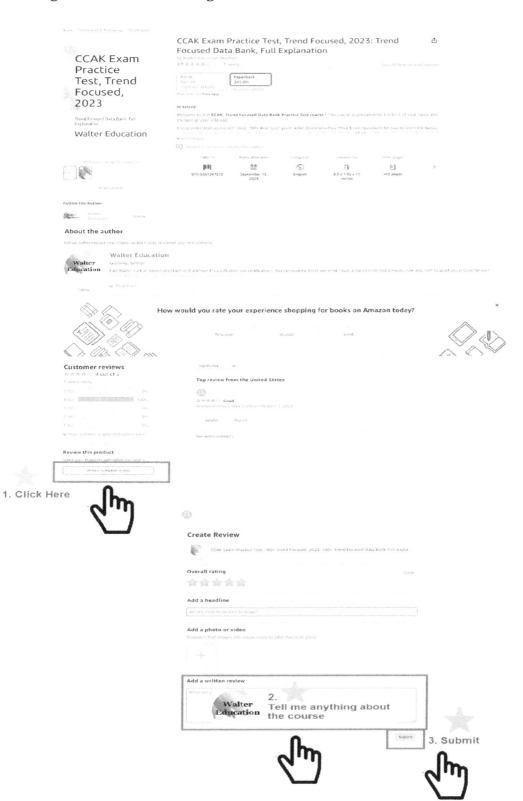

1. Click Here

2. Tell me anything about the course

3. Submit

Contents

This practice test covers will over 1200+ Real-Live-Exam-Alike Questions from topics across the 4 critical domains for the CRISC certificate plus Bonus Section of CRISC relevant questions from other ISACA certifications. You can learn both the Core and Advance knowledge.

What is covered on the CRISC exam?

The Certified in Risk and Information Systems Control (CRISC) exam consists of 150 questions covering 4 job practice domains, all testing your knowledge and ability on real-life job practices leveraged by expert professionals.

Below are the key domains, subtopics and tasks candidates will be tested on:

26% Domain 1 > Governance

20% Domain 2 > IT Risk Assessment

32% Domain 3 > Risk Response and Reporting

22% Domain 4 > Information Technology and Security

This practice test has been made with reference to the official guidelines and the exam weight in each domain.

In this Course:

You will go through a journey to acquire Core and Advance concepts and knowledge of the 4 critical domains by doing the practice test. I hope you enjoy it and get your **CRISC** exam passed.

Beside doing the practice test, I would suggest you to do as much simulation test / question as you could to get yourself well prepared for the exam. More practice test will be released soon. Stay tuned and Good Luck.

Please feel free to visit my other courses. Thank you for your hardworking and study.

What is CRISC and why CRISC?

A Certified in Risk and Information Systems Control (CRISC) certification will make you a Risk Management expert. Studying a proactive approach based on Agile methodology, you'll learn how to enhance your company's business resilience, deliver stakeholder value and optimize Risk Management across the enterprise.

CRISC benefit you:

4 TOP PAYING CERTIFICATION WORLDWIDE
52% EXPERIENCED ON-THE-JOB IMPROVEMENT

Are you Ready to get the CRISC Certification?

About Walter

Greetings, talents!

I am Walter. I am an expert at obtaining IT and non-IT qualification and certifications. You can read my Bio to see what I have acquired in my last 20 years. I am now here to assist you prepare for your exams at the lowest cost and in the shortest amount of time possible.

As I believe that everyone is talented and intelligent. Together, we will discuss the most efficient methods to "**Hack**" the learning process and "**Pass**" your exams without squandering your most valuable assets - **money and time.**

You will find the **best values** through join my course, get the exam **passed**, get the qualification and certifications and be a **Rocket** in achieving the **rocket-high** success in your career path. You will definitely out-perform all of your peers and you will be much more confidence when you talk to your peer and you know **you have achieved something that they didn't!**

You must approach each practice test question as a "Simulation of Real Exam Question" on this voyage. Here, I will provide the precise response to the query. I will also provide you the **FULL** explanation for EACH practice question.

You must investigate why the correct answer is correct and challenge it if you disagree. This is the only method to learn quickly, in-depth, and most importantly, to develop a capacity for self-learning. This WILL be the most valuable weapon in your arsenal for career success.

Believe me, I have *Been there,* and I have *Done that* before.

BIO

Walter Education ("Walter" or "Walter Education Team") is formed by a group of experienced and knowledgeable consultants and auditors. Walter has over 20 years of experience in the industry. Walter has worked as senior management at several major financial institutions in Key Financial Centers across the world.

CISA, CISSP, CRISC, CIA, CAMS, ISO 27001 LA, CEH, Scrum Master, GIAC Security, ITIL, CCIE Routing and Switching, COBIT, CPA and numerous other professional certifications and qualifications are held by Walter.

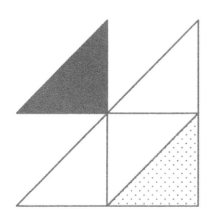

Visit Our Udemy
ONLINE COURSE

Search

Walter Education

www.udemy.com/user/Walter-Education

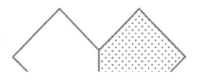

My Profile in Udemy:

I have a number of **Exam Practice Test Courses** held at Udemy for you to learn and study via a Real-Live-Exam-Alike environment and simulation.

My Homepage: http://waltereducation.com

Udemy: https://www.udemy.com/user/walter-education

Amazon: https://www.amazon.com/author/waltereducation

 udemy.com/user/walter-education/

INSTRUCTOR

Walter Education - Investing in You

- Never Give Up, Never Stop Learning

About me

Greetings, talents!

I am Walter. I am an expert at obtaining IT and non-IT qualification and certifications. You can read my **Bio** to see what I have acquired in my last 20 years. I am now here to assist you prepare for your exams at the lowest cost and in the shortest amount of time possible.

As I believe that everyone is talented and intelligent. Together, we will discuss the most efficient methods to "Hack" the learning process and "Pass" your exams without squandering your most valuable assets - money and time.

Show more ∨

My courses (17)

CSSLP (New Syllabus) Practice Test B-Trends Focus, Oct 2023
Walter Education - Investing in You
625 questions • All Levels
$44.99
New

CSSLP (New Syllabus) Practice Test A-General Focus, Oct 2023
Walter Education - Investing in You
625 questions • All Levels
$39.99
New

Discount Codes for my other Practice Test courses in Udemy:

Please feel free to click the links below to **enjoy discounts:**

ISACA

- CCAK Exam Practice Test, Trend Focused, SEP 2023
  - https://www.udemy.com/course/ccak-exam-practice-test-trend-focused-sep-2023/?referralCode=530219636B779BA4772B
- CISM - ISACA Practice Test A - Core Focus, SEP 2023, New
  - https://www.udemy.com/course/cism-isaca-practice-test-a-core-focus-sep-2023-new/?referralCode=3B6C4E08B23039069E19
- CISM - ISACA Practice Test B - Trends Focus, SEP 2023, New
  - https://www.udemy.com/course/cism-isaca-practice-test-b-trends-focus-sep-2023-new/?referralCode=9E7E1E6527BDA1797922
- **CGEIT 900+ Practice Test, 2023**
  - https://www.udemy.com/course/buy1-get-3-cgeit-900-practice-test-2023-ccsp-ccak/?referralCode=4BF5FF0AAF7B61F47E6D
- **CRISC 1200+ Practice Test, SEP 202**
  - https://www.udemy.com/course/crisc-1200-practice-test-2023-isaca-cisa-cism-cissp-ccak/?referralCode=C913D8A69A91ED9ABB99
- **CDPSE 900+ Practice Test, 2023**
  - https://www.udemy.com/course/cdpse-900-practice-test-2023-full-explanation-cisa-cgeit/?referralCode=F62D674CA2DB5D05CC8C
- **CCAK CCSP CCSKv4 3in1 Practice Test 2023 updated**
  - https://www.udemy.com/course/ccsp-ccskv4-ccak-bundle-3in1-practice-test-2023-updated/?referralCode=ED588D079804F9530244

ISC2

- CISSP-ISSMP Practice Test A - Core Focus, SEP 2023, New
  - https://www.udemy.com/course/cissp-issmp-practice-test-a-core-focus-sep-2023-new/?referralCode=6D5233F6FD3691F9BAD2
- CISSP-ISSMP Practice Test B - Trends Focus, SEP 2023, New
  - https://www.udemy.com/course/cissp-issmp-practice-test-b-trends-focus-sep-2023-new/?referralCode=D374F92DE9D3FCAF27DB
- **CSSLP (New Syllabus) Practice Test, Trend Focus, SEP 2023**
  - **https://www.udemy.com/course/csslp-new-syllabus-practice-test-trend-focus-sep-2023/?referralCode=33AD3DA51E351807C96E**
- **CSSLP (New Syllabus) Practice Test, General Focus, SEP 2023**
  - **https://www.udemy.com/course/csslp-new-syllabus-practice-test-general-focus-sep-2023/?referralCode=C6FC805F549D2580B901CCAK Exam Practice Test, Trend Focused, SEP 2023**
- CSSLP (New Syllabus) Practice Test C- Mock Exams SEP 2023

- https://www.udemy.com/course/csslp-new-syllabus-mock-exams-sep-2023/?referralCode=A4073301648B86362ABD
- **CGRC Practice Test, Set A Data Bank, Learn & Exam, SEP 2023**
  - https://www.udemy.com/course/cgrc-practice-test-set-a-data-bank-learn-exam-sep-2023/?referralCode=E545B726352EFFA1F3D9
- **CGRC Practice Test, Set B Trend Focused, SEP 2023**
  - https://www.udemy.com/course/cgrc-practice-test-set-b-trend-focused-sep-2023/?referralCode=F59A22C25057683C4E04
- **CCSP 900+ Practice Test, 2023**
  - https://www.udemy.com/course/ccsp-certified-cloud-security-professional-practice-test-o/?referralCode=C0C572F978F539E57251

IAPP

- CIPT, Certified Information Privacy Technologists, SEP 2023
  - https://www.udemy.com/course/cipt-certified-information-privacy-technologists-sep-2023/?referralCode=FC0A8099E3A173BDC6AC

CSA

- CCSKv4 900+ Practice Test 2023
  - https://www.udemy.com/course/ccskv4-900-practice-test-2023-full-explanation-ccspccak/?referralCode=E6ADB4B80C52206F55DF

Visit Our Amazon Book Store

WalterEducation.com

Visit Walter's author page:

http://WalterEducation.com

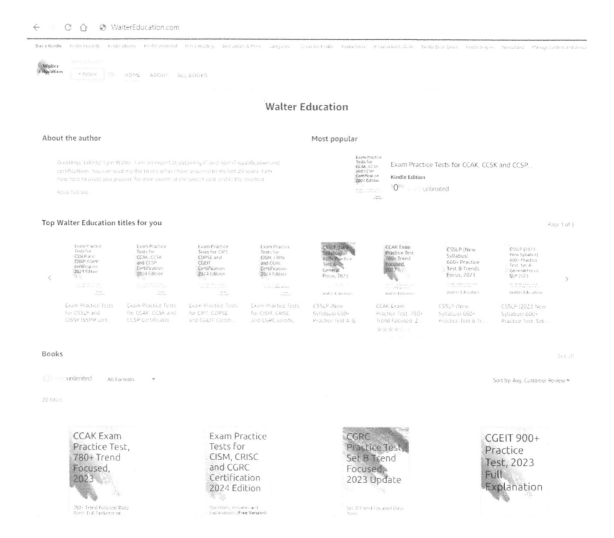

Simulation of CRISC Exam

Question Number: 1

Question: The CIO has requested a review of user access controls across critical systems to reduce risk. Which of the following is the BEST approach for the risk practitioner?

Option 1: Review entitlements against policy

Option 2: Conduct access certification

Option 3: Implement MFA globally

Option 4: Rescind excessive privileges

Correct Response: 2

Explanation: Access certification involves reviewing and confirming user access is appropriate, which helps reduce risk.

Knowledge Area: Exam_Sim

Question Number: 2

Question: Which process involves communicating risk-related info between stakeholders to support strategy and objectives?

Option 1: Risk identification

Option 2: Risk monitoring

Option 3: Risk governance

Option 4: Risk communication

Correct Response: 4

Explanation: Risk communication facilitates sharing risk insights between stakeholders to align on priorities.

Knowledge Area: Exam_Sim

Question Number: 3

Question: Which process involves determining risk likelihood and potential impacts to help prioritize responses?

Option 1: Risk analysis

Option 2: Risk framing

Option 3: Risk treatment

Option 4: Risk assessment

Correct Response: 4

Explanation: Risk assessment evaluates probability and impact to help rank risks.

Knowledge Area: Exam_Sim

Question Number: 4

Question: Jill is performing qualitative risk analysis for a project using risk urgency assessment. Which artifact will NOT help with this activity?

Option 1: Risk register

Option 2: Scope baseline

Option 3: Stakeholder analysis

Option 4: Progress reports

Correct Response: 4

Explanation: Progress reports track status but don't help assess risk impacts.

Knowledge Area: Exam_Sim

Question Number: 5

Question: A company is migrating systems to a new IaaS cloud provider. What is the most important step before deployment?

Option 1: Update security policies

Option 2: Conduct provider due diligence

Option 3: Train administrative staff

Option 4: Implement encryption

Correct Response: 2

Explanation: Due diligence on the provider's security is critical before migrating.

Knowledge Area: Exam_Sim

Question Number: 6

Question: To reduce operational risks from compliance gaps, what should an organization do first?

Option 1: Strengthen access controls

Option 2: Perform risk assessments

Option 3: Update risk registry

Option 4: Improve monitoring

Correct Response: 2

Explanation: Assessing risks guides optimal compliance responses.

Knowledge Area: Exam_Sim

Question Number: 7

Question: A project manager wants to reduce potential financial losses from supply chain disruptions. What is the most effective risk mitigation?

Option 1: Dual source critical components

Option 2: Improve inventory forecasting

Option 3: Increase safety stock levels

Option 4: Negotiate supplier discounts

Correct Response: 1

Explanation: Dual sourcing critical items mitigates supply chain risk.

Knowledge Area: Exam_Sim

Question Number: 8

Question: What provides the most valuable input when assessing disaster recovery capabilities?

Option 1: More systems meeting RTOs

Option 2: Fewer systems needing plans

Option 3: More tested systems

Option 4: Less systems with long RTOs

Correct Response: 2

Explanation: The number of systems with long RTOs highlights gaps.

Knowledge Area: Exam_Sim

Question Number: 9

Question: An organization is adopting a new cloud infrastructure platform. What activity will provide the most risk insights before migrating applications?

Option 1: Review vendor security policy compliance

Option 2: Conduct due diligence on provider security controls

Option 3: Update internal security and architecture standards

Option 4: Train staff on new administration procedures

Correct Response: 2

Explanation: Conducting thorough due diligence on the cloud provider's security controls and architecture before adopting the platform will provide valuable risk insights.

Knowledge Area: Exam_Sim

Question Number: 10

Question: To optimize resources for risk management, what input should guide the focus areas?

Option 1: Industry benchmarking results

Option 2: Risk register totals

Option 3: Senior management concerns

Option 4: Assessment of risk appetite and tolerance

Correct Response: 4

Explanation: Aligning risk management focus with organizational risk appetite and tolerance designated by senior leaders will help optimize resource allocation.

Knowledge Area: Exam_Sim

Question Number: 11

Question: A supply chain manager wants to reduce financial risks from potential component shortages. What option would be most effective?

Option 1: Increase inventory at distribution centers

Option 2: Improve demand forecasting accuracy

Option 3: Dual source critical materials and parts

Option 4: Negotiate volume discounts with suppliers

Correct Response: 3

Explanation: Dual sourcing key components through alternate suppliers reduces supply chain disruption risks.

Knowledge Area: Exam_Sim

Question Number: 12

Question: What data provides the most valuable input when evaluating disaster recovery capabilities?

Option 1: Higher percentage of systems meeting RTOs

Option 2: Fewer systems requiring disaster recovery plans

Option 3: More systems undergoing testing

Option 4: Lower percentage of systems with lengthy RTOs

Correct Response: 4

Explanation: A lower percentage of systems with lengthy recovery time objectives indicates gaps in disaster recovery capabilities.

Knowledge Area: Exam_Sim

Question Number: 13

Question: When implementing encryption, what is critical for assessing residual risk?

Option 1: Data retention rules

Option 2: Cloud architecture

Option 3: Destruction procedures

Option 4: Key management

Correct Response: 4

Explanation: Effective key management is crucial for managing encryption residual risk.

Knowledge Area: Exam_Sim

Question Number: 14

Question: Upon finding unlicensed software during an IT audit, what should the risk practitioner first do?

Option 1: Uninstall the software

Option 2: Procure licenses

Option 3: Report to management

Option 4: Restrict admin rights

Correct Response: 3

Explanation: The issue should be reported to management for appropriate action.

Knowledge Area: Exam_Sim

Question Number: 15

Question: How can risk management help justify additional investment in network resilience?

Option 1: Present related risk trends

Option 2: Compare to benchmarks

Option 3: Highlight ROI

Option 4: Show reduced risk exposure

Correct Response: 4

Explanation: Quantifying risk reduction demonstrates value gained.

Knowledge Area: Exam_Sim

Question Number: 16

Question: After internal audit finds IAM control gaps, what should the risk practitioner focus on?

Option 1: Replacing the system

Option 2: Training IAM staff

Option 3: Verifying risk owner awareness

Option 4: Performing added assessment

Correct Response: 3

Explanation: Ensuring risk owners understand the implications is critical.

Knowledge Area: Exam_Sim

Question Number: 17

Question: A business unit wants to accept the risk of weak password controls in a software application. What should be the response?

Option 1: Obtain an exception

Option 2: Proceed as planned

Option 3: Develop stronger passwords

Option 4: Select a more secure application

Correct Response: 4

Explanation: An alternative with stronger controls should be selected.

Knowledge Area: Exam_Sim

Question Number: 18

Question: To enable risk-based decisions on projects and resources, what information is most valuable for management?

Option 1: List of risk indicators

Option 2: Audit reports

Option 3: Risk register

Option 4: Project list

Correct Response: 3

Explanation: The risk register provides a consolidated risk profile.

Knowledge Area: Exam_Sim

Question Number: 19

Question: What is most important to communicate to management after an external audit finds control gaps?

Option 1: Training recommendations

Option 2: Mitigation plans

Option 3: Audit validation needs

Option 4: Impacts to risk profile

Correct Response: 4

Explanation: The risk profile impact highlights exposure from gaps.

Knowledge Area: Exam_Sim

Question Number: 20

Question: What metric evaluates and compares the efficiency of different IT investments?

Option 1: Total cost of ownership

Option 2: Redundancy level

Option 3: Return on investment

Option 4: Recovery time objective

Correct Response: 3

Explanation: ROI evaluates and compares the efficiency of investments.

Knowledge Area: Exam_Sim

Question Number: 21

Question: Who should a data loss risk at a cloud provider be assigned to?

Option 1: CRO

Option 2: Vendor manager

Option 3: Data owner

Option 4: Senior management

Correct Response: 3

Explanation: The data owner should be the risk owner.

Knowledge Area: Exam_Sim

Question Number: 22

Question: After an audit finds major control gaps at a cloud provider, what should happen next?

Option 1: Verify with a follow-up audit

Option 2: Review contract for penalties

Option 3: Analyze business impact

Option 4: Migrate data to new provider

Correct Response: 3

Explanation: The impact to the business should be analyzed first.

Knowledge Area: Exam_Sim

Question Number: 23

Question: What should be the main concern when fast time-to-market is a priority?

Option 1: Email rollback readiness

Option 2: Understaffed development

Option 3: Undetected phishing emails

Option 4: Help desk staff training

Correct Response: 2

Explanation: Insufficient development resources is the key risk.

Knowledge Area: Exam_Sim

Question Number: 24

Question: Who decides whether to accept the risk of no redundancy for a critical application?

Option 1: BC director

Option 2: App owner

Option 3: DR manager

Option 4: Data center manager

Correct Response: 2

Explanation: The business application owner decides on risk acceptance.

Knowledge Area: Exam_Sim

Question Number: 25

Question: Getting the right information to the right people when needed aligns with which risk?

Option 1: Integrity risk

Option 2: Availability risk

Option 3: Relevance risk

Option 4: Access risk

Correct Response: 3

Explanation: Ensuring information relevance addresses relevance risk.

Knowledge Area: Exam_Sim

Question Number: 26

Question: Upon finding a low-risk control gap during self-assessments, what should happen next?

Option 1: Accept the low risks

Option 2: Re-evaluate associated risks

Option 3: Assess risk tolerance

Option 4: Propose new controls

Correct Response: 4

Explanation: The linked risks should be re-evaluated.

Knowledge Area: Exam_Sim

Question Number: 27

Question: Employees not swiping their own badges but following others represents what?

Option 1: A vulnerability

Option 2: A threat

Option 3: An impact

Option 4: A control

Correct Response: 1

Explanation: It is a physical access vulnerability.

Knowledge Area: Exam_Sim

Question Number: 28

Question: Using a vendor for encryption services to secure cloud uploads is an example of which risk approach?

Option 1: Mitigation

Option 2: Avoidance

Option 3: Acceptance

Option 4: Transfer

Correct Response: 1

Explanation: It transfers some risk to a vendor.

Knowledge Area: Exam_Sim

Question Number: 29

Question: What information would be most important for assessing the risk impact when an internal audit report reveals that not all IT application databases have encryption in place?

Option 1: The reason some databases have not been encrypted

Option 2: A list of unencrypted databases which contain sensitive data

Option 3: The cost required to enforce encryption

Option 4: The number of users who can access sensitive data

Correct Response: 2

Explanation: A list of unencrypted databases which contain sensitive data would be the most important information for assessing the risk impact. It helps identify the extent of potential exposure and the level of sensitivity of the data, which are crucial factors in understanding the impact of the risk.

Knowledge Area: Exam_Sim

Question Number: 30

Question: When a business unit wants to use personal information for a purpose other than for which it was originally collected, what should be the FIRST consideration?

Option 1: Informed consent

Option 2: Data breach protection

Option 3: Cross border controls

Option 4: Business impact analysis (BI

Correct Response: 1

Explanation: The FIRST consideration when a business unit wants to use personal information for a different purpose should be obtaining informed consent. Informed consent ensures that individuals are aware of and agree to the new use of their personal information, which is essential for legal and ethical practices.

Knowledge Area: Exam_Sim

Question Number: 31

Question: What term refers to the type of loss when unauthorized changes are made to a website?

Option 1: Loss of confidentiality

Option 2: Loss of integrity

Option 3: Loss of availability

Option 4: Loss of revenue

Correct Response: 2

Explanation: Loss of integrity refers to the type of loss that occurs when unauthorized changes are made to a website. It compromises the accuracy, completeness, or reliability of the information contained on the website.

Knowledge Area: Exam_Sim

Question Number: 32

Question: Why should project team members be involved in the Identify Risk process?

Option 1: They are the individuals who will need a sense of ownership and responsibility for the risk events.

Option 2: They are the individuals who will have the best responses for identified risk events within the project.

Option 3: They are the individuals who are most affected by the risk events.

Option 4: They are the individuals who will most likely cause and respond to the risk events.

Correct Response: 1

Explanation: Project team members should be involved in the Identify Risk process because they are the individuals who will need a sense of ownership and responsibility for the risk events. Their involvement ensures that risks are adequately addressed, and their expertise and perspectives are valuable in identifying and responding to the risks effectively.

Knowledge Area: Exam_Sim

Question Number: 33

Question: What control best limits access to sensitive data?

Option 1: Logon attempt monitoring

Option 2: Forced password changes

Option 3: Challenge response system

Option 4: Need-to-know access

Correct Response: 4

Explanation: Need-to-know access limits exposure.

Knowledge Area: Exam_Sim

Question Number: 34

Question: Who owns the risk for an outsourced SaaS application?

Option 1: Provider's IT manager

Option 2: Provider's risk manager

Option 3: Organization's process manager

Option 4: Organization's vendor manager

Correct Response: 3

Explanation: The organization's process owner is the risk owner.

Knowledge Area: Exam_Sim

Question Number: 35

Question: An employee taking a sensitive file offsite indicates failure of which control?

Option 1: Background checks

Option 2: Awareness training

Option 3: Access controls

Option 4: Policy management

Correct Response: 2

Explanation: It shows inadequate security awareness training.

Knowledge Area: Exam_Sim

Question Number: 36

Question: If risk mitigation differs from the approved plan, what should happen first?

Option 1: Revert the mitigation

Option 2: Validate mitigation adequacy

Option 3: Notify the CRO

Option 4: Update the risk register

Correct Response: 2

Explanation: The mitigation should be validated.

Knowledge Area: Exam_Sim

Question Number: 37

Question: If risk is now below appetite, what should be recommended?

Option 1: Reduce scenarios

Option 2: Optimize controls

Option 3: Realign appetite

Option 4: Cut risk budget

Correct Response: 2

Explanation: The control environment should be optimized.

Knowledge Area: Exam_Sim

Question Number: 38

Question: After allowing cyber insurance to lapse, how should the risk be reported?

Option 1: Mitigated

Option 2: Transferred

Option 3: Avoided

Option 4: Accepted

Correct Response: 4

Explanation: The risk has been accepted until new insurance.

Knowledge Area: Exam_Sim

Question Number: 39

Question: For outsourced IT security, who should own the controls?

Option 1: Organization's risk function

Option 2: Provider's audit function

Option 3: Organization's IT management

Option 4: Provider's security team

Correct Response: 1

Explanation: The organization retains responsibility.

Knowledge Area: Exam_Sim

Question Number: 40

Question: After a process change reduces risk, what should happen first?

Option 1: Reallocate resources

Option 2: Review KRIs

Option 3: Conduct analysis

Option 4: Update register

Correct Response: 3

Explanation: Analysis should validate reduced risk.

Knowledge Area: Exam_Sim

Question Number: 41

Question: What risk impacts multiple enterprises across an industry?

Option 1: Reporting risk

Option 2: Operational risk

Option 3: Contagious risk

Option 4: Systemic risk

Correct Response: 4

Explanation: Systemic risk affects multiple enterprises.

Knowledge Area: Exam_Sim

Question Number: 42

Question: Who is best suited to prioritize risks from loss of private data?

Option 1: Regulators

Option 2: Auditors

Option 3: Security management

Option 4: Process owners

Correct Response: 3

Explanation: Process owners know risks and impacts.

Knowledge Area: Exam_Sim

Question Number: 43

Question: After social engineering attacks, what should be the main goal of a risk awareness program?

Option 1: Communicate consequences

Option 2: Implement best practices

Option 3: Reduce risk appetite

Option 4: Reduce risk exposure

Correct Response: 4

Explanation: Reducing risk exposure should be the priority.

Knowledge Area: Exam_Sim

Question Number: 44

Question: When updating a risk register, what is most important to capture?

Option 1: Assessment methodology

Option 2: Assigned risk manager

Option 3: Assessment team

Option 4: Risk treatment plans

Correct Response: 4

Explanation: Documenting treatment plans is critical.

Knowledge Area: Exam_Sim

Question Number: 45

Question: An organization is permitting access to data from personal mobile devices. What is the most important factor when evaluating this risk?

Option 1: Amount of data accessed

Option 2: Device management capabilities

Option 3: Data classification level

Option 4: Type of personal device

Correct Response: 3

Explanation: The classification level of the data being accessed from personal devices is the most important factor when assessing the risk.

Knowledge Area: Exam_Sim

Question Number: 46

Question: In a mature risk management program, what best indicates the IT risk profile is current?

Option 1: Compliance manual

Option 2: Management assertion

Option 3: Risk questionnaire

Option 4: Risk register

Correct Response: 2

Explanation: Regular updates to the risk register provide the best evidence that the IT risk profile reflects the current state.

Knowledge Area: Exam_Sim

Question Number: 47

Question: What best provides early warning that employee network access removal per SLAs is not happening?

Option 1: Analyze access logs

Option 2: Update multifactor authentication

Option 3: Revise SLAs

Option 4: Monitor key metrics

Correct Response: 4

Explanation: Tracking key performance metrics around access removal provides early warning of issues meeting SLAs.

Knowledge Area: Exam_Sim

Question Number: 48

Question: How should training effectiveness be assessed after required security awareness training?

Option 1: Audit training materials

Option 2: Perform vulnerability testing

Option 3: Conduct social engineering

Option 4: Administer a training quiz

Correct Response: 3

Explanation: Social engineering testing best assesses real-world effectiveness of security awareness training.

Knowledge Area: Exam_Sim

Question Number: 49

Question: After accounts were created without approvals, what should be recommended first?

Option 1: Comprehensive compliance review

Option 2: Develop an incident response plan

Option 3: Inform management of breach

Option 4: Investigate root cause

Correct Response: 4

Explanation: Investigating the root cause of the noncompliance issue should be addressed first.

Knowledge Area: Exam_Sim

Question Number: 50

Question: When planning global social media advertising data collection, what is the key business risk?

Option 1: Data analysis ineffectiveness

Option 2: Industry restrictions

Option 3: Country-specific tailoring

Option 4: Regulatory differences

Correct Response: 4

Explanation: Differing regulations across countries is the main risk consideration.

Knowledge Area: Exam_Sim

Question Number: 51

Question: What should you primarily use to justify a specific risk mitigation activity?

Option 1: Budget needs

Option 2: Technical report

Option 3: Vulnerability assessment

Option 4: Business case

Correct Response: 4

Explanation: Developing a strong business case is the most important justification for a risk mitigation.

Knowledge Area: Exam_Sim

Question Number: 52

Question: If the risk register has not been updated in a year, what should happen first?

Option 1: Redesign risk management

Option 2: Outsource risk updates

Option 3: Initiate risk reviews

Option 4: Replace old register

Correct Response: 3

Explanation: Key risk factors should be reviewed to identify necessary updates.

Knowledge Area: Exam_Sim

Question Number: 53

Question: Who should own the risk of a problematic technology?

Option 1: Business process owner

Option 2: CFO

Option 3: CRO

Option 4: IT system owner

Correct Response: 4

Explanation: The system owner should own technology risks.

Knowledge Area: Exam_Sim

Question Number: 54

Question: When evaluating controls on a critical system, what is most important?

Option 1: Control system cost

Option 2: Additional control benefits

Option 3: ALE of system

Option 4: Business impact frequency

Correct Response: 3

Explanation: ALE determines expected loss from gaps.

Knowledge Area: Exam_Sim

Question Number: 55

Question: How to verify management addressed external audit issues?

Option 1: Inspect audit docs

Option 2: Review action plans

Option 3: Observe controls

Option 4: Interview owners

Correct Response: 3

Explanation: Observing enhanced controls verifies remediation.

Knowledge Area: Exam_Sim

Question Number: 56

Question: What process addresses risk priorities and budgets resources?

Option 1: Identify risks

Option 2: Qualitative analysis

Option 3: Monitor and control risk

Option 4: Plan risk response

Correct Response: 4

Explanation: Risk response planning allocates resources.

Knowledge Area: Exam_Sim

Question Number: 57

Question: What is the most important risk management training topic for leadership?

Option 1: Strategic initiatives

Option 2: Resource allocation

Option 3: Risk appetite and tolerance

Option 4: Responsibilities

Correct Response: 3

Explanation: Understanding risk appetite is critical.

Knowledge Area: Exam_Sim

Question Number: 58

Question: Before implementing regulatory changes, what should happen first?

Option 1: Review risk profile

Option 2: Conduct a gap analysis

Option 3: Engage legal department

Option 4: Implement controls

Correct Response: 2

Explanation: A gap analysis identifies required changes.

Knowledge Area: Exam_Sim

Question Number: 59

Question: Unusual internal firewall activity indicates which control compromised?

Option 1: Data validation

Option 2: Identification

Option 3: Authentication

Option 4: Data integrity

Correct Response: 3

Explanation: It likely represents authentication gaps.

Knowledge Area: Exam_Sim

Question Number: 60

Question: Supply chain disruptions primarily impact which risk type?

Option 1: Compliance risk

Option 2: Strategic risk

Option 3: Financial risk

Option 4: Reputation risk

Correct Response: 3

Explanation: Disruptions present financial and revenue risk.

Knowledge Area: Exam_Sim

Question Number: 61

Question: After implementing IoT devices, new risks were identified. What is the primary reason to report this to risk owners?

Option 1: Recommend IoT policy changes

Option 2: Add new risk controls

Option 3: Reevaluate IoT use

Option 4: Confirm risk impacts

Correct Response: 3

Explanation: Reporting to risk owners confirms the impact of new IoT risks to the profile.

Knowledge Area: Exam_Sim

Question Number: 62

Question: Which is NOT an indicator of risk priority during qualitative analysis?

Option 1: Symptoms

Option 2: Warning signs

Option 3: Risk rating

Option 4: Project cost

Correct Response: 4

Explanation: Project cost does not indicate inherent risk priority.

Knowledge Area: Exam_Sim

Question Number: 63

Question: If a control owner says an existing control has degraded over time, what should be recommended?

Option 1: Implement compensating controls

Option 2: Discuss mitigation with owner

Option 3: Certify control after documenting

Option 4: Escalate to management

Correct Response: 2

Explanation: Mitigation options should be discussed with the risk owner.

Knowledge Area: Exam_Sim

Question Number: 64

Question: After a social engineering security breach, what is the best prevention?

Option 1: Require access badges

Option 2: Employ security guards

Option 3: Install cameras

Option 4: Conduct awareness training

Correct Response: 4

Explanation: Awareness training helps prevent social engineering.

Question Number: 65

Question: How should compliance to device vulnerability plans be validated?

Option 1: Rescan user environment

Option 2: Require policy acceptance

Option 3: Review training assessments

Option 4: Survey device owners

Correct Response: 1

Explanation: Rescanning validates control implementation.

Knowledge Area: Exam_Sim

Question Number: 66

Question: What control ensures users have appropriate but minimal access rights?

Option 1: Access control

Option 2: ID and authentication

Option 3: Audit and accountability

Option 4: System and comms protection

Correct Response: 1

Explanation: Access controls provide need-to-know access.

Knowledge Area: Exam_Sim

Question Number: 67

Question: What best indicates an improved risk-aware culture after security training?

Option 1: Fewer access resets

Option 2: More reported incidents

Option 3: Fewer help desk calls

Option 4: More identified system flaws

Correct Response: 2

Explanation: More willingness to report shows awareness.

Knowledge Area: Exam_Sim

Question Number: 68

Question: How can risk management best address cyber risks?

Option 1: Conduct executive training

Option 2: Follow industry practices

Option 3: Use risk framework

Option 4: Define responsibilities

Correct Response: 3

Explanation: The risk framework optimally governs cyber risk.

Knowledge Area: Exam_Sim

Question Number: 69

Question: The primary concern with production data in a test environment is:

Option 1: Test environment security

Option 2: Data availability

Option 3: Data readability

Option 4: Data sensitivity

Correct Response: 4

Explanation: Data sensitivity is the main concern.

Knowledge Area: Exam_Sim

Question Number: 70

Question: After an unsuccessful DR test, what should happen next?

Option 1: Update the BIA

Option 2: Prioritize noted issues

Option 3: Identify needed controls

Option 4: Communicate results

Correct Response: 3

Explanation: Issues should be prioritized for remediation.

Knowledge Area: Exam_Sim

Question Number: 71

Question: After a malware incident, the most effective response is to perform a:

Option 1: Vulnerability assessment

Option 2: Root cause analysis

Option 3: Impact assessment

Option 4: Gap analysis

Correct Response: 2

Explanation: A root cause analysis will best inform a treatment plan.

Knowledge Area: Exam_Sim

Question Number: 72

Question: Which monitoring tool aspect ensures scalability?

Option 1: Customizability

Option 2: Sustainability

Option 3: Impact on performance

Option 4: Scalability

Correct Response: 4

Explanation: Scalability allows growth alignment.

Knowledge Area: Exam_Sim

Question Number: 73

Question: What is the most appropriate risk response?

Option 1: Any option

Option 2: Insuring

Option 3: Accepting

Option 4: Avoiding

Correct Response: 3

Explanation: Acceptance is often the best initial option.

Knowledge Area: Exam_Sim

Question Number: 74

Question: Who should own the risk from an identified control gap?

Option 1: CISO

Option 2: Risk manager

Option 3: Process owner

Option 4: Control owner

Correct Response: 3

Explanation: The process owner should own the risk.

Knowledge Area: Exam_Sim

Question Number: 75

Question: To engage stakeholders in a risk report, it should:

Option 1: Include benchmarks

Option 2: Publish on-demand

Option 3: Link to needs

Option 4: Provide a roadmap

Correct Response: 3

Explanation: Linking information to needs engages them.

Knowledge Area: Exam_Sim

Question Number: 76

Question: To minimize analytics risk from bad data, what helps most?

Option 1: Benchmark practices

Option 2: Review IP agreements

Option 3: Assess data sources

Option 4: Evaluate strategies

Correct Response: 3

Explanation: Reviewing data sources is critical.

Knowledge Area: Exam_Sim

Question Number: 77

Question: If a vulnerability is being actively exploited, the best response is to:

Option 1: Assess the vuln process

Option 2: Conduct self-assessment

Option 3: Reassess target risk

Option 4: Do vulnerability scanning

Correct Response: 4

Explanation: Scanning will reveal if assets are exposed.

Knowledge Area: Exam_Sim

Question Number: 78

Question: If code rework tickets exceed thresholds, what should be recommended?

Option 1: Implement training

Option 2: Do code reviews

Option 3: Perform root cause analysis

Option 4: Use version control

Correct Response: 3

Explanation: A root cause analysis will reveal reasons.

Knowledge Area: Exam_Sim

Question Number: 79

Question: What operational risk ensures quality is not overshadowed by cost?

Option 1: Info security risk

Option 2: Contract liability risk

Option 3: Project activity risk

Option 4: Profitability risk

Correct Response: 2

Explanation: It focuses on quality over cost-cutting.

Knowledge Area: Exam_Sim

Question Number: 80

Question: What is most important to include in a risk report to management?

Option 1: Decreased key controls

Option 2: Changes in design

Option 3: Increased residual risk

Option 4: Changes in ownership

Correct Response: 3

Explanation: Increases in residual risk are critical.

Knowledge Area: Exam_Sim

Question Number: 81

Question: What is the best method to revoke employee system access?

Option 1: Reconcile logins

Option 2: Remove access at exit

Option 3: HR system revokes access

Option 4: Reconcile to access list

Correct Response: 2

Explanation: Exiting access removal is ideal.

Knowledge Area: Exam_Sim

Question Number: 82

Question: What is most important when identifying provider risk scenarios?

Option 1: Purchasing agreements

Option 2: Process mapping

Option 3: Open vendor issues

Option 4: Supplier surveys

Correct Response: 3

Explanation: Current vendor issues highlight risks.

Knowledge Area: Exam_Sim

Question Number: 83

Question: What best indicates approaching unacceptable risk levels?

Option 1: ROI

Option 2: Risk register

Option 3: Cause/effect diagram

Option 4: Risk indicator

Correct Response: 3

Explanation: Risk indicators provide early warnings.

Knowledge Area: Exam_Sim

Question Number: 84

Question: What audit finding should raise most concern about a data center?

Option 1: Unassigned ownership

Option 2: Non-redundancy

Option 3: Lack of communication

Option 4: Incomplete KRIs

Correct Response: 2

Explanation: Lack of redundancy poses continuity risk.

Knowledge Area: Exam_Sim

Question Number: 85

Question: Which is NOT an input to quantitative risk analysis?

Option 1: Risk register

Option 2: Cost plan

Option 3: Enterprise factors

Option 4: Risk management plan

Correct Response: 3

Explanation: The cost plan is not an input.

Knowledge Area: Exam_Sim

Question Number: 86

Question: Before allowing instant messaging, what should mitigate data leakage risk?

Option 1: Access control list

Option 2: Usage policy

Option 3: IDS

Option 4: Data extraction tool

Correct Response: 2

Explanation: A usage policy sets appropriate expectations.

Knowledge Area: Exam_Sim

Question Number: 87

Question: What is most important to provide internal audit during planning?

Option 1: Closed actions

Option 2: Risk assessments

Option 3: Vulnerability report

Option 4: Generic scenarios

Correct Response: 2

Explanation: Current risk assessment results inform audits.

Knowledge Area: Exam_Sim

Question Number: 88

Question: Who is ultimately accountable for outsourced IT security operations?

Option 1: The organization's management

Option 2: Third party management

Option 3: Vendor management office

Option 4: Control operators

Correct Response: 2

Explanation: The organization retains accountability.

Knowledge Area: Exam_Sim

Question Number: 89

Question: What is the most important outsourced data center SLA metric?

Option 1: Systems hosted

Option 2: Response time

Option 3: Availability

Option 4: Recovery inclusion

Correct Response: 3

Explanation: Availability percentage is critical.

Knowledge Area: Exam_Sim

Question Number: 90

Question: When identifying risk scenario reviewers, the most important factor is:

Option 1: Senior management

Option 2: Process accountability

Option 3: Independence

Option 4: Authority to select mitigation

Correct Response: 3

Explanation: Reviewers should be process accountable.

Knowledge Area: Exam_Sim

Question Number: 91

Question: Upon learning of a compliance gap, the next step should be to:

Option 1: Notify executives

Option 2: Identify mitigation

Option 3: Assess likelihood and impact

Option 4: Determine penalties

Correct Response: 3

Explanation: Assessing the risk supports response decisions.

Knowledge Area: Exam_Sim

Question Number: 92

Question: If an organization is non-compliant, the best action is to:

Option 1: Modify assurance activities

Option 2: Conduct a gap analysis

Option 3: Collaborate to meet compliance

Option 4: Identify needed controls

Correct Response: 2

Explanation: A gap analysis defines required actions.

Knowledge Area: Exam_Sim

Question Number: 93

Question: What risk register element is most impacted by changing risk appetite?

Option 1: Inherent risk

Option 2: Velocity

Option 3: Likelihood and impact

Option 4: KRI thresholds

Correct Response: 4

Explanation: Changing appetite affects acceptable KRI levels.

Knowledge Area: Exam_Sim

Question Number: 94

Question: After finding terminated employees with account access, the first step should be to:

Option 1: Develop access policies

Option 2: Disable user access

Option 3: Perform risk assessment

Option 4: Do root cause analysis

Correct Response: 2

Explanation: Disabling access immediately reduces risk exposure.

Knowledge Area: Exam_Sim

Question Number: 95

Question: What is most helpful to understand a new system's risk impact?

Option 1: Review mitigations

Option 2: Hire consultants

Option 3: Conduct gap analysis

Option 4: Perform risk assessment

Correct Response: 4

Explanation: An assessment reveals how it affects the profile.

Knowledge Area: Exam_Sim

Question Number: 96

Question: For effective risk ownership, what is most important?

Option 1: Senior oversight

Option 2: Segregation of duties

Option 3: Decision authority

Option 4: IT system alignment

Correct Response: 3

Explanation: Authority enables risk management actions.

Knowledge Area: Exam_Sim

Question Number: 97

Question: What is the best KPI showing IT policy alignment?

Option 1: Support costs

Option 2: Exceptions

Option 3: Inquiries

Option 4: Breach costs

Correct Response: 3

Explanation: Exceptions indicate misalignment.

Knowledge Area: Exam_Sim

Question Number: 98

Question: What role initiates projects in system development lifecycle?

Option 1: CIO

Option 2: CRO

Option 3: Sponsor

Option 4: Business management

Correct Response: 3

Explanation: The project sponsor charters initiatives.

Knowledge Area: Exam_Sim

Question Number: 99

Question: How can brand misuse on the internet be mitigated?

Option 1: Monitor usage

Option 2: Search for violations

Option 3: Use DLP

Option 4: Training and awareness

Correct Response: 4

Explanation: Targeted training reduces malicious actions.

Knowledge Area: Exam_Sim

Question Number: 100

Question: With ineffective security controls, the first action should be to:

Option 1: Request risk acceptance

Option 2: Report in next audit

Option 3: Deploy compensating controls

Option 4: Assess impact

Correct Response: 4

Explanation: Understanding the impact guides next steps.

Knowledge Area: Exam_Sim

Question Number: 101

Question: What gives executives the best data for risk decisions from an assessment?

Option 1: Maturity assessment

Option 2: Qualitative results

Option 3: Quantitative results

Option 4: Desired state comparison

Correct Response: 3

Explanation: Quantitative data provides the most insight.

Knowledge Area: Exam_Sim

Question Number: 102

Question: What is the most effective KRI for BYOD risk?

Option 1: Enrolled devices

Option 2: Budget allocation

Option 3: Policy signoffs

Option 4: Incident origin

Correct Response: 4

Explanation: Incident source monitors real issues.

Knowledge Area: Exam_Sim

Question Number: 103

Question: What risk refers to lower than expected investment returns?

Option 1: Project ownership risk

Option 2: Integrity risk

Option 3: Expense risk

Option 4: Relevance risk

Correct Response: 4

Explanation: Relevance risk reflects return shortfalls.

Knowledge Area: Exam_Sim

Question Number: 104

Question: What process ensures risk responses stay on track?

Option 1: Risk management

Option 2: Risk response tracking

Option 3: Risk response integration

Option 4: Risk response implementation

Correct Response: 3

Explanation: Tracking keeps responses on schedule.

Knowledge Area: Exam_Sim

Question Number: 105

Question: When does blame on IT often occur in projects?

Option 1: Threat identification

Option 2: Misalignment with appetite

Option 3: System failure

Option 4: Finger-pointing culture

Correct Response: 3

Explanation: Mismatched appetite perceptions cause blaming.

Knowledge Area: Exam_Sim

Question Number: 106

Question: What is the best KPI for incident response maturity?

Option 1: Resolved incidents

Option 2: Escalated incidents

Option 3: Identified incidents

Option 4: Recurring incidents

Correct Response: 4

Explanation: Recurrences indicate process gaps.

Knowledge Area: Exam_Sim

Question Number: 107

Question: When using a penetration tester, what is the most important control?

Option 1: Sign NDA

Option 2: Define scope

Option 3: Require insurance

Option 4: Vendor background check

Correct Response: 3

Explanation: A defined scope prevents business disruption.

Knowledge Area: Exam_Sim

Question Number: 108

Question: What should be the primary focus after deciding to mitigate a risk?

Option 1: Confirm likelihood reduction

Option 2: Monitor control effectiveness

Option 3: Update risk register

Option 4: Ensure acceptable design

Correct Response: 2

Explanation: Effectiveness monitoring ensures results.

Knowledge Area: Exam_Sim

Question Number: 109

Question: The amount of risk an organization accepts is called:

Option 1: Hedging

Option 2: Tolerance

Option 3: Aversion

Option 4: Appetite

Correct Response: 4

Explanation: Risk appetite reflects accepted risk levels.

Knowledge Area: Exam_Sim

Question Number: 110

Question: When is it most important to involve stakeholders in bottom-up risk scenarios?

Option 1: Updating risk register

Option 2: Identifying controls

Option 3: Validating scenarios

Option 4: Documenting scenarios

Correct Response: 3

Explanation: Validation ensures alignment and completeness.

Knowledge Area: Exam_Sim

Question Number: 111

Question: After finding a control design gap, what should happen next?

Option 1: Re-evaluate KRIs

Option 2: Invoke response plan

Option 3: Document in register

Option 4: Modify control design

Correct Response: 4

Explanation: The control design should be remediated.

Knowledge Area: Exam_Sim

Question Number: 112

Question: What is the best KPI for IT asset management effectiveness?

Option 1: Assets procured

Option 2: Assets disposed

Option 3: Unpatched assets

Option 4: Assets without owners

Correct Response: 4

Explanation: Ownership reflects accountability.

Knowledge Area: Exam_Sim

Question Number: 113

Question: What is most important in regulatory and risk updates?

Option 1: Recommended KRIs

Option 2: Change costs

Option 3: Noncompliance risk

Option 4: Remediation timeframe

Correct Response: 3

Explanation: The risk of noncompliance is critical.

Knowledge Area: Exam_Sim

Question Number: 114

Question: How should compliance impact on objectives be evaluated?

Option 1: Map to policies

Option 2: Impact analysis

Option 3: Gap analysis

Option 4: Stakeholder communication

Correct Response: 2

Explanation: An impact analysis quantifies effects.

Knowledge Area: Exam_Sim

Question Number: 115

Question: What is an objective of the COSO ERM model?

Option 1: Risk assessment

Option 2: Control environment

Option 3: Financial reporting

Option 4: Monitoring

Correct Response: 2

Explanation: The control environment is a key goal.

Knowledge Area: Exam_Sim

Question Number: 116

Question: How can new system control effectiveness be confirmed?

Option 1: Review KPIs

Option 2: Interview owners

Option 3: Conduct testing

Option 4: Post-implementation review

Correct Response: 4

Explanation: A review validates controls operate.

Knowledge Area: Exam_Sim

Question Number: 117

Question: When control costs exceed ALE, it indicates the:

Option 1: Risk is inefficiently controlled

Option 2: Control is ineffective

Option 3: Risk is efficiently controlled

Option 4: Control is weak

Correct Response: 3

Explanation: Costs exceeding ALE show efficient control.

Knowledge Area: Exam_Sim

Question Number: 118

Question: When reporting risks to management, what is most important?

Option 1: Assets with highest risk

Option 2: Action plans and owners

Option 3: Losses compared to treatment

Option 4: Recent assessment results

Correct Response: 2

Explanation: Loss vs treatment cost enables decisions.

Knowledge Area: Exam_Sim

Question Number: 119

Question: What serves as the starting point for the IT continuity strategy?

Option 1: Index of Disaster Information

Option 2: Availability Testing Schedule

Option 3: Business Continuity Strategy

Option 4: Disaster Guideline

Correct Response: 3

Explanation: The business strategy guides IT continuity.

Knowledge Area: Exam_Sim

Question Number: 120

Question: What examines how strengths can offset weaknesses?

Option 1: Expert judgment

Option 2: Brainstorming

Option 3: SWOT analysis

Option 4: Delphi technique

Correct Response: 3

Explanation: A SWOT analysis looks at offsetting factors.

Knowledge Area: Exam_Sim

Question Number: 121

Question: How can control implementation be validated?

Option 1: Implement KRIs

Option 2: Test control design

Option 3: Test environment

Option 4: Implement KPIs

Correct Response: 2

Explanation: Testing the design verifies effectiveness.

Knowledge Area: Exam_Sim

Question Number: 122

Question: After a risk exceeds tolerance, the next step is to:

Option 1: Develop compensation

Option 2: Allocate resources

Option 3: Identify responses

Option 4: Do cost-benefit analysis

Correct Response: 1

Explanation: Develop compensation

Knowledge Area: Exam_Sim

Question Number: 123

Question: Who helps understand IT impact on objectives?

Option 1: IT management

Option 2: Senior management

Option 3: Internal audit

Option 4: Process owners

Correct Response: 4

Explanation: Process owners know operational impacts.

Knowledge Area: Exam_Sim

Question Number: 124

Question: What demonstrates evaluation of risk alternatives?

Option 1: Trend analysis

Option 2: Control chart

Option 3: Decision tree

Option 4: Sensitivity analysis

Correct Response: 3

Explanation: A decision tree maps out options.

Knowledge Area: Exam_Sim

Question Number: 125

Question: After identifying high data loss probability, the next step should be to:

Option 1: Enhance awareness

Option 2: Increase reporting

Option 3: Buy insurance

Option 4: Do control assessment

Correct Response: 4

Explanation: Assessing controls will reveal response options.

Knowledge Area: Exam_Sim

Question Number: 126

Question: What is the best justification for a GRC solution?

Option 1: Ensure compliance

Option 2: Close audit findings

Option 3: Demonstrate commitment

Option 4: Enable risk decisions

Correct Response: 4

Explanation: It facilitates risk-aware choices.

Knowledge Area: Exam_Sim

Question Number: 127

Question: With many vulnerabilities found, what should happen next?

Option 1: Handle as risks

Option 2: Prioritize by impact

Option 3: Analyze controls

Option 4: Evaluate threats, impacts, costs

Correct Response: 4

Explanation: A risk approach considers multiple facets.

Knowledge Area: Exam_Sim

Question Number: 128

Question: What is most important when selecting KRIs?

Option 1: Availability of data

Option 2: Prediction capability

Option 3: Automated reporting

Option 4: Data aggregation

Correct Response: 2

Explanation: Ongoing data availability enables monitoring.

Knowledge Area: Exam_Sim

Question Number: 129

Question: What component examines risks in change requests?

Option 1: Risk monitoring

Option 2: Configuration management

Option 3: Integrated change control

Option 4: Scope change control

Correct Response: 3

Explanation: Integrated change control governs all changes.

Knowledge Area: Exam_Sim

Question Number: 130

Question: At what maturity are appetite and tolerance episodic?

Option 1: Level 1

Option 2: Level 2

Option 3: Level 3

Option 4: Level 4

Correct Response: 1

Explanation: Level 1 has ad hoc appetite application.

Knowledge Area: Exam_Sim

Question Number: 131

Question: What best addresses piggybacking risk?

Option 1: Security training

Option 2: Biometric locks

Option 3: Two-factor authentication

Option 4: ID badges

Correct Response: 4

Explanation: ID badges enable access validation.

Knowledge Area: Exam_Sim

Question Number: 132

Question: How can hard drive disposal risk be reduced?

Option 1: Require IT confirmation

Option 2: Use accredited vendor

Option 3: Encrypt drives

Option 4: Require degaussing

Correct Response: 3

Explanation: An accredited vendor provides assurance.

Knowledge Area: Exam_Sim

Question Number: 133

Question: After identifying high data loss probability, the next step should be to:

Option 1: Enhance awareness

Option 2: Increase reporting

Option 3: Buy insurance

Option 4: Do control assessment

Correct Response: 4

Explanation: Assessing controls will reveal response options.

Knowledge Area: Exam_Sim

Question Number: 134

Question: What is the best justification for a GRC solution?

Option 1: Ensure compliance

Option 2: Close audit findings

Option 3: Demonstrate commitment

Option 4: Enable risk decisions

Correct Response: 4

Explanation: It facilitates risk-aware choices.

Knowledge Area: Exam_Sim

Question Number: 135

Question: With many vulnerabilities found, what should happen next?

Option 1: Handle as risks

Option 2: Prioritize by impact

Option 3: Analyze controls

Option 4: Evaluate threats, impacts, costs

Correct Response: 4

Explanation: A risk approach considers multiple facets.

Knowledge Area: Exam_Sim

Question Number: 136

Question: What is most important when selecting KRIs?

Option 1: Availability of data

Option 2: Prediction capability

Option 3: Automated reporting

Option 4: Data aggregation

Correct Response: 2

Explanation: Ongoing data availability enables monitoring.

Knowledge Area: Exam_Sim

Question Number: 137

Question: What component examines risks in change requests?

Option 1: Risk monitoring

Option 2: Configuration management

Option 3: Integrated change control

Option 4: Scope change control

Correct Response: 3

Explanation: Integrated change control governs all changes.

Knowledge Area: Exam_Sim

Question Number: 138

Question: At what maturity are appetite and tolerance episodic?

Option 1: Level 1

Option 2: Level 2

Option 3: Level 3

Option 4: Level 4

Correct Response: 1

Explanation: Level 1 has ad hoc appetite application.

Knowledge Area: Exam_Sim

Question Number: 139

Question: What best addresses piggybacking risk?

Option 1: Security training

Option 2: Biometric locks

Option 3: Two-factor authentication

Option 4: ID badges

Correct Response: 4

Explanation: ID badges enable access validation.

Knowledge Area: Exam_Sim

Question Number: 140

Question: How can hard drive disposal risk be reduced?

Option 1: Require IT confirmation

Option 2: Use accredited vendor

Option 3: Encrypt drives

Option 4: Require degaussing

Correct Response: 3

Explanation: An accredited vendor provides assurance.

Knowledge Area: Exam_Sim

Question Number: 141

Question: Why use qualitative residual risk measures for new threats?

Option 1: Regulatory alignment

Option 2: Expert judgment

Option 3: Easier updating

Option 4: Less monitoring

Correct Response: 3

Explanation: Qualitative incorporates judgment better.

Knowledge Area: Exam_Sim

Question Number: 142

Question: If preventive controls cannot be implemented, the first action is to:

Option 1: Upgrade technology

Option 2: Monitor risk

Option 3: Evaluate alternatives

Option 4: Redefine process

Correct Response: 2

Explanation: Alternatives should be explored before changes.

Knowledge Area: Exam_Sim

Question Number: 143

Question: When risk exceeds appetite, the best action is to:

Option 1: Maintain controls

Option 2: Analyze controls

Option 3: Review tolerance

Option 4: Execute response

Correct Response: 4

Explanation: The response plan addresses the gap.

Knowledge Area: Exam_Sim

Question Number: 144

Question: What most indicates ineffective risk actions?

Option 1: Breach occurs

Option 2: Unauthorized changes

Option 3: Recurring exceptions

Option 4: Sample validation

Correct Response: 2

Explanation: Recurring issues show ineffectiveness.

Knowledge Area: Exam_Sim

Question Number: 145

Question: What is most important for effective metrics reporting?

Option 1: Audits

Option 2: Incident management

Option 3: Reporting process

Option 4: Incident procedures

Correct Response: 3

Explanation: The reporting process enables action.

Knowledge Area: Exam_Sim

Question Number: 146

Question: With offshore cloud data storage, the primary concern is:

Option 1: Data validation

Option 2: Data aggregation

Option 3: Data quality

Option 4: Data privacy

Correct Response: 2

Explanation: Offshore increases privacy risks.

Knowledge Area: Exam_Sim

Question Number: 147

Question: What term describes the expected value from taking a risk?

Option 1: Risk premium

Option 2: Certain value assurance

Option 3: Certainty equivalent

Option 4: Risk value guarantee

Correct Response: 3

Explanation: Certainty equivalent is the expected value.

Knowledge Area: Exam_Sim

Question Number: 148

Question: After more emergency changes, the best action is to:

Option 1: Reconfigure infrastructure

Option 2: Conduct root cause analysis

Option 3: Evaluate control impact

Option 4: Validate processes

Correct Response: 2

Explanation: Analysis reveals reasons for the changes.

Knowledge Area: Exam_Sim

Question Number: 149

Question: What is most important to communicate when implementing risk management?

Option 1: Regulatory compliance

Option 2: Desired risk level

Option 3: Best practices

Option 4: Risk ownership

Correct Response: 3

Explanation: The desired level sets expectations.

Knowledge Area: Exam_Sim

Question Number: 150

Question: With multiple risk owners, what is most important?

Option 1: Treatment plan updates

Option 2: Consistent assessments

Option 3: Escalation procedures

Option 4: Risk/control alignment

Correct Response: 2

Explanation: Consistent assessments ensure coherence.

Knowledge Area: Exam_Sim

Question Number: 151

Question: What helps ensure mitigated risk stays acceptable?

Option 1: Risk owner reviews

Option 2: Profile updates

Option 3: Control testing participation

Option 4: Effectiveness monitoring

Correct Response: 4

Explanation: Ongoing monitoring maintains awareness.

Knowledge Area: Exam_Sim

Question Number: 152

Question: What best informs risk decisions in control reporting?

Option 1: Audit plan

Option 2: Implementation spend

Option 3: Deployment status

Option 4: Testing deficiencies

Correct Response: 4

Explanation: Deficiencies highlight issues.

Knowledge Area: Exam_Sim

Question Number: 153

Question: What component generates threats in scenarios?

Option 1: Assets

Option 2: Timing

Option 3: Events

Option 4: Actors

Correct Response: 4

Explanation: Actors, internal or external, drive threats.

Knowledge Area: Exam_Sim

Question Number: 154

Question: What improves risk indicator buy-in?

Option 1: Lag indicator

Option 2: Root cause

Option 3: Lead indicator

Option 4: Stakeholder

Correct Response: 4

Explanation: Stakeholder input enables engagement.

Knowledge Area: Exam_Sim

Question Number: 155

Question: A reciprocal DR agreement applies what treatment?

Option 1: Avoidance

Option 2: Mitigation

Option 3: Acceptance

Option 4: Transfer

Correct Response: 4

Explanation: It transfers risk through sharing.

Knowledge Area: Exam_Sim

Question Number: 156

Question: What best prevents unauthorized data retrieval?

Option 1: Single sign-on

Option 2: Digital signatures

Option 3: Access policy enforcement

Option 4: Segregation of duties

Correct Response: 3

Explanation: An access policy restricts visibility.

Knowledge Area: Exam_Sim

Question Number: 157

Question: When evaluating control adequacy, the PRIMARY focus should be:

Option 1: Residual risk level

Option 2: Risk appetite

Option 3: Cost-benefit analysis

Option 4: Sensitivity analysis

Correct Response: 3

Explanation: Cost-benefit analysis determines efficient mitigation.

Knowledge Area: Exam_Sim

Question Number: 158

Question: Regarding KRI monitoring, the GREATEST concern is:

Option 1: Excessive log retention

Option 2: Encrypted log transmission

Option 3: Pre-analysis log modification

Option 4: Limited data sources

Correct Response: 3

Explanation: Modified logs undermine analysis.

Knowledge Area: Exam_Sim

Question Number: 159

Question: For resource allocation, the most helpful input is:

Option 1: Pen testing results

Option 2: Case studies

Option 3: Audit findings

Option 4: Assessments

Correct Response: 3

Explanation: Assessments show exposure levels to guide mitigation.

Knowledge Area: Exam_Sim

Question Number: 160

Question: A key project success factor is:

Option 1: Motivation

Option 2: Political/cultural awareness

Option 3: Communication

Option 4: Influencing

Correct Response: 3

Explanation: Effective communication enables collaboration.

Knowledge Area: Exam_Sim

Question Number: 161

Question: Expert judgment for risks provides:

Option 1: Contingent strategies

Option 2: Risk transfer

Option 3: External guidance

Option 4: Risk acceptance

Correct Response: 3

Explanation: Experts give informed recommendations.

Knowledge Area: Exam_Sim

Question Number: 162

Question: The GREATEST generic risk concern is:

Option 1: Higher costs

Option 2: Irrelevant factors

Option 3: Lack of inherent risk

Option 4: No quantification

Correct Response: 3

Explanation: Irrelevant factors undermine analysis.

Knowledge Area: Exam_Sim

Question Number: 163

Question: Risk training should focus on:

Option 1: Security incidents

Option 2: Staff responsibilities

Option 3: Policy exceptions

Option 4: Risk profiles

Correct Response: 4

Explanation: Incidents make risks tangible to staff.

Knowledge Area: Exam_Sim

Question Number: 164

Question: Numerically analyzing risk impact is:

Option 1: Monitoring risks

Option 2: Qualitative assessment

Option 3: Identifying risks

Option 4: Quantitative assessment

Correct Response: 4

Explanation: This defines the quantitative process.

Knowledge Area: Exam_Sim

Question Number: 165

Question: For a system go-live, the most important factor is:

Option 1: Resource availability

Option 2: Documentation completeness

Option 3: Variance from cost

Option 4: Testing results

Correct Response: 4

Explanation: Testing confirms readiness and functionality.

Knowledge Area: Exam_Sim

Question Number: 166

Question: For BYOD, the best data loss protection is:

Option 1: Strong passwords

Option 2: Remote monitoring

Option 3: Pen testing

Option 4: Encryption and wipe

Correct Response: 4

Explanation: Encryption and wiping protect lost devices.

Knowledge Area: Exam_Sim

Question Number: 167

Question: To effectively monitor KRIs, the most critical element is:

Option 1: Escalation procedures

Option 2: Automated data feeds

Option 3: Threshold definitions

Option 4: Controls monitoring

Correct Response: 2

Explanation: Automated data enables real-time tracking.

Knowledge Area: Exam_Sim

Question Number: 168

Question: To incorporate IT risks into enterprise risk, it is best to:

Option 1: Get business approval of IT risk appetite

Option 2: Assess IT risks enterprise-wide

Option 3: Develop KRIs for IT risks

Option 4: Put IT risks in business context

Correct Response: 4

Explanation: Business context creates relevance.

Knowledge Area: Exam_Sim

Question Number: 169

Question: Recurring security exceptions likely indicate:

Option 1: Decreased threats

Option 2: Ineffective governance

Option 3: Lack of mitigation

Option 4: Poor service delivery

Correct Response: 2

Explanation: Governance should ensure policy compliance.

Knowledge Area: Exam_Sim

Question Number: 170

Question: The best KPI for vulnerability management is:

Option 1: Escalated vulnerabilities

Option 2: Identified vulnerabilities

Option 3: Reopened vulnerabilities

Option 4: Remediated vulnerabilities

Correct Response: 4

Explanation: Remediation percentage indicates success.

Knowledge Area: Exam_Sim

Question Number: 171

Question: A force majeure risk event will likely trigger:

Option 1: Acceptance

Option 2: Mitigation

Option 3: Enhancement

Option 4: Transference

Correct Response: 1

Explanation: Force majeure leads to risk acceptance.

Knowledge Area: Exam_Sim

Question Number: 172

Question: For a critical system, the most important control factor is:

Option 1: Available budget

Option 2: Number of vulnerabilities

Option 3: Level of acceptable risk

Option 4: Number of threats

Correct Response: 3

Explanation: Controls should align to risk appetite.

Knowledge Area: Exam_Sim

Question Number: 173

Question: To ensure risk register completeness, most important is reviewing:

Option 1: Risk mitigation

Option 2: Vulnerability results

Option 3: Cost-benefit analysis

Option 4: Assessment results

Correct Response: 4

Explanation: Assessments identify risks for inclusion.

Knowledge Area: Exam_Sim

Question Number: 174

Question: For wearable technology risks, the first step is:

Option 1: Assess potential risk

Option 2: Monitor usage

Option 3: Identify potential risk

Option 4: Develop awareness

Correct Response: 3

Explanation: Identification frames subsequent actions.

Knowledge Area: Exam_Sim

Question Number: 175

Question: The best IT service availability KPI is:

Option 1: Mean time to recover

Option 2: Planned downtime

Option 3: Unplanned downtime

Option 4: Mean time between failures

Correct Response: 3

Explanation: Unplanned downtime shows interruptions.

Knowledge Area: Exam_Sim

Question Number: 176

Question: Global risk standards are primarily useful for:

Option 1: Gap identification

Option 2: Continuous improvement

Option 3: Regulatory compliance

Option 4: Culture building

Correct Response: 3

Explanation: Standards provide compliance guidance.

Knowledge Area: Exam_Sim

Question Number: 177

Question: The most useful IAM efficiency KPI is:

Option 1: Password resets

Option 2: Tickets created

Option 3: Provisioning time

Option 4: Account lockout time

Correct Response: 3

Explanation: Provisioning time impacts productivity.

Knowledge Area: Exam_Sim

Question Number: 178

Question: Risk analysis results should be quantitative or qualitative based on:

Option 1: Organizational tolerance

Option 2: Management needs

Option 3: Framework used

Option 4: Assessment results

Correct Response: 4

Explanation: Actual results guide ideal presentation.

Knowledge Area: Exam_Sim

Question Number: 179

Question: Updating the risk register primarily:

Option 1: Maintains compliance

Option 2: Mitigates factors

Option 3: Enables decisions

Option 4: Validates appetite

Correct Response: 3

Explanation: It provides timely information for decisions.

Knowledge Area: Exam_Sim

Question Number: 180

Question: IT and business risk strategy coordination is likely owned by:

Option 1: CIO

Option 2: Internal audit director

Option 3: CFO

Option 4: Security director

Correct Response: 1

Explanation: The CIO oversees technology risks.

Knowledge Area: Exam_Sim

Question Number: 181

Question: Process awareness enables a risk practitioner to:

Option 1: Establish guidelines

Option 2: Identify risk sources

Option 3: Understand control design

Option 4: Perform BIAs

Correct Response: 4

Explanation: It reveals potential risk origins.

Knowledge Area: Exam_Sim

Question Number: 182

Question: SWOT analysis helps identify risk from:

Option 1: Standard procedures

Option 2: Benchmarking

Option 3: Control gaps

Option 4: Business changes

Correct Response: 4

Explanation: It assesses internal and external factors.

Knowledge Area: Exam_Sim

Question Number: 183

Question: IT control effectiveness is best indicated by:

Option 1: Risk heat maps

Option 2: Internal audits

Option 3: KPIs

Option 4: Penetration testing

Correct Response: 3

Explanation: KPIs provide real-time monitoring.

Knowledge Area: Exam_Sim

Question Number: 184

Question: An appropriate monthly backup KRI is:

Option 1: Backup completion rate

Option 2: Backup size change

Option 3: Restore test failures

Option 4: Restore time

Correct Response: 4

Explanation: Failed restores show reliability issues.

Knowledge Area: Exam_Sim

Question Number: 185

Question: KCIs primarily evaluate controls to:

Option 1: Raise awareness

Option 2: Ensure objectives

Option 3: Identify vulnerabilities

Option 4: Monitor risk exposure

Correct Response: 3

Explanation: KCIs reveal control weaknesses.

Knowledge Area: Exam_Sim

Question Number: 186

Question: ERM oversight of IT risk is most valuable for:

Option 1: Focusing on risk impact

Option 2: Aligning IT to strategy

Option 3: Enabling risk resources

Option 4: Prioritizing customers

Correct Response: 2

Explanation: It aligns technology risk management.

Knowledge Area: Exam_Sim

Question Number: 187

Question: An operational audit assesses:

Option 1: Administrative controls

Option 2: Specialized controls

Option 3: Financial controls

Option 4: Productivity controls

Correct Response: 4

Explanation: It focuses on operational efficiency.

Knowledge Area: Exam_Sim

Question Number: 188

Question: Anti-virus effectiveness is best measured by:

Option 1: Update frequency

Option 2: Alert quantity

Option 3: Definition currency

Option 4: False positives

Correct Response: 3

Explanation: Current definitions ensure protection.

Knowledge Area: Exam_Sim

Question Number: 189

Question: When developing a risk register, focus on:

Option 1: Risk management strategy

Option 2: Risk identification

Option 3: Risk monitoring

Option 4: Response planning

Correct Response: 2

Explanation: The register captures identified risks.

Knowledge Area: Exam_Sim

Question Number: 190

Question: Stakeholder KRI selection benefits include:

Option 1: Risk treatment optimization

Option 2: Obtaining risk owner buy-in

Option 3: Leveraging metrics

Option 4: Improving awareness

Correct Response: 3

Explanation: It drives engagement and adoption.

Knowledge Area: Exam_Sim

Question Number: 191

Question: Best risk tolerance adherence comes from:

Option 1: Avoiding big losses

Option 2: Increasing resources

Option 3: Defining expectations

Option 4: Communicating audits

Correct Response: 3

Explanation: Clear policy expectations enable compliance.

Knowledge Area: Exam_Sim

Question Number: 192

Question: Backup effectiveness is best measured by:

Option 1: Recovery requests

Option 2: Monitoring reports

Option 3: Allocation of resources

Option 4: Recurring failures

Correct Response: 4

Explanation: Failures indicate issues.

Knowledge Area: Exam_Sim

Question Number: 193

Question: The risk register primarily supports:

Option 1: Risk process

Option 2: Risk profile

Option 3: Risk strategy

Option 4: Risk map

Correct Response: 3

Explanation: It provides data for risk profiling.

Knowledge Area: Exam_Sim

Question Number: 194

Question: Key for risk response strategy is:

. Option 1: Probability definition

Option 2: Cost of controls

Option 3: Appetite

Option 4: Tolerance

Correct Response: 3

Explanation: Appetite guides appropriate responses.

Knowledge Area: Exam_Sim

Question Number: 195

Question: A policy forbidding personal email use is an:

Option 1: Anti-harassment policy

Option 2: Intellectual property policy

Option 3: Acceptable use policy

Option 4: Privacy policy

Correct Response: 3

Explanation: An AUP covers appropriate usage

Knowledge Area: Exam_Sim

Question Number: 196

Question: What type of assessment would help determine vulnerabilities in an organization's critical assets?

Option 1: Threat assessment

Option 2: Vulnerability assessment

Option 3: Risk assessment

Option 4: Penetration testing

Correct Response: 2

Explanation: A vulnerability assessment specifically looks for weaknesses in critical assets that could be exploited by threats, making it the best choice to identify vulnerabilities.

Knowledge Area: Exam_Sim

Question Number: 197

Question: Which of the following is the BEST way to promote a risk-aware culture?

Option 1: Mandating risk training

Option 2: Establishing risk tolerances

Option 3: Implementing financial controls

Option 4: Hiring a risk officer

Correct Response: 2

Explanation: Setting risk tolerances helps define acceptable levels of risk for staff, promoting awareness of how much risk can be taken.

Knowledge Area: Exam_Sim

Question Number: 198

Question: To improve visibility into cybersecurity risks, what should be included in a risk register?

Option 1: Mitigations

Option 2: Inherent risks

Option 3: Residual risks

Option 4: Threat events

Correct Response: 3

Explanation: Documenting residual risk shows what risks remain after controls, giving visibility into areas needing improvement.

Knowledge Area: Exam_Sim

Question Number: 199

Question: Which risk analysis method uses scenarios to estimate potential losses from threats?

Option 1: HERA

Option 2: Failure modes and effects analysis

Option 3: Annualized loss expectancy

Option 4: Three lines of defense

Correct Response: 3

Explanation: ALE analysis looks at potential loss scenarios to quantify possible losses from threats manifesting.

Knowledge Area: Exam_Sim

Question Number: 200

Question: What is a PRIMARY benefit of qualitative risk analysis?

Option 1: It is easy to automate

Option 2: It provides quantifiable results

Option 3: It gives contextual insights

Option 4: It requires minimal resources

Correct Response: 3

Explanation: Qualitative analysis provides subjective but important context around risks that quantitative data lacks.

Knowledge Area: Exam_Sim

HELP US IMPROVE!

WE WANT YOUR FEEDBACK

Amazing!

You have been studying very hard to this stage.

How is your exam preparation so far? Can the practice test meet your needs and expectation? I desperately desire your voice.

Please kindly consider

1. Visiting my exam practice test books and consider purchasing them to assist you to pass your target exam, though the direct links provided at the beginning of this book
2. Visiting my exam practice test courses held at Udemy though the direct links provided at the beginning of this book
3. Leaving a positive review and feedback to me though the direct book review links provided at the next page.

Keep going! See you at the end of the book.

Warm regards,

Walter

Or the **Links at Amazon Book Store:**

CRISC 1200+ Practice Test, 2023 (Exam Simulation and Core & Advanced Knowledge)	
Paperback Review URL:	- https://www.amazon.com/review/create-review?&asin=B0CJ43R78T
Kindle eBook Review URL:	- https://www.amazon.com/review/create-review?&asin=B0CJ72JJLY

Direct URLs to visit all Walter's Practice Tests at Amazon

Visit Walter's author page:
http://WalterEducation.com

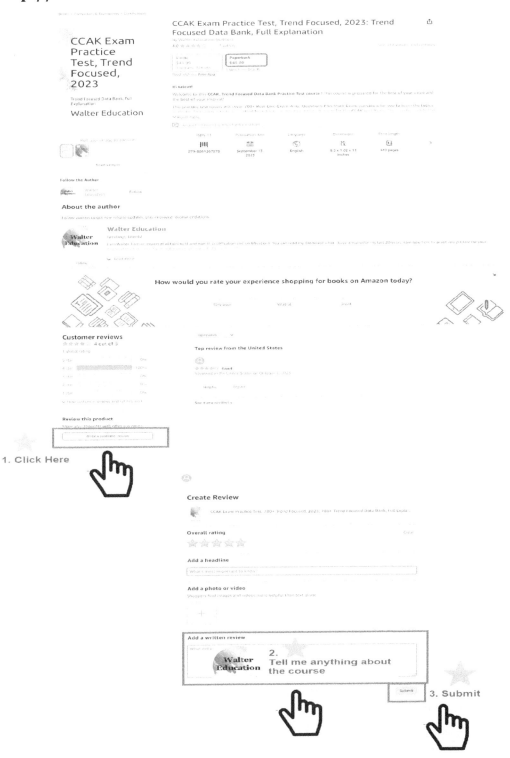

1. Click Here

2. Tell me anything about the course

3. Submit

Question Number: 201

Question: Which control activity BEST deters social engineering?

Option 1: Role-based access controls

Option 2: Background checks

Option 3: Security awareness training

Option 4: Encryption

Correct Response: 3

Explanation: Training makes staff aware of social engineering, improving their ability to detect and deter it.

Knowledge Area: Exam_Sim

Question Number: 202

Question: Which metric can indicate the effectiveness of an organization's vulnerability management program?

Option 1: Time to patch vulnerabilities

Option 2: Number of malware infections

Option 3: Number of security events

Option 4: Number of exploited vulnerabilities

Correct Response: 4

Explanation: Exploited vulnerabilities show if patches were effective in preventing vulnerabilities from being exploited.

Knowledge Area: Exam_Sim

Question Number: 203

Question: What should be done AFTER implementing a risk response?

Option 1: Conduct a cost-benefit analysis

Option 2: Identify the risk owner

Option 3: Monitor the risk

Option 4: Calculate residual risk

Correct Response: 3

Explanation: Post-implementation monitoring verifies if the response is working as intended.

Knowledge Area: Exam_Sim

Question Number: 204

Question: Which of the following actions assures management that the organization's objectives are protected from the occurrence of risk events?

Option 1: Comprehensive risk assessments

Option 2: Effective risk treatment measures

Option 3: Continuous risk monitoring

Option 4: Clear risk communication and reporting

Correct Response: 4

Explanation: Clear risk communication and reporting assures management that the organization's objectives are protected from the occurrence of risk events. By effectively communicating and reporting risks, management can make informed decisions, implement appropriate risk treatment measures, and ensure alignment with organizational objectives.

Knowledge Area: Exam_Sim

Question Number: 205

Question: A change management process has recently been updated with new testing procedures. The NEXT course of action is to:

Option 1: Communicate the changes to relevant stakeholders

Option 2: Implement the updated procedures immediately

Option 3: Review the impact of the changes on existing processes

Option 4: Conduct training on the new testing procedures

Correct Response: 1

Explanation: The next course of action after updating the change management process with new testing procedures is to communicate the changes to relevant stakeholders. Effective communication ensures that all stakeholders are informed about the changes, understand their roles and responsibilities, and can adapt their processes accordingly. This helps in maintaining a smooth transition and minimizing potential disruptions.

Knowledge Area: Exam_Sim

Question Number: 206

Question: After undertaking a risk assessment of a production system, the MOST appropriate action is for the risk manager to:

Option 1: Develop a risk treatment plan

Option 2: Document the risk assessment findings

Option 3: Implement risk mitigation measures

Option 4: Review and update risk assessment periodically

Correct Response: 1

Explanation: The most appropriate action for the risk manager after undertaking a risk assessment of a production system is to develop a risk treatment plan. Based on the assessment findings, the risk manager can prioritize and plan for risk mitigation measures, allocate resources, and establish timelines for implementation. The risk treatment plan helps in addressing identified risks effectively and reducing their potential impact.

Knowledge Area: Exam_Sim

Question Number: 207

Question: Which of the following is the FIRST step in managing the risk associated with the leakage of confidential data?

Option 1: Conduct a data classification assessment

Option 2: Implement access controls and encryption measures

Option 3: Develop and enforce data handling policies

Option 4: Identify the sources and potential causes of data leakage

Correct Response: 1

Explanation: The first step in managing the risk associated with the leakage of confidential data is to conduct a data classification assessment. This involves identifying and categorizing data based on its sensitivity and criticality. By understanding the value and sensitivity of data, organizations can prioritize their protection efforts and implement appropriate access controls, encryption measures, and data handling policies.

Knowledge Area: Exam_Sim

Question Number: 208

Question: After a risk has been identified, who is in the BEST position to select the appropriate risk treatment option?

Option 1: Risk owner

Option 2: Risk analyst

Option 3: Risk committee

Option 4: Senior management

Correct Response: 1

Explanation: The risk owner is in the best position to select the appropriate risk treatment option after identifying a risk. As the individual responsible for the management and mitigation of the risk, the risk owner has the necessary knowledge and authority to evaluate the available options, consider the organization's objectives and risk appetite, and make an informed decision regarding the most suitable risk treatment option.

Knowledge Area: Exam_Sim

Question Number: 209

Question: Which of the following is the MOST important technology control to reduce the likelihood of fraudulent payments committed internally?

Option 1: Segregation of duties

Option 2: Access controls

Option 3: Encryption

Option 4: Intrusion detection systems

Correct Response: 1

Explanation: Segregation of duties is the most important technology control to reduce the likelihood of fraudulent payments committed internally. By implementing segregation of duties, organizations ensure that multiple individuals are involved in critical financial processes, reducing the risk of collusion and unauthorized actions. This control helps in maintaining accountability, detecting and preventing fraudulent activities, and safeguarding the integrity of financial transactions.

Knowledge Area: Exam_Sim

Question Number: 210

Question: Which of the following is the BEST indication that an organization is following a mature risk management process?

Option 1: Regular risk assessments and updates

Option 2: Comprehensive risk documentation

Option 3: Integration of risk management with strategic planning

Option 4: Active involvement of senior management

Correct Response: 3

Explanation: The best indication that an organization is following a mature risk management process is the active involvement of senior management. When senior management is actively engaged in risk management activities, including setting risk appetite, providing necessary resources, and promoting a risk-aware culture, it demonstrates the organization's commitment to effective risk management. This involvement fosters a proactive approach to risk and helps in integrating risk management with strategic planning processes.

Knowledge Area: Exam_Sim

Question Number: 211

Question: Which of the following BEST ensures that a firewall is configured in compliance with an enterprise's security policy?

Option 1: Regularly review and update the firewall configuration

Option 2: Conduct periodic penetration testing

Option 3: Implement change control procedures

Option 4: Perform regular security audits

Correct Response: 1

Explanation: The best approach to ensure that a firewall is configured in compliance with an enterprise's security policy is to regularly review and update the firewall configuration. Regular reviews help to ensure that the firewall rules and settings align with the organization's security policy and requirements. By keeping the configuration up to date, organizations can address emerging threats, vulnerabilities, and compliance requirements effectively.

Knowledge Area: Exam_Sim

Question Number: 212

Question: Which of the following actions ensures that a firewall is configured in compliance with an enterprise's security policy?

Option 1: Regularly review and update firewall configurations

Option 2: Conduct vulnerability scans on the firewall

Option 3: Implement intrusion detection systems

Option 4: Perform regular security audits

Correct Response: 1

Explanation: Regularly reviewing and updating firewall configurations ensures that the firewall is aligned with the enterprise's security policy. By regularly reviewing the configurations, organizations can identify and address any deviations or vulnerabilities, ensuring that the firewall remains effective in protecting the network against potential threats.

Knowledge Area: Exam_Sim

Question Number: 213

Question: Which of the following business requirements is most closely related to the need for resilient business and information systems processes?

Option 1: Business continuity planning

Option 2: Financial risk management

Option 3: Regulatory compliance

Option 4: Supplier management

Correct Response: 1

Explanation: The business requirement most closely related to the need for resilient business and information systems processes is business continuity planning. Business continuity planning involves identifying potential disruptions, developing strategies to ensure continuous operations, and implementing measures to minimize the impact of disruptions. It aims to maintain essential functions and protect critical assets during and after disruptive events.

Knowledge Area: Exam_Sim

Question Number: 214

Question: Which of the following methods involves the use of predictive or diagnostic analytical tools for exposing risk factors?

Option 1: Data mining

Option 2: Penetration testing

Option 3: Business process modeling

Option 4: Gap analysis

Correct Response: 1

Explanation: The method that involves the use of predictive or diagnostic analytical tools for exposing risk factors is data mining. Data mining involves analyzing large datasets to identify patterns, correlations, and anomalies that may indicate potential risks. By applying data mining techniques, organizations can gain insights into risk factors and make informed decisions to mitigate those risks.

Knowledge Area: Exam_Sim

Question Number: 215

Question: When updating the risk register after a risk assessment, what is the most important information to include?

Option 1: Identified risks and their likelihood and impact

Option 2: Actions taken to mitigate risks

Option 3: Current risk levels and trends

Option 4: Roles and responsibilities of risk owners

Correct Response: 1

Explanation: The most important information to include when updating the risk register after a risk assessment is the identified risks and their likelihood and impact. This information provides a comprehensive overview of the risks the organization faces and allows for informed decision-making regarding risk treatment and mitigation strategies. It helps prioritize resources and efforts to address the most significant risks.

Knowledge Area: Exam_Sim

Question Number: 216

Question: When determining which control deficiencies are most significant, what provides the most useful information?

Option 1: Impact analysis

Option 2: Risk assessment reports

Option 3: Control testing results

Option 4: Incident reports

Correct Response: 2

Explanation: When determining which control deficiencies are most significant, risk assessment reports provide the most useful information. Risk assessment reports offer insights into the likelihood and potential impact of identified control deficiencies. They enable organizations to prioritize remediation efforts based on the level of risk exposure and ensure that resources are allocated effectively to address the most significant control deficiencies.

Knowledge Area: Exam_Sim

Question Number: 217

Question: A risk heat map is most commonly used as part of an IT risk analysis to facilitate risk:

Option 1: Visualization and communication

Option 2: Quantification and modeling

Option 3: Assessment and prioritization

Option 4: Mitigation and treatment

Correct Response: 1

Explanation: A risk heat map is most commonly used as part of an IT risk analysis to facilitate risk visualization and communication. By visually representing risks based on their likelihood and impact, a risk heat map provides a clear and concise overview of the risk landscape. It helps stakeholders understand complex risk information, enables effective communication, and supports decision-making regarding risk response and mitigation strategies.

Knowledge Area: Exam_Sim

Question Number: 218

Question: Which approach would most effectively enable a business operations manager to identify events exceeding risk thresholds?

Option 1: Establishing key risk indicators (KRIs)

Option 2: Implementing robust internal controls

Option 3: Conducting regular risk assessments

Option 4: Enhancing business continuity planning

Correct Response: 1

Explanation: Establishing key risk indicators (KRIs) would most effectively enable a business operations manager to identify events exceeding risk thresholds. KRIs are measurable metrics that provide early warning signs of potential risks and allow for proactive risk management. By monitoring KRIs, the manager can identify deviations from acceptable risk levels and take timely actions to mitigate risks.

Knowledge Area: Exam_Sim

Question Number: 219

Question: Who is best suited to determine whether a new control properly mitigates data loss risk within a system?

Option 1: Information security officer

Option 2: Risk management committee

Option 3: Internal auditor

Option 4: Control owner

Correct Response: 1

Explanation: The information security officer is best suited to determine whether a new control properly mitigates data loss risk within a system. As the individual responsible for ensuring the confidentiality, integrity, and availability of information, the information security officer possesses the expertise to evaluate controls and assess their effectiveness in addressing data loss risks. They play a crucial role in aligning controls with best practices and regulatory requirements.

Knowledge Area: Exam_Sim

---------- --------------------------------

Question Number: 220

Question: When reviewing existing controls during a risk assessment, what should raise concerns about potential ineffectiveness in mitigating risks?

Option 1: Manual processes

Option 2: Frequency of testing

Option 3: Limited automation

Option 4: Gaps in coverage

Correct Response: 4

Explanation: Control gaps and weak enforcement indicate risk mitigation deficiencies.

Knowledge Area: Exam_Sim

Question Number: 221

Question: What should an organization do first when assessing the maturity of their internal control environment?

Option 1: Analyze audit findings

Option 2: Conduct control testing

Option 3: Interview process owners

Option 4: Establish assessment metrics

Correct Response: 3

Explanation: Defining metrics provides objectives to evaluate control maturity.

Knowledge Area: Exam_Sim

Question Number: 222

Question: What IT key risk indicator would provide the most meaningful insights into capacity risks and constraints?

Option 1: Help desk ticket volume

Option 2: Threat alerts

Option 3: System availability

Option 4: Workload utilization

Correct Response: 4

Explanation: Workload and utilization metrics give visibility into capacity.

Knowledge Area: Exam_Sim

Question Number: 223

Question: If a risk assessment identified an ineffective key control on a critical system, what should the risk practitioner do next?

Option 1: Remove access

Option 2: Log issue for future change

Option 3: Initiate an audit

Option 4: Implement compensating controls

Correct Response: 4

Explanation: Prompt compensating controls mitigate the weak control exposure.

Knowledge Area: Exam_Sim

Question Number: 224

Question: When monitoring a client-facing application, what is most important to ensure continually?

Option 1: Costs stay within budget

Option 2: Vulnerability scans performed

Option 3: Audit logs are reviewed

Option 4: Performance is analyzed

Correct Response: 4

Explanation: Proactive monitoring ensures availability and user experience.

Knowledge Area: Exam_Sim

Question Number: 225

Question: What is the highest risk of having inadequately defined data and system ownership?

Option 1: Non-compliance

Option 2: Difficulty integrating acquisitions

Option 3: Excessive privilege creep

Option 4: Gaps in responsibilities

Correct Response: 4

Explanation: Undefined owners lead to responsibility gaps and actions not taken.

Knowledge Area: Exam_Sim

Question Number: 226

Question: What is the best practice for identifying changes in an organization's overall risk profile?

Option 1: Review static risk register

Option 2: Conduct audits on known issues

Option 3: Monitor existing KRIs

Option 4: Perform refreshed risk assessments

Correct Response: 4

Explanation: Updated risk assessments reliably detect evolving profiles.

Knowledge Area: Exam_Sim

Question Number: 227

Question: Which role typically serves as part of the second line of defense in the three lines model?

Option 1: Business unit manager

Option 2: External consultant

Option 3: Chief Information Officer

Option 4: Information security team

Correct Response: 4

Explanation: Infosec aligns with standardized second line RM functions.

Knowledge Area: Exam_Sim

Question Number: 228

Question: When implementing user activity log monitoring, the primary consideration should be ensuring controls align to policy, legal, and risk management objectives to balance oversight with minimal business disruption.

Option 1: Storage capacity planning

Option 2: Log format standardization

Option 3: Real-time alerting

Option 4: Objective alignment

Correct Response: 4

Explanation: Objective alignment guides log controls.

Knowledge Area: Exam_Sim

Question Number: 229

Question: Realistic scenarios including identified threats, vulnerable assets, and potential impacts should be included in risk analysis scenarios to provide targeted insights.

Option 1: Hypothetical situations

Option 2: Recent incidents

Option 3: Worst-case extrapolations

Option 4: Realistic components

Correct Response: 4

Explanation: Realistic scenarios provide relevant insights.

Knowledge Area: Exam_Sim

Question Number: 230

Question: The greatest concern with an incident response plan is lack of testing and validation of its effectiveness in actual response situations requiring activation.

Option 1: Incomplete documentation

Option 2: Untrained staff

Option 3: No third-party integration

Option 4: Lack of testing

Correct Response: 4

Explanation: Untested plans risk failure in response.

Knowledge Area: Exam_Sim

Question Number: 231

Question: Business process modeling linking objectives, risks, and controls visualizes how risk management aligns to and enables strategic goals.

Option 1: Risk heat maps

Option 2: Risk-control matrices

Option 3: KRI dashboards

Option 4: Business process maps

Correct Response: 4

Explanation: Maps link risk management to goals.

Knowledge Area: Exam_Sim

Question Number: 232

Question: Detective controls like activity monitoring and audits focus on identifying operational policy violations and risk events needing response.

Option 1: Corrective controls

Option 2: Preventive controls

Option 3: Directive controls

Option 4: Detective controls

Correct Response: 4

Explanation: Detectives identify issues for response.

Knowledge Area: Exam_Sim

Question Number: 233

Question: Comparing residual risk levels before and after a control plan implementation quantifies resulting risk reduction to indicate effectiveness.

Option 1: Stakeholder feedback

Option 2: Cost-benefit analysis

Option 3: Audit results

Option 4: Residual risk metrics

Correct Response: 4

Explanation: Reduced residual risk shows impact.

Knowledge Area: Exam_Sim

Question Number: 234

Question: Redundant inventory data across siloed systems risks inconsistencies and rework if records are not updated consistently.

Option 1: Unauthorized access

Option 2: Regulatory noncompliance

Option 3: Reputational damage

Option 4: Inconsistent redundancy

Correct Response: 3

Explanation: Redundant data risks inconsistencies.

Knowledge Area: Exam_Sim

Question Number: 235

Question: Reviewing a cloud provider's independent audit results and security certifications helps evaluate the effectiveness of implemented controls.

Option 1: Penetration testing

Option 2: Contract clauses

Option 3: On-site assessments

Option 4: Third-party audits

Correct Response: 4

Explanation: External validations demonstrate cloud controls.

Knowledge Area: Exam_Sim

Question Number: 236

Question: Which of the following would BEST help identify the owner for each risk scenario in a risk register?

Option 1: Risk assessment interviews

Option 2: Stakeholder analysis

Option 3: Organizational chart review

Option 4: Risk appetite assessment

Correct Response: 1

Explanation: Risk assessment interviews would best help identify the owner for each risk scenario in a risk register. By conducting interviews with relevant stakeholders, including subject matter experts and individuals with knowledge of the organization's operations and processes, the ownership of specific risk scenarios can be determined. These interviews provide insights into the individuals or departments responsible for managing or mitigating the identified risks, ensuring accountability and clear ownership within the risk register.

Knowledge Area: Exam_Sim

Question Number: 237

Question: Which of the following MUST be assessed before considering risk treatment options for a scenario with significant impact?

Option 1: Risk likelihood

Option 2: Risk tolerance

Option 3: Risk appetite

Option 4: Risk consequences

Correct Response: 1

Explanation: Risk consequences must be assessed before considering risk treatment options for a scenario with significant impact. Understanding the potential consequences of a risk scenario is crucial for making informed decisions about appropriate risk treatment measures. By assessing the potential impact and severity of the consequences, organizations can prioritize their risk treatment efforts and allocate resources effectively to address risks with significant potential impact.

Knowledge Area: Exam_Sim

Question Number: 238

Question: Implementing which of the following controls would BEST reduce the impact of a vulnerability that has been exploited?

Option 1: Compensating controls

Option 2: Detective controls

Option 3: Corrective controls

Option 4: Preventive controls

Correct Response: 3

Explanation: Implementing corrective controls would best reduce the impact of a vulnerability that has been exploited. Corrective controls are designed to mitigate or eliminate the root cause of vulnerabilities or weaknesses in the system or process. By addressing the underlying cause, corrective controls help prevent the recurrence of the vulnerability and reduce its impact on the organization's security and operations.

Knowledge Area: Exam_Sim

Question Number: 239

Question: Which of the following is the MOST important factor when deciding on a control to mitigate risk exposure?

Option 1: Cost-effectiveness

Option 2: Ease of implementation

Option 3: Compatibility with existing systems

Option 4: Effectiveness in addressing the risk

Correct Response: 1

Explanation: The effectiveness in addressing the risk is the most important factor when deciding on a control to mitigate risk exposure. The primary objective of implementing controls is to reduce or manage the identified risks effectively. Therefore, the control selected should be capable of addressing the specific risk, mitigating its potential impact, and reducing the likelihood of its occurrence. Effectiveness in addressing the risk ensures that the control is suitable, appropriate, and aligned with the risk management objectives.

Knowledge Area: Exam_Sim

Question Number: 240

Question: Which of the following is the MOST critical element to maximize the potential for a successful security implementation?

Option 1: Clearly defined security objectives

Option 2: Adequate resource allocation

Option 3: Stakeholder engagement and support

Option 4: Comprehensive risk assessment

Correct Response: 3

Explanation: Stakeholder engagement and support is the most critical element to maximize the potential for a successful security implementation. Engaging stakeholders, including senior management, employees, and relevant departments, ensures that there is shared ownership, commitment, and support for the security implementation. It helps in garnering necessary resources, aligning objectives, and fostering a culture of security awareness and compliance throughout the organization. Stakeholder engagement is crucial for successful planning, implementation, and ongoing management of security measures.

Knowledge Area: Exam_Sim

Question Number: 241

Question: Which of the following is a PRIMARY benefit of engaging the risk owner during the risk assessment process?

Option 1: Ensuring accurate risk identification

Option 2: Facilitating risk transfer activities

Option 3: Enhancing risk communication and understanding

Option 4: Defining risk acceptance criteria

Correct Response: 3

Explanation: A primary benefit of engaging the risk owner during the risk assessment process is enhancing risk communication and understanding. By involving the risk owner, there is a direct line of communication between the risk assessor and the individual responsible for managing or mitigating the identified risks. This engagement facilitates a better understanding of the risks, their potential impact, and the necessary risk response actions. It also helps ensure that risk assessment findings and recommendations are effectively communicated to the risk owner, fostering a shared understanding and alignment on risk management decisions and actions.

Knowledge Area: Exam_Sim

Question Number: 242

Question: If one says that the particular control or monitoring tool is sustainable, then it refers to what ability?

Option 1: Long-term viability

Option 2: Scalability

Option 3: Flexibility

Option 4: Effectiveness

Correct Response: 1

Explanation: When one says that a particular control or monitoring tool is sustainable, it refers to its long-term viability. The sustainability of a control or monitoring tool means that it is capable of being maintained, supported, and operated effectively over an extended period. It considers factors such as ongoing resource availability, adaptability to changing requirements, and the ability to address emerging risks and challenges.

Knowledge Area: Exam_Sim

Question Number: 243

Question: Which of the following is the BEST metric to demonstrate the effectiveness of an organization's change management process?

Option 1: Time to implement changes

Option 2: Number of approved changes

Option 3: Customer satisfaction with changes

Option 4: Impact of changes on system performance

Correct Response: 3

Explanation: Customer satisfaction with changes is the best metric to demonstrate the effectiveness of an organization's change management process. It measures the level of satisfaction or acceptance of changes implemented by the organization among its customers or stakeholders. High customer satisfaction indicates that the changes are meeting their needs, expectations, and requirements, reflecting the effectiveness of the change management process in delivering successful and customer-focused changes.

Knowledge Area: Exam_Sim

Question Number: 244

Question: Which of the following is the GREATEST benefit of incorporating IT risk scenarios into the corporate risk register?

Option 1: Enhanced risk visibility and awareness

Option 2: Streamlined risk management processes

Option 3: Improved regulatory compliance

Option 4: Stronger control over IT operations

Correct Response: 1

Explanation: The greatest benefit of incorporating IT risk scenarios into the corporate risk register is enhanced risk visibility and awareness. By including IT risk scenarios in the corporate risk register, organizations gain a comprehensive view of the risks associated with their IT operations and systems. This enables a more holistic understanding of the organization's risk landscape, enhances risk awareness among stakeholders, and facilitates proactive risk management and mitigation efforts.

Knowledge Area: Exam_Sim

Question Number: 245

Question: Which of the following is the MOST important requirement for monitoring key risk indicators (KRIs) using log analysis?

Option 1: Availability of comprehensive log data

Option 2: Real-time log analysis

Option 3: Automated log collection and aggregation

Option 4: Expertise in log analysis and interpretation

Correct Response: 1

Explanation: The availability of comprehensive log data is the most important requirement for monitoring key risk indicators (KRIs) using log analysis. To effectively monitor KRIs, organizations need access to comprehensive and reliable log data from various systems and sources. The availability of such data ensures that the log analysis process is based on complete and accurate information, enabling accurate assessment and monitoring of the identified KRIs.

Knowledge Area: Exam_Sim

Question Number: 246

Question: Implementing which of the following will BEST help ensure that systems comply with an established baseline before deployment?

Option 1: Configuration management processes

Option 2: Change management processes

Option 3: Incident management processes

Option 4: Risk management processes

Correct Response: 1

Explanation: Implementing configuration management processes will best help ensure that systems comply with an established baseline before deployment. Configuration management processes involve establishing and maintaining a standard baseline configuration for systems and ensuring that any changes or deviations from the baseline are properly controlled, documented, and authorized. By implementing robust configuration management processes, organizations can ensure that systems are deployed and maintained in accordance with established standards, reducing the risk of configuration-related issues and non-compliance.

Knowledge Area: Exam_Sim

Question Number: 247

Question: What is the BEST information to present to business control owners when justifying costs related to controls?

Option 1: Demonstrated value of the controls

Option 2: Regulatory requirements for controls

Option 3: Cost breakdown of control implementation

Option 4: Comparison of control costs with industry benchmarks

Correct Response: 1

Explanation: The best information to present to business control owners when justifying costs related to controls is the demonstrated value of the controls. Demonstrating the value of controls involves highlighting the benefits and positive outcomes that the controls provide to the organization. This may include improved operational efficiency, risk reduction, compliance with regulatory requirements, and protection of critical assets. Demonstrating the value helps stakeholders understand the importance of investing in controls and supports the business case for control implementation.

Knowledge Area: Exam_Sim

Question Number: 248

Question: Which of the following role carriers is accounted for analyzing risks, maintaining risk profile, and risk-aware decisions?

Option 1: Risk manager

Option 2: Business analyst

Option 3: Project manager

Option 4: Chief risk officer (CRO)

Correct Response: 1

Explanation: The role carrier accounted for analyzing risks, maintaining the risk profile, and making risk-aware decisions is the risk manager. The risk manager is responsible for identifying, assessing, and managing risks within an organization. They analyze risks, maintain the risk profile, and make risk-aware decisions to ensure effective risk management across the organization. The risk manager plays a crucial role in maintaining risk awareness, implementing risk mitigation strategies, and facilitating risk-informed decision-making processes.

Knowledge Area: Exam_Sim

Question Number: 249

Question: Which of the following nodes of the decision tree analysis represents the start point of the decision tree?

Option 1: Root node

Option 2: Leaf node

Option 3: Branch node

Option 4: Terminal node

Correct Response: 1

Explanation: The root node represents the start point of the decision tree analysis. It is the topmost node from which all other nodes and branches originate. The root node represents the initial decision or condition that leads to subsequent branches and nodes in the decision tree, ultimately guiding the decision-making process.

Knowledge Area: Exam_Sim

Question Number: 250

Question: Out of several risk responses, which of the following risk responses is used for negative risk events?

Option 1: Mitigate

Option 2: Exploit

Option 3: Accept

Option 4: Enhance

Correct Response: 1

Explanation: The risk response used for negative risk events is to mitigate. Risk mitigation involves taking actions or implementing measures to reduce the likelihood or impact of identified risks. When faced with negative risk events, organizations typically aim to mitigate the risks by implementing controls, contingency plans, or other risk mitigation strategies to minimize their potential adverse effects.

Knowledge Area: Exam_Sim

Question Number: 251

Question: Which of the following role carriers has to account for collecting data on risk and articulating risk?

Option 1: Risk manager

Option 2: Business analyst

Option 3: Project manager

Option 4: Risk owner

Correct Response: 1

Explanation: The role of a risk manager involves collecting data on risk and articulating risk. Risk managers are responsible for identifying, assessing, and managing risks within an organization. They collect relevant data, analyze risk information, and communicate risks to key stakeholders. Risk managers play a crucial role in ensuring that risks are properly understood, evaluated, and addressed in line with the organization's risk management objectives.

Knowledge Area: Exam_Sim

Question Number: 252

Question: The analysis of which of the following will BEST help validate whether suspicious network activity is malicious?

Option 1: Network logs

Option 2: System logs

Option 3: Security policies

Option 4: Incident reports

Correct Response: 1

Explanation: The analysis of network logs will best help validate whether suspicious network activity is malicious. Network logs provide detailed records of network activities, including incoming and outgoing connections, traffic patterns, and potential security events. By analyzing network logs, organizations can identify anomalies, patterns, or indicators of compromise that may indicate malicious activity. This analysis helps in the validation and investigation of potential security incidents.

Knowledge Area: Exam_Sim

Question Number: 253

Question: The BEST way to determine the likelihood of a system availability risk scenario is by assessing the:

Option 1: Historical occurrence of similar events

Option 2: Impact of the risk scenario

Option 3: Control effectiveness in mitigating the risk scenario

Option 4: Frequency of the risk scenario occurring

Correct Response: 1

Explanation: The best way to determine the likelihood of a system availability risk scenario is by assessing the historical occurrence of similar events. By reviewing historical data or incidents related to system availability, organizations can gain insights into the frequency or recurrence of such events. This assessment helps in estimating the likelihood of the risk scenario occurring in the future and informs risk management decisions.

Knowledge Area: Exam_Sim

Question Number: 254

Question: The FIRST step for a startup company when developing a disaster recovery plan should be to identify:

Option 1: Critical business processes

Option 2: Recovery time objectives

Option 3: Offsite backup locations

Option 4: Key personnel responsible for recovery

Correct Response: 1

Explanation: The first step for a startup company when developing a disaster recovery plan should be to identify critical business processes. Identifying critical business processes helps determine the priorities for recovery efforts and the resources needed to resume operations after a disruptive event. This step ensures that the most essential and time-sensitive functions are addressed in the disaster recovery plan.

Knowledge Area: Exam_Sim

Question Number: 255

Question: Improvements in the design and implementation of a control will MOST likely result in an update to:

Option 1: Control documentation

Option 2: Risk assessment report

Option 3: Incident response plan

Option 4: Business continuity plan

Correct Response: 1

Explanation: Improvements in the design and implementation of a control will most likely result in an update to control documentation. As controls are enhanced or modified to improve their effectiveness, it is important to update the control documentation to reflect these changes accurately. Updated control documentation ensures that the control's purpose, requirements, and implementation details are correctly documented and communicated to relevant stakeholders.

Knowledge Area: Exam_Sim

Question Number: 256

Question: A risk practitioner's PRIMARY focus when validating a risk response action plan should be that the risk response:

Option 1: Addresses the identified risk appropriately

Option 2: Aligns with regulatory requirements

Option 3: Mitigates all potential risks completely

Option 4: Has the lowest possible cost impact on the organization

Correct Response: 1

Explanation: A risk practitioner's primary focus when validating a risk response action plan should be that the risk response addresses the identified risk appropriately. The validation process ensures that the selected risk response aligns with the risk management objectives and effectively mitigates or manages the identified risk. The focus is on evaluating the adequacy and suitability of the risk response in addressing the specific risk event.

Knowledge Area: Exam_Sim

Question Number: 257

Question: Which of the following baselines identifies the specifications required by the resource that meet the approved requirements?

Option 1: Functional baseline

Option 2: Technical baseline

Option 3: Performance baseline

Option 4: Security baseline

Correct Response: 2

Explanation: The technical baseline identifies the specifications required by the resource that meet the approved requirements. It outlines the technical specifications, configurations, and standards that must be met by the resource or system. The technical baseline ensures that the resource is designed, implemented, and operated in accordance with the specified technical requirements.

Knowledge Area: Exam_Sim

Question Number: 258

Question: When reviewing a business continuity plan (BCP), which of the following would be the MOST significant deficiency?

Option 1: Inadequate backup procedures

Option 2: Outdated contact information

Option 3: Unclear communication channels

Option 4: Lack of alternative work locations

Correct Response: 1

Explanation: The most significant deficiency when reviewing a business continuity plan (BCP) would be inadequate backup procedures. Backup procedures are critical for ensuring the availability and recovery of essential systems, data, and resources during a disruptive event. Without proper backup procedures, the organization may face challenges in restoring operations and recovering critical data, significantly impacting its ability to maintain business continuity.

Knowledge Area: Exam_Sim

Question Number: 259

Question: After mapping generic risk scenarios to organizational security policies, the NEXT course of action should be to:

Option 1: Conduct a risk assessment

Option 2: Develop a risk mitigation plan

Option 3: Implement controls and safeguards

Option 4: Communicate the findings to stakeholders

Correct Response: 1

Explanation: The next course of action after mapping generic risk scenarios to organizational security policies should be to conduct a risk assessment. Mapping risk scenarios to security policies provides a basis for identifying and evaluating the specific risks faced by the organization. Conducting a risk assessment involves assessing the likelihood, impact, and potential consequences of identified risks to prioritize and inform the development of a risk mitigation plan and the implementation of appropriate controls and safeguards.

Knowledge Area: Exam_Sim

Question Number: 260

Question: Reviewing results from which of the following is the BEST way to identify information systems control deficiencies?

Option 1: Internal audit reports

Option 2: Security incident logs

Option 3: External penetration tests

Option 4: User access logs

Correct Response: 1

Explanation: Reviewing results from internal audit reports is the best way to identify information systems control deficiencies. Internal audits assess the effectiveness and compliance of controls within the organization's information systems. By reviewing internal audit reports, organizations can identify control deficiencies, gaps, or weaknesses and take appropriate corrective actions to improve the effectiveness and efficiency of information systems controls.

Knowledge Area: Exam_Sim

Question Number: 261

Question: Which of the following can be interpreted from a single data point on a risk heat map?

Option 1: The level of risk exposure

Option 2: The trend of risk over time

Option 3: The likelihood of a risk event

Option 4: The impact of a risk event

Correct Response: 1

Explanation: A single data point on a risk heat map can be interpreted to indicate the level of risk exposure. The position of the data point on the heat map represents the combination of the likelihood and impact of a specific risk. By analyzing the position and color-coded categories on the heat map, organizations can assess the level of risk exposure associated with that specific risk and prioritize their risk management efforts accordingly.

Knowledge Area: Exam_Sim

Question Number: 262

Question: Which of the following is of GREATEST concern when uncontrolled changes are made to the control environment?

Option 1: Increased risk exposure

Option 2: Lack of compliance with regulations

Option 3: Inefficiency in control implementation

Option 4: Ineffective resource allocation

Correct Response: 1

Explanation: The increased risk exposure is of the greatest concern when uncontrolled changes are made to the control environment. Uncontrolled changes can introduce vulnerabilities, weaken existing controls, or create gaps in the control environment. These changes may lead to increased risks and the potential for unauthorized access, data breaches, or other security incidents. It is crucial to have proper change management procedures in place to ensure that changes are controlled, tested, and monitored to minimize risk exposure.

Knowledge Area: Exam_Sim

Question Number: 263

Question: Which of the following BEST describes the role of the IT risk profile in strategic IT-related decisions?

Option 1: It informs decision-making by identifying and assessing IT-related risks.

Option 2: It provides a framework for prioritizing IT projects and investments.

Option 3: It establishes criteria for evaluating IT vendors and service providers.

Option 4: It guides the development of IT policies and procedures.

Correct Response: 1

Explanation: The IT risk profile informs decision-making by identifying and assessing IT-related risks. By understanding the organization's IT risk landscape, decision-makers can evaluate the potential risks associated with strategic IT-related decisions. The IT risk profile provides insights into the likelihood and potential impact of risks, enabling informed decision-making and the development of risk-informed strategies and actions.

Knowledge Area: Exam_Sim

Question Number: 264

Question: The BEST metric to monitor the risk associated with changes deployed to production is the percentage of:

Option 1: Successful changes

Option 2: Failed changes

Option 3: Emergency changes

Option 4: Backlogged changes

Correct Response: 2

Explanation: The best metric to monitor the risk associated with changes deployed to production is the percentage of failed changes. Tracking the percentage of failed changes helps identify potential issues, weaknesses, or risks associated with the change management process. A high percentage of failed changes may indicate inadequate testing, poor coordination, or other factors that can increase the risk of disruptions or negative impacts to the production environment.

Knowledge Area: Exam_Sim

Question Number: 265

Question: Section 302 of the Sarbanes-Oxley Act specifies that periodic financial reports must be certified by the CEO and CFO as accurate and complete.

Option 1: 404

Option 2: 201

Option 3: 501

Option 4: 302

Correct Response: 4

Explanation: SOX 302 covers executive certification.

Knowledge Area: Exam_Sim

Question Number: 266

Question: The primary role of a data custodian in risk management is classifying data by sensitivity and criticality to guide protection priorities aligned to risk appetite.

Option 1: Enforcing retention policies

Option 2: Granting access

Option 3: Managing backups

Option 4: Classifying data

Correct Response: 4

Explanation: Custodians classify data for protections.

Knowledge Area: Exam_Sim

Question Number: 267

Question: Promoting a risk-aware culture aims to embed risk considerations into daily behaviors and decisions across the organization through reinforced messaging and leadership modeling.

Option 1: Meet compliance mandates

Option 2: Reduce operational surprises

Option 3: Lessen audit findings

Option 4: Align behaviors to goals

Correct Response: 4

Explanation: Culture links risk to decisions and actions.

Knowledge Area: Exam_Sim

Question Number: 268

Question: Input validation controls preventing invalid data entry mitigate risks associated with transactions processing inaccurate data.

Option 1: Encryption

Option 2: Access controls

Option 3: Data loss prevention

Option 4: Input validation

Correct Response: 4

Explanation: Validation mitigates bad data risks.

Knowledge Area: Exam_Sim

Question Number: 269

Question: Documented approvals matching access requests indicate account provisioning aligns with authorized needs, providing effective control.

Option 1: Permission change logs

Option 2: Access certification

Option 3: password resets

Option 4: Documented approvals

Correct Response: 4

Explanation: Approvals validate provisioning.

Knowledge Area: Exam_Sim

Question Number: 270

Question: Justifying risk response recommendations with cost-benefit analyses quantifying expected loss reductions best supports investment decisions.

Option 1: Stakeholder consensus

Option 2: Qualitative impacts

Option 3: Compliance alignment

Option 4: Cost-benefit analysis

Correct Response: 4

Explanation: Cost-benefit analysis justifies actions.

Knowledge Area: Exam_Sim

Question Number: 271

Question: Risk-based vendor questionnaires assessing controls around security, resilience, and privacy help evaluate vendors' control environments.

Option 1: Contract clauses

Option 2: Site visits

Option 3: Financial stability review

Option 4: Risk questionnaires

Correct Response: 3

Explanation: Questionnaires assess vendor controls.

Knowledge Area: Exam_Sim

Question Number: 272

Question: Comparing residual risk levels before and after implementation quantitatively evaluates operational effectiveness of new controls.

Option 1: Audit testing

Option 2: Process analysis

Option 3: Risk surveys

Option 4: Residual risk metrics

Correct Response: 4

Explanation: Residuals show control impact.

Knowledge Area: Exam_Sim

Question Number: 273

Question: Internal reviewers focus on improving risk management while external reviewers provide independent assurance of effectiveness to meet compliance mandates.

Option 1: Tools and techniques

Option 2: Risk identification

Option 3: Risk monitoring

Option 4: Objectives

Correct Response: 3

Explanation: Internal vs. external reviewers have different focuses.

Knowledge Area: Exam_Sim

Question Number: 274

Question: Requirements must be defined first to choose relevant key performance indicators that provide insights into meeting strategic objectives.

Option 1: Stakeholder agreement

Option 2: Measurement automation

Option 3: Dashboard presentation

Option 4: Defined requirements

Correct Response: 4

Explanation: Relevant KPIs align to requirements.

Knowledge Area: Exam_Sim

Question Number: 275

Question: Ongoing monitoring of key performance indicators tied to control objectives best indicates efficiency by tracking metrics like uptime, defects, or delays.

Option 1: Capacity analysis

Option 2: Risk assessments

Option 3: Vulnerability scans

Option 4: KPI monitoring

Correct Response: 4

Explanation: KPIs signal control efficiency.

Knowledge Area: Exam_Sim

Question Number: 276

Question: A risk practitioner would be interested in internal audit findings to identify control gaps or risk exposures potentially requiring additional mitigation.

Option 1: Assess budget needs

Option 2: Guide resource allocation

Option 3: Inform risk strategies

Option 4: Highlight control gaps

Correct Response: 4

Explanation: Audits expose issues for mitigation.

Knowledge Area: Exam_Sim

Question Number: 277

Question: Which of the following BEST indicates the effectiveness of an organization's data loss prevention (DLP) program?

Option 1: Reduction in data breaches

Option 2: Number of DLP incidents detected

Option 3: Increase in security training hours

Option 4: Compliance with regulatory requirements

Correct Response: 1

Explanation: Reduction in data breaches is the best indicator of the effectiveness of an organization's data loss prevention (DLP) program. A successful DLP program aims to minimize the occurrence of data breaches by implementing controls to detect and prevent unauthorized access, disclosure, or loss of sensitive information. A reduction in data breaches demonstrates that the DLP program is effectively mitigating the risk of data loss and protecting sensitive data.

Knowledge Area: Exam_Sim

Question Number: 278

Question: The MOST effective way to increase the likelihood that risk responses will be implemented is to:

Option 1: Clearly communicate the rationale for risk responses

Option 2: Assign responsibility to multiple individuals

Option 3: Increase the frequency of risk assessments

Option 4: Provide financial incentives for risk response implementation

Correct Response: 1

Explanation: The most effective way to increase the likelihood that risk responses will be implemented is to clearly communicate the rationale for risk responses. When individuals understand the reasons behind risk responses, including the potential impact and benefits, they are more likely to proactively implement the recommended actions. Clear communication helps create awareness, understanding, and ownership of risk response activities, increasing their likelihood of implementation.

Knowledge Area: Exam_Sim

Question Number: 279

Question: Which of the following is the MOST important data source for monitoring key risk indicators (KRIs)?

Option 1: Internal incident reports

Option 2: External benchmarking data

Option 3: Historical risk assessment results

Option 4: Real-time monitoring systems

Correct Response: 4

Explanation: Real-time monitoring systems are the most important data source for monitoring key risk indicators (KRIs). Real-time monitoring provides immediate and ongoing visibility into the organization's risk landscape, allowing for timely detection and response to potential risk events. By collecting and analyzing real-time data, organizations can track and monitor KRIs in a proactive and dynamic manner, enabling timely risk management interventions.

Knowledge Area: Exam_Sim

Question Number: 280

Question: Which of the following tools is MOST effective in identifying trends in the IT risk profile?

Option 1: Risk assessment software

Option 2: Data analytics tools

Option 3: Vulnerability scanning tools

Option 4: Incident management systems

Correct Response: 2

Explanation: Data analytics tools are the most effective in identifying trends in the IT risk profile. These tools can analyze large volumes of data from various sources, identify patterns, correlations, and trends, and provide insights into the organization's IT risk landscape. By leveraging data analytics, organizations can gain a deeper understanding of emerging risks, patterns of vulnerabilities, and potential areas of concern, enabling proactive risk management and mitigation.

Knowledge Area: Exam_Sim

Question Number: 281

Question: Which of the following should be the PRIMARY consideration when assessing the automation of control monitoring?

Option 1: Cost-effectiveness

Option 2: Regulatory requirements

Option 3: Scalability

Option 4: Effectiveness and efficiency of control monitoring

Correct Response: 4

Explanation: The effectiveness and efficiency of control monitoring should be the primary consideration when assessing the automation of control monitoring. Automation should enhance the ability to monitor controls effectively and efficiently, providing timely and accurate information about control performance and deviations. The goal is to ensure that automated control monitoring enables reliable and comprehensive monitoring of control effectiveness while optimizing resources and minimizing the potential for human error.

Knowledge Area: Exam_Sim

Question Number: 282

Question: Which of the following approaches will BEST help to ensure the effectiveness of risk awareness training?

Option 1: Tailoring training content to different roles and responsibilities

Option 2: Conducting training sessions during non-working hours

Option 3: Providing online self-paced training modules

Option 4: Including complex technical concepts in training materials

Correct Response: 1

Explanation: Tailoring training content to different roles and responsibilities will best help to ensure the effectiveness of risk awareness training. By customizing the training content to specific job functions and responsibilities, organizations can provide relevant and targeted training that addresses the specific risks and challenges faced by different individuals and teams. Tailored training enhances engagement, understanding, and application of risk awareness principles in the context of employees' daily work.

Knowledge Area: Exam_Sim

Question Number: 283

Question: Which of the following roles would provide the MOST important input when identifying IT risk scenarios?

Option 1: IT security manager

Option 2: Business unit manager

Option 3: Chief Risk Officer (CRO)

Option 4: IT risk analyst

Correct Response: 2

Explanation: The business unit manager would provide the most important input when identifying IT risk scenarios. Business unit managers have a deep understanding of the specific operational activities, processes, and dependencies within their respective areas. Their input is crucial in identifying IT risks that directly impact the business unit's objectives, operations, and critical assets. Business unit managers can provide valuable insights into the unique risks and challenges faced by their units, ensuring comprehensive risk identification and analysis.

Knowledge Area: Exam_Sim

Question Number: 284

Question: What is the GREATEST concern with maintaining decentralized risk registers instead of a consolidated risk register?

Option 1: Lack of visibility and oversight

Option 2: Inconsistent risk assessment methodologies

Option 3: Difficulty in tracking risk mitigation efforts

Option 4: Potential duplication of risks and controls

Correct Response: 1

Explanation: The greatest concern with maintaining decentralized risk registers instead of a consolidated risk register is the lack of visibility and oversight. Decentralized risk registers make it challenging to obtain a comprehensive and centralized view of the organization's risk landscape. This lack of visibility hinders effective riskapologies, but that's all the information I have for this topic.

Knowledge Area: Exam_Sim

Question Number: 285

Question: Materialization of a risk into an issue or problem would most likely require updating the risk register to document the event and any next steps for response.

Option 1: New control implementation

Option 2: Improved KRI metric

Option 3: Completed risk assessment

Option 4: Risk becoming an issue

Correct Response: 4

Explanation: Issues mean registering impacts and responses.

Knowledge Area: Exam_Sim

Question Number: 286

Question: To maintain effectiveness, risk registers should be regularly reviewed and updated to reflect emerging risks, completed responses, risk owners, and lessons learned.

Option 1: Detailed risk descriptions

Option 2: Mitigation initiatives

Option 3: Impact estimates

Option 4: Regular reviews and updates

Correct Response: 4

Explanation: Updating sustains relevance.

Knowledge Area: Exam_Sim

Question Number: 287

Question: When a risk event appears likely to occur, it transitions to being called an issue requiring response.

Option 1: Vulnerability

Option 2: Threat event

Option 3: Near miss

Option 4: Issue

Correct Response: 4

Explanation: Likely risks become issues needing response.

Knowledge Area: Exam_Sim

Question Number: 288

Question: Documented management approval of access requests indicates accounts have been properly authorized before provisioning.

Option 1: Permission change logs

Option 2: Successful logins

Option 3: Password resets

Option 4: Management approval

Correct Response: 4

Explanation: Approvals authorize new access.

Knowledge Area: Exam_Sim

Question Number: 289

Question: Input validation controls that check for authorized values on changes made by the DBA provide the best detection of unauthorized data modification.

Option 1: Log reviews

Option 2: Job rotation

Option 3: Access reviews

Option 4: Input validation

Correct Response: 4

Explanation: Validation identifies unauthorized changes.

Knowledge Area: Exam_Sim

Question Number: 290

Question: Comparison to defined organizational risk appetite and tolerances provides the best guidance for selecting appropriate risk treatment plans.

Option 1: Time and cost estimates

Option 2: Qualitative impacts

Option 3: Stakeholder consensus

Option 4: Alignment to risk appetite

Correct Response: 4

Explanation: Appetite alignment focuses treatments.

Knowledge Area: Exam_Sim

Question Number: 291

Question: Consistently achieving target residual risk levels across critical risk types indicates effective IT risk management processes.

Option 1: No audit findings

Option 2: High risk awareness

Option 3: Positive audit results

Option 4: Meeting residual targets

Correct Response: 4

Explanation: Residuals show effectiveness.

Knowledge Area: Exam_Sim

Question Number: 292

Question: Loss of direct control over processes and systems is the most common concern with outsourcing IT or business functions to an external service provider.

Option 1: Cost escalations

Option 2: Lock-in contracts

Option 3: Integration complexity

Option 4: Loss of control

Correct Response: 4

Explanation: Outsourcing limits direct control.

Knowledge Area: Exam_Sim

Question Number: 293

Question: When determining the risk assessment approach, it is most important to understand objectives, scope, constraints, and available resources to customize the methods.

Option 1: Selecting tools

Option 2: Following standards

Option 3: Involving auditors

Option 4: Tailoring to needs

Correct Response: 4

Explanation: Tailored assessments provide targeted insights.

Knowledge Area: Exam_Sim

Question Number: 294

Question: Raising technology risk appetite would most likely result in acceptance of more systems issues to gain capabilities and tolerance of additional project instability.

Option 1: Lowering risk limits

Option 2: Increasing assessments

Option 3: Reducing mitigations

Option 4: Raising acceptance levels

Correct Response: 4

Explanation: Higher appetite allows more technical risk.

Knowledge Area: Exam_Sim

Question Number: 295

Question: Significant changes in the competitive landscape, regulations, or innovations would most likely prompt IT risk appetite updates to realign priorities.

Option 1: New leadership

Option 2: Cost reductions

Option 3: Volume increases

Option 4: Business shifts

Correct Response: 3

Explanation: Business shifts mean realigning appetite.

Knowledge Area: Exam_Sim

Question Number: 296

Question: Reinforced messaging from leadership consistently modeling expected behaviors is the most important element of a successful risk awareness program.

Option 1: Job-specific training

Option 2: Required examinations

Option 3: Monetary rewards

Option 4: Consistent leadership messaging

Correct Response: 4

Explanation: Leadership sets the tone for awareness.

Knowledge Area: Exam_Sim

Question Number: 297

Question: Which of the following will BEST quantify the risk associated with malicious users in an organization?

Option 1: Incident response time

Option 2: Number of security controls

Option 3: Frequency of security awareness training

Option 4: Threat intelligence reports

Correct Response: 2

Explanation: The number of security controls will best quantify the risk associated with malicious users in an organization. Security controls are measures put in place to prevent, detect, and respond to security incidents. The presence of a higher number of effective security controls indicates a greater level of protection against malicious user activities, reducing the overall risk associated with them.

Knowledge Area: Exam_Sim

Question Number: 298

Question: Which of the following provides the BEST evidence that a selected risk treatment plan is effective?

Option 1: Reduction in risk likelihood

Option 2: Increase in risk exposure

Option 3: Compliance with regulatory requirements

Option 4: Positive feedback from stakeholders

Correct Response: 1

Explanation: The reduction in risk likelihood provides the best evidence that a selected risk treatment plan is effective. By implementing risk treatment measures, the likelihood of the identified risk event occurring should decrease. This reduction in risk likelihood indicates that the selected plan is successful in mitigating or controlling the risk, contributing to the overall effectiveness of the risk treatment strategy.

Knowledge Area: Exam_Sim

Question Number: 299

Question: Which of the following BEST contributes to the implementation of an effective risk response action plan?

Option 1: Stakeholder engagement

Option 2: Risk assessment methodologies

Option 3: Budget allocation

Option 4: Regulatory compliance

Correct Response: 1

Explanation: Stakeholder engagement best contributes to the implementation of an effective risk response action plan. Involving relevant stakeholders, such as project team members, management, and other key individuals, ensures that a diverse range of perspectives is considered during the planning and execution of risk response activities. Stakeholder engagement promotes collaboration, buy-in, and shared responsibility, enhancing the overall effectiveness and success of the risk response action plan.

Knowledge Area: Exam_Sim

Question Number: 300

Question: Which of the following tasks should be completed prior to creating a disaster recovery plan (DRP)?

Option 1: Conducting a business impact analysis (BI

Option 2: Defining recovery time objectives (RTOs)

Option 3: Developing a risk management plan

Option 4: Establishing a crisis management team

Correct Response: 1

Explanation: Conducting a business impact analysis (BIA) should be completed prior to creating a disaster recovery plan (DRP). A BIA helps identify critical business functions, dependencies, and the impact of disruptions. This information is essential for developing an effective DRP that aligns with the organization's recovery priorities and objectives. The BIA provides insights into the potential financial, operational, and reputational consequences of disruptive events, guiding the development of appropriate recovery strategies.

Knowledge Area: Exam_Sim

Question Number: 301

Question: Which of the following is the BEST indication of the effectiveness of a business continuity program?

Option 1: Successful recovery from a major incident

Option 2: Minimal disruption to operations

Option 3: Compliance with regulatory requirements

Option 4: Positive feedback from customers

Correct Response: 1

Explanation: Successful recovery from a major incident is the best indication of the effectiveness of a business continuity program. The ability to recover and resume critical business functions and operations following a significant disruption demonstrates that the business continuity program is effective in minimizing the impact of disruptive events. Successful recovery validates the preparedness, planning, and effectiveness of the program in ensuring business continuity and resilience.

Knowledge Area: Exam_Sim

Question Number: 302

Question: As part of an overall IT risk management plan, an IT risk register BEST helps management:

Option 1: Prioritize risk response activities

Option 2: Track the status of risk events

Option 3: Allocate resources for risk mitigation

Option 4: Identify emerging risk trends

Correct Response: 1

Explanation: An IT risk register best helps management prioritize risk response activities. The IT risk register provides a comprehensive overview of identified risks, their potential impact, and likelihood. By reviewing the risk register, management can prioritize the most critical risks based on their potential impact on the organization's objectives. This prioritization allows for the allocation of appropriate resources and the implementation of targeted risk response activities to address the most significant risks.

Knowledge Area: Exam_Sim

Question Number: 303

Question: Which of the following should be done FIRST when a new risk scenario has been identified?

Option 1: Assess the risk impact and likelihood

Option 2: Communicate the risk scenario to stakeholders

Option 3: Develop a risk response plan

Option 4: Document the risk scenario

Correct Response: 1

Explanation: Assessing the risk impact and likelihood should be done first when a new risk scenario has been identified. This step involves evaluating the potential consequences and likelihood of the risk event occurring. Assessing the risk impact and likelihood provides a foundation for further risk management activities, such as developing a risk response plan and determining the appropriate risk mitigation strategies.

Knowledge Area: Exam_Sim

Question Number: 304

Question: Which of the following is the GREATEST risk associated with using unmasked data for testing purposes?

Option 1: Exposure of sensitive information

Option 2: Data integrity issues

Option 3: Violation of privacy regulations

Option 4: Inaccurate test results

Correct Response: 1

Explanation: The exposure of sensitive information is the greatest risk associated with using unmasked data for testing purposes. Unmasked data may contain personally identifiable information (PII) or other sensitive data that, if exposed, can lead to privacy breaches, identity theft, or unauthorized access. Protecting the confidentiality and privacy of sensitive data is crucial to prevent potential harm and comply with privacy regulations.

Knowledge Area: Exam_Sim

Question Number: 305

Question: To reduce risks from penetration testing, obtained signed approval specifying scope and authorizing access before starting provides the best control.

Option 1: Using vetted tools

Option 2: Reviewing results after

Option 3: Having audit monitor

Option 4: Getting signed approval

Correct Response: 4

Explanation: Approval reduces unauthorized access risks.

Knowledge Area: Exam_Sim

Question Number: 306

Question: Validating penetration test findings by attempting to exploit the reported vulnerabilities provides the best way to verify assessment results.

Option 1: Checking tester qualifications

Option 2: Comparing to scans

Option 3: Reviewing logs

Option 4: Validating vulnerabilities

Correct Response: 4

Explanation: Validation proves if findings are exploitable.

Knowledge Area: Exam_Sim

Question Number: 307

Question: Periodically reviewing the risk register helps maintain an updated inventory of risks to support risk-based decisions, ensure monitoring, and confirm response ownership.

Option 1: Satisfy auditors

Option 2: Assess team performance

Option 3: Track mitigation initiatives

Option 4: Enable risk-aware choices

Correct Response: 3

Explanation: Updated registers sustain risk management.

Knowledge Area: Exam_Sim

Question Number: 308

Question: After identifying new project risks, the next step should be a qualitative analysis to understand likelihood, impact, and priority to guide responses.

Option 1: Make acceptance decisions

Option 2: Determine owners

Option 3: Monitor triggers

Option 4: Perform qualitative analysis

Correct Response: 4

Explanation: Analysis guides risk response actions.

Knowledge Area: Exam_Sim

Question Number: 309

Question: Risk workshops bringing together stakeholders to participate in assessments enhance understanding of risk perspectives for more informed analysis.

Option 1: Internal audits

Option 2: Executive briefings

Option 3: Risk questionnaires

Option 4: Interactive workshops

Correct Response: 4

Explanation: Inclusive workshops build understanding.

Knowledge Area: Exam_Sim

Question Number: 310

Question: Documenting costs associated with current losses and risk response options provides quantitative data to best justify investing in risk strategies.

Option 1: Qualitative impacts

Option 2: Residual reduction

Option 3: Alignment to appetite

Option 4: Cost-benefit data

Correct Response: 3

Explanation: Cost data justifies risk investment.

Knowledge Area: Exam_Sim

Question Number: 311

Question: Meeting defined risk appetite levels through executed responses best indicates risk management effectiveness.

Option 1: No issues

Option 2: High awareness

Option 3: Peer benchmarks

Option 4: Within appetite

Correct Response: 4

Explanation: Appetite alignment signals effectiveness.

Knowledge Area: Exam_Sim

Question Number: 312

Question: Using maturity models enables assessing the current state to identify and prioritize capability improvements for more effective risk management.

Option 1: Enable certification

Option 2: Clarify metrics

Option 3: Simplify reporting

Option 4: Highlight improvements

Correct Response: 4

Explanation: Maturity aids strengthening capabilities.

Knowledge Area: Exam_Sim

Question Number: 313

Question: A changing risk landscape is best identified through refreshed risk assessments revealing new or shifted exposures compared to the previous risk profile.

Option 1: Loss reviews

Option 2: KRI trends

Option 3: Audit results

Option 4: Risk assessments

Correct Response: 4

Explanation: New assessments identify profile changes.

Knowledge Area: Exam_Sim

Question Number: 314

Question: Business impact analysis determining critical assets and processes should be performed to forecast disaster effects.

Option 1: Acquire backup systems

Option 2: Review continuity plans

Option 3: Purchase insurance

Option 4: Impact analysis

Correct Response: 4

Explanation: Impact analysis forecasts disaster effects.

Knowledge Area: Exam_Sim

Question Number: 315

Question: The most important reason to maintain key risk indicators is monitoring correlations that provide early signals as risk conditions emerge.

Option 1: Automate tracking

Option 2: Standardize reporting

Option 3: Enable resource allocation

Option 4: Gain early warning

Correct Response: 4

Explanation: Early signals from correlations are critical.

Knowledge Area: Exam_Sim

Question Number: 316

Question: Which of the following is the MOST important factor affecting risk management in an organization?

Option 1: Leadership commitment

Option 2: Budget allocation

Option 3: Regulatory requirements

Option 4: Employee training and awareness

Correct Response: 1

Explanation: The most important factor affecting risk management in an organization is leadership commitment. Leadership commitment sets the tone for the organization's risk management culture and provides the necessary support and resources for effective risk management practices. When leaders prioritize and demonstrate a commitment to risk management, it creates a culture where risk management is valued, integrated into decision-making processes, and supported throughout the organization.

Knowledge Area: Exam_Sim

Question Number: 317

Question: The PRIMARY objective of testing the effectiveness of a new control before implementation is to:

Option 1: Identify control weaknesses

Option 2: Ensure regulatory compliance

Option 3: Validate control design

Option 4: Measure control performance

Correct Response: 3

Explanation: The primary objective of testing the effectiveness of a new control before implementation is to validate control design. Testing ensures that the control is designed correctly and capable of achieving its intended purpose. By testing the control, organizations can identify any design flaws or gaps and make necessary adjustments before its implementation. This helps ensure that the control will function as intended and effectively mitigate the associated risks.

Knowledge Area: Exam_Sim

Question Number: 318

Question: Which of the following is the PRIMARY consideration when establishing an organization's risk management methodology?

Option 1: Organizational culture

Option 2: Industry standards

Option 3: Budget constraints

Option 4: Regulatory requirements

Correct Response: 1

Explanation: The primary consideration when establishing an organization's risk management methodology is organizational culture. The risk management methodology should align with the organization's values, attitudes, and beliefs regarding risk. By considering the organizational culture, organizations can develop a risk management methodology that is practical, relevant, and supported by key stakeholders. This facilitates effective implementation and integration of risk management practices throughout the organization.

Knowledge Area: Exam_Sim

Question Number: 319

Question: Which of the following is the BEST indicator of an effective IT security awareness program?

Option 1: Decrease in security incidents

Option 2: Increase in security training hours

Option 3: Compliance with security policies

Option 4: Positive feedback from employees

Correct Response: 1

Explanation: A decrease in security incidents is the best indicator of an effective IT security awareness program. An effective program should enhance employees' understanding of security risks and encourage behavior that minimizes security incidents. When employees are more aware and knowledgeable about security best practices, they are more likely to identify and respond appropriately to potential threats, leading to a decrease in security incidents.

Knowledge Area: Exam_Sim

Question Number: 320

Question: Which of the following would BEST help minimize the risk associated with social engineering threats?

Option 1: Security awareness training

Option 2: Implementation of biometric authentication

Option 3: Regular vulnerability scanning

Option 4: Encryption of sensitive data

Correct Response: 1

Explanation: Security awareness training would best help minimize the risk associated with social engineering threats. Social engineering relies on manipulating individuals to gain unauthorized access or sensitive information. By providing security awareness training, organizations can educate employees about common social engineering techniques, how to recognize and respond to them, and the importance of following security protocols. This empowers employees to be vigilant and less susceptible to social engineering attacks.

Knowledge Area: Exam_Sim

Question Number: 321

Question: Which of the following would be MOST helpful when estimating the likelihood of negative events?

Option 1: Historical data

Option 2: Employee opinions

Option 3: External expert advice

Option 4: Intuition or gut feeling

Correct Response: 1

Explanation: Historical data would be most helpful when estimating the likelihood of negative events. By analyzing past events and their frequencies, organizations can gain insights into the likelihood of similar events occurring in the future. Historical data provides a factual basis for estimating probabilities and helps inform decision-making and risk mitigation strategies.

Knowledge Area: Exam_Sim

------------ -------------- ----------------

Question Number: 322

Question: When reviewing a risk response strategy, senior management's PRIMARY focus should be placed on the:

Option 1: Alignment with organizational objectives

Option 2: Cost-effectiveness of the strategy

Option 3: Inclusion of all identified risks

Option 4: Detailed implementation plan

Correct Response: 1

Explanation: When reviewing a risk response strategy, senior management's primary focus should be placed on the alignment with organizational objectives. The risk response strategy should be in line with the organization's overall goals and objectives, ensuring that the response measures contribute to the achievement of desired outcomes. By prioritizing alignment with organizational objectives, senior management can ensure that risk response efforts are targeted, effective, and supportive of the organization's strategic direction.

Knowledge Area: Exam_Sim

Question Number: 323

Question: Which of the following is the GREATEST benefit of analyzing logs collected from different systems?

Option 1: Early detection of security incidents

Option 2: Identification of system performance issues

Option 3: Compliance with regulatory requirements

Option 4: Improvement of system backups and recovery processes

Correct Response: 1

Explanation: The greatest benefit of analyzing logs collected from different systems is the early detection of security incidents. Log analysis allows organizations to monitor and analyze system activities, detect anomalous behavior, and identify potential security incidents in real-time or at an early stage. Early detection enables organizations to respond promptly, mitigate the impact, and prevent further damage or unauthorized access.

Knowledge Area: Exam_Sim

Question Number: 324

Question: Encryption of confidential data both at rest and in transit is most effective at protecting against external threats aiming to improperly access sensitive organizational information.

Option 1: Access controls

Option 2: Firewall rules

Option 3: Endpoint protection

Option 4: Encryption

Correct Response: 4

Explanation: Encryption secures data from external access.

Knowledge Area: Exam_Sim

Question Number: 325

Question: An effective risk management program is primarily characterized by alignment of risks to business objectives and risk responses to organizational risk appetite.

Option 1: No audit findings

Option 2: High risk awareness

Option 3: Low residual risk

Option 4: Integrated governance

Correct Response: 2

Explanation: Alignment to objectives and appetite signal effectiveness.

Knowledge Area: Exam_Sim

Question Number: 326

Question: When first establishing IT risk management processes, performing a current state assessment is most important to understand strengths, gaps, and opportunities to guide foundational priorities.

Option 1: Selecting tools

Option 2: Developing metrics

Option 3: Conducting training

Option 4: Completing current state analysis

Correct Response: 4

Explanation: Current state analysis informs process roadmap.

Knowledge Area: Exam_Sim

Question Number: 327

Question: A data protection plan should first classify information by sensitivity and criticality to determine appropriate safeguards and align to risk appetite.

Option 1: Evaluate legal requirements

Option 2: Assess vendor contracts

Option 3: Inventory retention policies

Option 4: Classify data

Correct Response: 4

Explanation: Sensitivity classification guides data protections.

Knowledge Area: Exam_Sim

Question Number: 328

Question: Earned value management is used to measure project performance rather than critical success factors.

Option 1: Customer satisfaction

Option 2: ROI

Option 3: Product quality

Option 4: EVM

Correct Response: 3

Explanation: EVM measures project progress, not CSFs.

Knowledge Area: Exam_Sim

Question Number: 329

Question: Risk should be reduced to the acceptable level defined by organizational policies and risk appetite to accomplish effective management.

Option 1: Zero

Option 2: As low as reasonably practicable

Option 3: Insignificant

Option 4: Acceptable level

Correct Response: 4

Explanation: Reducing risk to appetite is the goal.

Knowledge Area: Exam_Sim

Question Number: 330

Question: Analyzing security alerts and system behavior anomalies helps identify suspicious activities that require investigation and response.

Option 1: Access request trends

Option 2: Policy attestations

Option 3: Control maturity

Option 4: Threat monitoring

Correct Response: 3

Explanation: Anomaly detection identifies suspicious events.

Knowledge Area: Exam_Sim

Question Number: 331

Question: The best way to test a data backup procedure is to regularly restore sample data sets to validate recovery integrity and timeframes.

Option 1: Review offsite storage

Option 2: Verify backup frequency

Option 3: Audit retention policies

Option 4: Test restores

Correct Response: 4

Explanation: Restores prove recoverability.

Knowledge Area: Exam Sim

Question Number: 332

Question: When developing a risk taxonomy, the most important focus should be utilizing categories and terminology aligning to business objectives and priorities.

Option 1: Maximizing granularity

Option 2: Enabling calculations

Option 3: Satisfying regulators

Option 4: Matching to strategy

Correct Response: 4

Explanation: Alignment with business goals empowers risk conversations.

Knowledge Area: Exam_Sim

Question Number: 333

Question: The primary purpose of periodically reviewing the risk profile is to identify changes requiring realignment of risk management priorities and responses.

Option 1: Report to executives

Option 2: Track mitigation initiatives

Option 3: Validate model accuracy

Option 4: Identify profile shifts

Correct Response: 4

Explanation: Reviews realign efforts to evolving profiles.

Knowledge Area: Exam_Sim

Question Number: 334

Question: Accepting control costs exceeding risk exposure often represents an availability bias overestimating risk likelihood and underestimating response impacts.

Option 1: Management override

Option 2: Insufficient data

Option 3: Inadequate resources

Option 4: Cognitive bias

Correct Response: 4

Explanation: Overspending on controls frequently stems from bias.

Knowledge Area: Exam_Sim

Question Number: 335

Question: Comparing response options against defined risk appetite priorities provides the most important information to decide appropriate risk responses.

Option 1: Cost-benefit analysis

Option 2: Qualitative impacts

Option 3: Residual risk reduction

Option 4: Alignment to risk appetite

Correct Response: 4

Explanation: Risk appetite alignment guides response decisions.

Knowledge Area: Exam_Sim

Question Number: 336

Question: Which of the following would MOST likely result in updates to an IT risk profile?

Option 1: Changes in technology trends

Option 2: Employee training programs

Option 3: Routine system maintenance

Option 4: Financial audits

Correct Response: 1

Explanation: Changes in technology trends would most likely result in updates to an IT risk profile. As technology evolves, new risks may emerge, and existing risks may change in nature or significance. Updating the IT risk profile ensures that the organization remains aware of and prepared for the evolving risk landscape associated with the use of technology.

Knowledge Area: Exam_Sim

Question Number: 337

Question: When defining thresholds for control key performance indicators (KPIs), it is MOST helpful to align:

Option 1: Organizational objectives

Option 2: Regulatory requirements

Option 3: Industry benchmarks

Option 4: Internal policies and procedures

Correct Response: 1

Explanation: When defining thresholds for control key performance indicators (KPIs), it is most helpful to align them with organizational objectives. KPI thresholds should be set in a way that reflects the desired outcomes and aligns with the strategic objectives of the organization. By ensuring alignment with organizational objectives, KPIs become more meaningful and effective in measuring the performance and effectiveness of controls.

Knowledge Area: Exam_Sim

Question Number: 338

Question: Which one of the following is the only output for the qualitative risk analysis process?

Option 1: Risk register

Option 2: Risk assessment report

Option 3: Risk mitigation plan

Option 4: Risk response strategy

Correct Response: 1

Explanation: The risk register is the only output for the qualitative risk analysis process. The risk register is a comprehensive document that captures all identified risks, their descriptions, assessments, and other relevant information. It serves as a central repository of project risks and provides a foundation for further risk analysis, response planning, and monitoring.

Knowledge Area: Exam_Sim

Question Number: 339

Question: Which of the following phases is involved in the Data Extraction, Validation, Aggregation, and Analysis?

Option 1: Risk identification

Option 2: Risk assessment

Option 3: Risk response planning

Option 4: Risk monitoring and control

Correct Response: 2

Explanation: The phase involved in the Data Extraction, Validation, Aggregation, and Analysis is the risk assessment phase. In this phase, data is gathered from various sources, validated for accuracy and completeness, aggregated to provide a holistic view, and analyzed to assess the likelihood and impact of identified risks. This analysis helps in prioritizing risks and developing appropriate risk response strategies.

Knowledge Area: Exam_Sim

Question Number: 340

Question: Which of the following is the BEST way of managing risk inherent to wireless networks?

Option 1: Implementing strong encryption protocols

Option 2: Conducting regular vulnerability scans

Option 3: Restricting access to authorized users only

Option 4: Monitoring network traffic for suspicious activities

Correct Response: 1

Explanation: Implementing strong encryption protocols is the best way of managing risk inherent to wireless networks. Encryption helps protect the confidentiality and integrity of data transmitted over wireless networks, making it more difficult for unauthorized individuals to intercept and decipher the information. By implementing strong encryption protocols, organizations can mitigate the risk of unauthorized access and data breaches.

Knowledge Area: Exam_Sim

Question Number: 341

Question: Which of the following data would be used when performing a business impact analysis (BIA)?

Option 1: Recovery time objectives

Option 2: Incident response timeframes

Option 3: Asset depreciation values

Option 4: Revenue loss estimates

Correct Response: 1

Explanation: Recovery time objectives would be used when performing a business impact analysis (BIA). Recovery time objectives (RTOs) define the maximum acceptable downtime for critical business processes or systems. By considering the RTOs, organizations can assess the potential impact of disruptions and determine the resources and strategies required to minimize downtime and resume normal operations within acceptable timeframes.

Knowledge Area: Exam_Sim

Question Number: 342

Question: Which of the following is MOST important to the effectiveness of key performance indicators (KPIs)?

Option 1: Clear and measurable metrics

Option 2: Timely data collection

Option 3: Regular performance reporting

Option 4: Stakeholder involvement

Correct Response: 1

Explanation: Clear and measurable metrics are the most important aspect of the effectiveness of key performance indicators (KPIs). KPIs should be well-defined, specific, and quantifiable, enabling accurate measurement and tracking of performance against predetermined targets. Clear metrics ensure that KPIs provide meaningful and reliable information for decision-making and performance evaluation.

Knowledge Area: Exam_Sim

Question Number: 343

Question: To help ensure the success of a major IT project, it is MOST important to:

Option 1: Define clear project objectives

Option 2: Allocate sufficient budget

Option 3: Follow established project management methodologies

Option 4: Engage stakeholders throughout the project lifecycle

Correct Response: 1

Explanation: To help ensure the success of a major IT project, it is most important to define clear project objectives. Clear objectives provide a clear direction and purpose for the project, guiding decision-making, resource allocation, and project execution. Well-defined objectives help align project activities with the desired outcomes and facilitate effective project management and stakeholder engagement.

Knowledge Area: Exam_Sim

Question Number: 344

Question: Which of the following provides the BEST measurement of an organization's risk management maturity level?

Option 1: Risk assessment results

Option 2: Regulatory compliance status

Option 3: Incident response time

Option 4: Maturity model assessment

Correct Response: 4

Explanation: A maturity model assessment provides the best measurement of an organization's risk management maturity level. Maturity models evaluate an organization's risk management practices, processes, and capabilities against established criteria to determine their maturity level. This assessment helps identify strengths, weaknesses, and areas for improvement, enabling organizations to enhance their risk management practices and achieve higher levels of maturity.

Knowledge Area: Exam_Sim

Question Number: 345

Question: The BEST reason to classify IT assets during a risk assessment is to determine the:

Option 1: Potential impact of asset loss

Option 2: Frequency of asset usage

Option 3: Cost of asset maintenance

Option 4: Availability of asset backups

Correct Response: 1

Explanation: The best reason to classify IT assets during a risk assessment is to determine the potential impact of asset loss. Classifying IT assets helps identify their importance, criticality, and value to the organization. By understanding the potential impact of asset loss, organizations can prioritize their risk mitigation efforts, allocate resources effectively, and implement appropriate controls to protect valuable assets.

Knowledge Area: Exam_Sim

Question Number: 346

Question: Which of the following should be the PRIMARY focus of an IT risk awareness program?

Option 1: Understanding risk management concepts

Option 2: Identifying and reporting risks

Option 3: Mitigating risks through controls

Option 4: Aligning risks with business objectives

Correct Response: 1

Explanation: The primary focus of an IT risk awareness program should be on understanding risk management concepts. It is crucial to educate employees and stakeholders about the fundamentals of risk management, including risk identification, assessment, and mitigation. By building a strong foundation of risk management knowledge, individuals can become active participants in identifying, assessing, and addressing risks in their respective roles and responsibilities.

Knowledge Area: Exam_Sim

Question Number: 347

Question: Which of the following is MOST important to update when an organization's risk appetite changes?

Option 1: Risk assessment methodologies

Option 2: Risk response strategies

Option 3: Risk monitoring procedures

Option 4: Risk appetite statement

Correct Response: 4

Explanation: When an organization's risk appetite changes, the risk appetite statement is the most important element to update. The risk appetite statement outlines the organization's willingness to accept and manage risk within defined boundaries. By updating the risk appetite statement, organizations ensure that decision-making and risk management align with the new risk appetite, guiding actions and strategies to achieve the organization's objectives within the revised risk tolerance levels.

Knowledge Area: Exam_Sim

Question Number: 348

Question: Which of the following should be an element of the risk appetite of an organization?

Option 1: Risk tolerance thresholds

Option 2: Risk management team structure

Option 3: Risk assessment methodologies

Option 4: Risk monitoring tools

Correct Response: 1

Explanation: Risk tolerance thresholds should be an element of the risk appetite of an organization. Risk tolerance represents the acceptable level of risk that an organization is willing to tolerate while pursuing its objectives. By defining risk tolerance thresholds, organizations establish boundaries within which risks are considered acceptable, guiding decision-making and risk management efforts.

Knowledge Area: Exam_Sim

Question Number: 349

Question: Which of the following is the MOST effective key performance indicator (KPI) for change management?

Option 1: Percentage of successful changes implemented

Option 2: Average time for change approval

Option 3: Number of change requests received

Option 4: Stakeholder satisfaction with changes implemented

Correct Response: 1

Explanation: The most effective key performance indicator (KPI) for change management is the percentage of successful changes implemented. This KPI measures the efficiency and effectiveness of the change management process by assessing the proportion of changes that are implemented successfully without adverse impacts or disruptions. It reflects the organization's ability to plan, execute, and manage changes in a controlled and reliable manner.

Knowledge Area: Exam_Sim

Question Number: 350

Question: Which of the following is the MOST cost-effective way to test a business continuity plan?

Option 1: Full-scale simulation exercise

Option 2: Tabletop exercise

Option 3: Parallel testing

Option 4: Checklist review

Correct Response: 2

Explanation: The most cost-effective way to test a business continuity plan is through tabletop exercises. Tabletop exercises involve conducting scenario-based discussions and simulations of emergency situations without actually executing the recovery processes. They provide an opportunity for stakeholders to review and validate the plan, assess their roles and responsibilities, and identify areas for improvement in a controlled and interactive manner, without the costs associated with full-scale simulations or parallel testing.

Knowledge Area: Exam_Sim

Question Number: 351

Question: Which of the following helps ensure compliance with a non-repudiation policy requirement for electronic transactions?

Option 1: Digital signatures

Option 2: Firewalls

Option 3: Intrusion detection systems

Option 4: Encryption

Correct Response: 1

Explanation: Digital signatures help ensure compliance with a non-repudiation policy requirement for electronic transactions. Digital signatures provide a cryptographic mechanism to verify the integrity and authenticity of electronic documents or transactions, preventing the sender from denying their involvement or the validity of the transaction. They provide strong evidence of the origin and integrity of the data, ensuring non-repudiation and supporting the enforceability of electronic contracts or agreements.

Knowledge Area: Exam_Sim

Question Number: 352

Question: When approving risk response plans, the primary management consideration should be selecting cost-effective actions that reduce intolerable risks to acceptable levels.

Option 1: Ease of implementation

Option 2: Consensus agreement

Option 3: Maximum risk reduction

Option 4: Lowest cost options

Correct Response: 1

Explanation: Management focuses on efficient risk reduction.

Knowledge Area: Exam_Sim

Question Number: 353

Question: Data owners' top priority when establishing risk mitigation should be reducing intolerable risks to critical assets to align with organizational risk appetite.

Option 1: Meeting compliance mandates

Option 2: Enabling monitoring

Option 3: Optimizing resources

Option 4: Maximizing data access

Correct Response: 1

Explanation: Owners mitigate risks to critical data.

Knowledge Area: Exam_Sim

Question Number: 354

Question: A vulnerability scanner that checks for weak passwords exposed on the network is .

Option 1: Nessus

Option 2: Snort

Option 3: Wireshark

Option 4: NetFlow

Correct Response: 1

Explanation: Nessus scans for vulnerabilities like weak passwords.

Knowledge Area: Exam_Sim

Question Number: 355

Question: Using a probability and impact matrix helps produce a comprehensive qualitative analysis by defining ranked risk severity levels based on potential likelihoods and impacts.

Option 1: Decision trees

Option 2: Risk surveys

Option 3: Threat modeling

Option 4: EMV analysis

Correct Response: 1

Explanation: Matrices comprehensively classify risk severity.

Knowledge Area: Exam_Sim

Question Number: 356

Question: An organization's risk management maturity level provides the best measurement of the degree of formality, sophistication, and effectiveness of risk practices.

Option 1: Audit results

Option 2: KRI trends

Option 3: Threat intelligence

Option 4: Training attendance

Correct Response: 1

Explanation: Maturity level reflects risk program sophistication.

Knowledge Area: Exam_Sim

Question Number: 357

Question: Classifying IT assets by criticality and value best determines the potential business impact if an asset is compromised to focus responses on highest risks.

Option 1: System interconnections

Option 2: Data retention needs

Option 3: Backup requirements

Option 4: Access permissions

Correct Response: 1

Explanation: Asset classification evaluates potential impact.

Knowledge Area: Exam_Sim

Question Number: 358

Question: The primary focus of an IT risk awareness program should be fostering a culture that incorporates risk considerations into daily behaviors and decisions.

Option 1: Reduce errors

Option 2: Meet mandates

Option 3: Lessen skill gaps

Option 4: Enable faster reporting

Correct Response: 2

Explanation: Awareness aligns behaviors to risk culture.

Knowledge Area: Exam_Sim

Question Number: 359

Question: The organization's risk appetite statement should be updated when tolerance for key risk exposures changes to realign risk management priorities.

Option 1: Business strategy

Option 2: Technology landscape

Option 3: Regulatory environment

Option 4: Risk maturity level

Correct Response: 1

Explanation: Changing appetite changes risk priorities.

Knowledge Area: Exam_Sim

Question Number: 360

Question: Defined risk tolerances for specific risk types should be an element of an organization's documented risk appetite to guide decisions.

Option 1: Risk process maps

Option 2: Insurance policies

Option 3: Threat databases

Option 4: Risk workshop results

Correct Response: 2

Explanation: Tolerances guide risk-based decisions.

Knowledge Area: Exam_Sim

Question Number: 361

Question: The most effective KPI for change management is percentage of changes causing incidents in production to incentivize quality.

Option 1: Change request volume

Option 2: Emergency change rate

Option 3: Change task efficiency

Option 4: Stakeholder satisfaction

Correct Response: 1

Explanation: Incidents caused show change quality.

Knowledge Area: Exam_Sim

Question Number: 362

Question: Tabletop exercises simulating scenarios offer a cost-effective way to test business continuity plan viability compared to disruptive tests or expensive full recreations.

Option 1: Full continuity invocation

Option 2: Documented plans

Option 3: Staff awareness training

Option 4: Plan certifications

Correct Response: 1

Explanation: Simulations effectively test plans.

Knowledge Area: Exam_Sim

Question Number: 363

Question: Digitally signing transactions and retaining secure logs of all activity provides evidence needed to meet non-repudiation requirements.

Option 1: Role-based access controls

Option 2: Data loss prevention

Option 3: Network segmentation

Option 4: Annual audits

Correct Response: 1

Explanation: Signatures and logs prove non-repudiation.

Knowledge Area: Exam_Sim

Question Number: 364

Question: Which of the following activities would BEST contribute to promoting an organization-wide risk-aware culture?

Option 1: Regular risk assessments and reporting

Option 2: Mandatory risk management training

Option 3: Implementing robust risk mitigation controls

Option 4: Establishing a risk management committee

Correct Response: 1

Explanation: Regular risk assessments and reporting would best contribute to promoting an organization-wide risk-aware culture. By conducting regular assessments, organizations can identify and evaluate risks, raising awareness among employees and stakeholders. Reporting the outcomes of risk assessments promotes transparency and accountability, fostering a culture that recognizes the importance of risk management and encourages proactive risk mitigation actions.

Knowledge Area: Exam_Sim

Question Number: 365

Question: Which of the following attributes of a key risk indicator (KRI) is MOST important?

Option 1: Relevance to business objectives

Option 2: Availability of data sources

Option 3: Frequency of measurement

Option 4: Alignment with industry benchmarks

Correct Response: 1

Explanation: The most important attribute of a key risk indicator (KRI) is its relevance to business objectives. KRIs should directly reflect the critical risks that impact the achievement of business objectives. By focusing on relevant KRIs, organizations can effectively monitor and manage the risks that are most crucial to their success. Relevance ensures that KRIs provide meaningful insights and drive informed decision-making.

Knowledge Area: Exam_Sim

Question Number: 366

Question: Which of the following is the MOST effective way to mitigate identified risk scenarios?

Option 1: Risk acceptance

Option 2: Risk avoidance

Option 3: Risk transfer

Option 4: Risk mitigation

Correct Response: 4

Explanation: Risk mitigation is the most effective way to mitigate identified risk scenarios. Mitigation involves taking proactive actions to reduce the likelihood or impact of risks. By implementing risk mitigation strategies, organizations can address potential threats and minimize their adverse effects. Mitigation may involve implementing controls, developing contingency plans, or making process improvements to reduce the overall risk exposure.

Knowledge Area: Exam_Sim

Question Number: 367

Question: Which of the following is the MOST effective inhibitor of relevant and efficient communication?

Option 1: Lack of transparency

Option 2: Inadequate communication channels

Option 3: Language barriers

Option 4: Poor listening skills

Correct Response: 1

Explanation: Lack of transparency is the most effective inhibitor of relevant and efficient communication. When information is not transparently shared or withheld, it hinders effective communication. Transparency fosters open and honest communication, ensuring that relevant information is accessible to all stakeholders. Without transparency, misunderstandings, misalignment, and inefficiencies can arise, impeding effective risk communication and decision-making.

Knowledge Area: Exam_Sim

Question Number: 368

Question: Which of the following is the BEST course of action to reduce risk impact?

Option 1: Implementing risk mitigation controls

Option 2: Transferring risk to a third party

Option 3: Accepting the risk as unavoidable

Option 4: Avoiding the activities associated with the risk

Correct Response: 1

Explanation: Implementing risk mitigation controls is the best course of action to reduce risk impact. Risk mitigation involves taking specific actions to minimize the likelihood or impact of identified risks. By implementing effective controls, organizations can reduce the potential negative consequences associated with risks and enhance their ability to achieve objectives while minimizing the impact of uncertainties.

Knowledge Area: Exam_Sim

Question Number: 369

Question: Which of the following is MOST helpful in aligning IT risk with business objectives?

Option 1: Regular risk assessments and audits

Option 2: Collaboration between IT and business units

Option 3: Implementing advanced cybersecurity measures

Option 4: Utilizing risk management software

Correct Response: 2

Explanation: Collaboration between IT and business units is most helpful in aligning IT risk with business objectives. By fostering communication, cooperation, and shared understanding between IT and business stakeholders, organizations can ensure that IT risks are identified, assessed, and managed in a manner that supports and aligns with the overarching business objectives. This collaboration enables effective risk-informed decision-making and the integration of risk management into business processes.

Knowledge Area: Exam_Sim

Question Number: 370

Question: Documenting risk response strategies with assigned owners, steps, timeframes, and resource requirements in the risk register helps ensure efficient risk management through clarity.

Option 1: Sorting by priority

Option 2: Tracking with a risk board

Option 3: Weekly analysis meetings

Option 4: Monthly risk training

Correct Response: 1

Explanation: Documented responses enable efficient execution.

Knowledge Area: Exam_Sim

Question Number: 371

Question: Cross-functional steering committees with business and IT leaders that oversee technology initiatives would best mitigate risks from misalignment between IT and business objectives.

Option 1: IT service catalogs

Option 2: Vendor partnerships

Option 3: Reporting dashboards

Option 4: Cloud computing

Correct Response: 2

Explanation: Joint oversight aligns IT to business needs.

Knowledge Area: Exam_Sim

Question Number: 372

Question: Implementing a defense-in-depth strategy with preventive controls like firewalls, detection controls like IDS, and response plans provides the most effective recommendation for preventing cyber intrusions.

Option 1: Threat modeling

Option 2: Password complexity

Option 3: Annual penetration testing

Option 4: Cyber insurance

Correct Response: 1

Explanation: Layered controls prevent, detect, and respond.

Knowledge Area: Exam_Sim

Question Number: 373

Question: When initially identifying IT risks, focus should be on gathering information about the organization's core technologies, infrastructure, and systems before drilling into specific details.

Option 1: Staff capabilities

Option 2: Vendor dependencies

Option 3: Incident history

Option 4: Threat intelligence

Correct Response: 3

Explanation: Start by understanding the IT landscape at a high level.

Knowledge Area: Exam_Sim

Question Number: 374

Question: The primary objective of a risk awareness program is nurturing a culture focused on managing risks in alignment with organizational goals through consistent messaging from leadership.

Option 1: Reduce human errors

Option 2: Meet training mandates

Option 3: Lessen skill gaps

Option 4: Enable faster reporting

Correct Response: 2

Explanation: Awareness aligns behaviors to goals.

Knowledge Area: Exam_Sim

Question Number: 375

Question: Analyzing system logs provides visibility into unauthorized or anomalous activities to detect ineffective security controls, operational issues, or malicious threats requiring response.

Option 1: Calculate system uptime

Option 2: Identify capacity needs

Option 3: Set access permissions

Option 4: Detect intrusions

Correct Response: 4

Explanation: Log analysis detects problems needing response.

Knowledge Area: Exam_Sim

Question Number: 376

Question: A consistent approval workflow with documented justification requirements for granting access indicates an efficient and controlled access management process.

Option 1: Frequent reconciliations

Option 2: Provisioning timeframes

Option 3: End user surveys

Option 4: Policy attestations

Correct Response: 1

Explanation: Consistent justified approvals show efficiency.

Knowledge Area: Exam_Sim

Question Number: 377

Question: Enforcing password changes and access revocation when privileged users change roles best decreases exposure from compromised privileged credentials.

Option 1: Longer password expirations

Option 2: Increased complexity requirements

Option 3: Multi-factor authentication

Option 4: Permission recertification

Correct Response: 2

Explanation: Revocation on role changes limits exposure.

Knowledge Area: Exam_Sim

Question Number: 378

Question: Conducting disaster recovery exercises and tests to validate recovery readiness provides assurance that business resilience and continuity plans will be effective when needed.

Option 1: Documenting response procedures

Option 2: Securing backup facilities

Option 3: Reviewing insurance policies

Option 4: Training staff on plans

Correct Response: 1

Explanation: Tests prove recoverability capabilities.

Knowledge Area: Exam_Sim

Question Number: 379

Question: When developing a risk response, the highest priority should be selecting options that reduce risk to acceptable levels while supporting business objectives and resource constraints.

Option 1: Lowest cost options

Option 2: Fastest implementation

Option 3: Maximum risk reduction

Option 4: Consensus agreement

Correct Response: 1

Explanation: Responding must balance risk reduction with business needs.

Knowledge Area: Exam_Sim

Question Number: 380

Question: The inherent risk associated with an asset before controls reflects the potential impact and likelihood absent any mitigating measures.

Option 1: Residual risk

Option 2: Secondary risk

Option 3: Qualitative risk

Option 4: Inherent risk

Correct Response: 4

Explanation: Inherent risk is pre-control exposure.

Knowledge Area: Exam_Sim

Question Number: 381

Question: Service level agreements (SLAs) specifying required IT performance levels and metrics for monitoring indicate implemented IT requirements.

Option 1: User satisfaction surveys

Option 2: Uptime reports

Option 3: Audit findings

Option 4: Outage costs

Correct Response: 1

Explanation: SLAs define expected IT performance.

Knowledge Area: Exam_Sim

Question Number: 382

Question: The application's business owner is ultimately accountable for managing risks associated with high-risk application vulnerabilities.

Option 1: Security team

Option 2: Software vendor

Option 3: Project manager

Option 4: CISO

Correct Response: 1

Explanation: The business owner owns application risks.

Knowledge Area: Exam_Sim

Question Number: 383

Question: Risk management maturity level 1 has ad hoc practices, but still documents some policies, processes, and mitigation initiatives.

Option 1: No documentation

Option 2: KRI monitoring

Option 3: Continuous auditing

Option 4: Defined metrics

Correct Response: 2

Explanation: Level 1 has some documented practices.

Knowledge Area: Exam_Sim

Question Number: 384

Question: Consistent achievement of residual risk levels that align with organizational risk tolerances indicates an effective risk program.

Option 1: No audit findings

Option 2: High staff awareness

Option 3: Peer benchmarking

Option 4: Risk training attendance

Correct Response: 1

Explanation: Target residual risk levels show effectiveness.

Knowledge Area: Exam_Sim

Question Number: 385

Question: Changes should be promoted to production only after being tested, approved, and scheduled to minimize unplanned impacts.

Option 1: Requested by users

Option 2: Code is optimized

Option 3: Business case approved

Option 4: Vendor validated

Correct Response: 2

Explanation: Testing, approval, scheduling assure production readiness.

Knowledge Area: Exam_Sim

Question Number: 386

Question: An up-to-date risk register helps inform risk-based decisions and establish accountability through defined risk owners and response plans.

Option 1: Satisfy auditors

Option 2: Validate risk model

Option 3: Justify budgets

Option 4: Limit exposures

Correct Response: 2

Explanation: The register enables risk-aware decisions and ownership.

Knowledge Area: Exam_Sim

Question Number: 387

Question: Documenting control performance provides quantified metrics and trends demonstrating effectiveness to drive improvements in risk management over time.

Option 1: Meet compliance mandates

Option 2: Clarify business impact

Option 3: Enable quarterly reporting

Option 4: Identify audit priorities

Correct Response: 3

Explanation: Performance documentation provides risk insights.

Knowledge Area: Exam_Sim

Question Number: 388

Question: First line business unit managers should have accountability for monitoring controls within their operations to ensure effectiveness.

Option 1: External audit

Option 2: Internal audit

Option 3: Risk committee

Option 4: Senior management

Correct Response: 1

Explanation: First line directs day-to-day control operation.

Knowledge Area: Exam_Sim

Question Number: 389

Question: Strong change control processes that require justified scope changes best mitigate risks associated with uncontrolled project scope creep.

Option 1: Project manager discretion

Option 2: Progress tracking

Option 3: Status reporting

Option 4: Change control

Correct Response: 4

Explanation: Change control prevents uncontrolled scope changes.

Knowledge Area: Exam_Sim

Question Number: 390

Question: Expected monetary value analysis estimates potential loss from risks by quantifying probability, impact, and exposure to assign monetary values.

Option 1: Discount rates

Option 2: Qualitative analysis

Option 3: Auditor assessments

Option 4: Loss history reviews

Correct Response: 1

Explanation: EMV analysis monetizes probabilistic risk.

Knowledge Area: Exam_Sim

Question Number: 391

Question: Which of the following is the most accurate definition of a project risk?

Option 1: An uncertain event or condition that, if it occurs, may have a positive or negative effect on project objectives

Option 2: An unexpected event that always has a negative impact on project objectives

Option 3: A known event that always has a positive impact on project objectives

Option 4: A potential issue that may arise during project execution

Correct Response: 1

Explanation: The most accurate definition of a project risk is that it is an uncertain event or condition that, if it occurs, may have a positive or negative effect on project objectives. Risks can be both positive (opportunities) and negative (threats), and their occurrence is uncertain. Effective risk management involves identifying, assessing, and responding to these potential events to minimize their impact and maximize project success.

Knowledge Area: Exam_Sim

Question Number: 392

Question: Which of the following BEST measures the operational effectiveness of risk management capabilities?

Option 1: Number of identified risks

Option 2: Percentage of risks mitigated

Option 3: Timeliness of risk response actions

Option 4: Reduction in risk impact and likelihood over time

Correct Response: 4

Explanation: The operational effectiveness of risk management capabilities is best measured by the reduction in risk impact and likelihood over time. This indicates that the organization's risk management efforts are successfully identifying, assessing, and responding to risks, resulting in a reduced potential impact and likelihood of negative events. It demonstrates the effectiveness of risk management processes and controls in managing risks proactively.

Knowledge Area: Exam_Sim

Question Number: 393

Question: Which of the following is the final step in the policy development process?

Option 1: Policy implementation

Option 2: Policy review

Option 3: Policy approval

Option 4: Policy dissemination

Correct Response: 4

Explanation: The final step in the policy development process is policy dissemination. Once a policy has been approved, it needs to be effectively communicated and shared with all relevant stakeholders and individuals within the organization. Dissemination ensures that everyone is aware of the policy, understands its requirements, and can adhere to it in their respective roles and responsibilities.

Knowledge Area: Exam_Sim

Question Number: 394

Question: Which of the following serve as the authorization for a project to begin?

Option 1: Project charter

Option 2: Project plan

Option 3: Project budget

Option 4: Project schedule

Correct Response: 1

Explanation: The project charter serves as the authorization for a project to begin. It is a formal document that defines the project's objectives, scope, stakeholders, and other key aspects. The project charter is typically approved by the project sponsor or other relevant authority and provides the project manager with the necessary authority to initiate and lead the project.

Knowledge Area: Exam_Sim

Question Number: 395

Question: Which of the following is MOST important when developing key performance indicators (KPIs)?

Option 1: Alignment with organizational goals and objectives

Option 2: Availability of data sources

Option 3: Benchmarks with industry standards

Option 4: Inclusion of all project stakeholders

Correct Response: 1

Explanation: The most important factor when developing key performance indicators (KPIs) is their alignment with organizational goals and objectives. KPIs should be directly linked to the desired outcomes and success factors of the organization. By aligning KPIs with organizational goals, it ensures that they measure the critical areas that contribute to the overall success and effectiveness of the organization.

Knowledge Area: Exam_Sim

Question Number: 396

Question: Which of the following BEST measures the efficiency of an incident response process?

Option 1: Mean time to detect (MTT

Option 2: Mean time to respond (MTTR)

Option 3: Mean time between failures (MTBF)

Option 4: Mean time to recovery (MTTR)

Correct Response: 2

Explanation: The efficiency of an incident response process is best measured by the mean time to respond (MTTR). MTTR represents the average time taken to respond to an incident once it has been detected. A shorter MTTR indicates a more efficient incident response process, as it reflects a quicker and more effective response to mitigate the impact of incidents and restore normal operations.

Knowledge Area: Exam_Sim

----------------------- ---------------------

Question Number: 397

Question: Which of the following would BEST ensure that identified risk scenarios are addressed?

Option 1: Risk mitigation plan

Option 2: Risk identification checklist

Option 3: Risk register

Option 4: Risk assessment matrix

Correct Response: 1

Explanation: A risk mitigation plan would best ensure that identified risk scenarios are addressed. A risk mitigation plan outlines specific actions and measures to be taken to reduce the likelihood or impact of identified risks. It provides a structured approach to addressing risks, ensuring that appropriate risk response strategies are developed and implemented to manage and mitigate the identified risk scenarios effectively.

Knowledge Area: Exam_Sim

Question Number: 398

Question: Which of the following should be PRIMARILY considered while designing information systems controls?

Option 1: Regulatory compliance

Option 2: User convenience

Option 3: Cost-effectiveness

Option 4: Security and risk management

Correct Response: 4

Explanation: While all options are important, security and risk management should be primarily considered while designing information systems controls. Information systems controls aim to safeguard the confidentiality, integrity, and availability of data and systems, as well as mitigate risks associated with unauthorized access, data breaches, and system vulnerabilities. Security and risk management considerations are crucial to ensure the effectiveness and resilience of controls in protecting organizational assets.

Question Number: 399

Question: The most important objective of an information system control is to protect the confidentiality, integrity, and availability of data and systems that enable business objectives.

Option 1: Prevent threats

Option 2: Meet compliance

Option 3: Enable monitoring

Option 4: Reduce costs

Correct Response: 1

Explanation: Controls primarily secure CIA supporting business goals.

Knowledge Area: Exam_Sim

Question Number: 400

Question: The first step in the risk assessment process is establishing the context by defining objectives, scope, methodology, participants, and protocols to provide foundational understanding.

Option 1: Identifying risks

Option 2: Analyzing risks

Option 3: Evaluating controls

Option 4: Calculating impacts

Correct Response: 2

Explanation: Context setting is the critical first risk assessment step.

Knowledge Area: Exam_Sim

Amazing!

You have been studying very hard to this stage.

How is your exam preparation so far? Can the practice test meet your needs and expectation? I desperately desire your voice.

Please kindly consider

1. Visiting my exam practice test books and consider purchasing them to assist you to pass your target exam, though the direct links provided at the beginning of this book
2. Visiting my exam practice test courses held at Udemy though the direct links provided at the beginning of this book
3. Leaving a positive review and feedback to me though the direct book review links provided at the next page.

Keep going! See you at the end of the book.

Warm regards,

Walter

Or the **Links at Amazon Book Store:**

CRISC 1200+ Practice Test, 2023 (Exam Simulation and Core & Advanced Knowledge)	
Paperback Review URL:	- https://www.amazon.com/review/create-review?&asin=B0CJ43R78T
Kindle eBook Review URL:	- https://www.amazon.com/review/create-review?&asin=B0CJ72JJLY

Direct URLs to visit all Walter's Practice Tests at Amazon

Visit Walter's author page:
http://WalterEducation.com

Question Number: 401

Question: Entity-based risks under the COSO ERM framework fall under the Governance and Culture risk dimension focused on behaviors, integrity, and oversight.

Option 1: Strategy

Option 2: Operations

Option 3: Reporting

Option 4: Compliance

Correct Response: 1

Explanation: Entity risks relate to governance and culture.

Knowledge Area: Exam_Sim

Question Number: 402

Question: Formally integrating risk management responsibilities into job descriptions and processes would best facilitate effective risk practices across the organization.

Option 1: Centralized reporting tools

Option 2: External risk consultants

Option 3: Quarterly risk training

Option 4: Timely issue escalation

Correct Response: 1

Explanation: Integrated responsibilities drive broad adoption.

Knowledge Area: Exam_Sim

Question Number: 403

Question: A key benefit of well-designed key risk indicators is providing early warnings of emerging risk conditions through correlation to risk factors before impacts fully materialize.

Option 1: Automated tracking

Option 2: Quantified measures

Option 3: Dashboard visualization

Option 4: Response guidance

Correct Response: 2

Explanation: Early warnings from correlations to risk is critical.

Knowledge Area: Exam_Sim

Question Number: 404

Question: The greatest advantage of implementing risk management is enabling informed decisions aligned to organizational risk appetite to drive performance while protecting value.

Option 1: Reduced uncertainties

Option 2: Improved budgeting

Option 3: Compliance assurance

Option 4: Audit readiness

Correct Response: 1

Explanation: Enables risk-aware decision making.

Knowledge Area: Exam_Sim

Question Number: 405

Question: Establishing a code of conduct addresses detterent controls by defining expected employee behaviors and integrity standards within the organizational culture.

Option 1: Corrective

Option 2: Preventive

Option 3: Detective

Option 4: Directive

Correct Response: 4

Explanation: Codes of conduct are deterrent cultural controls.

Knowledge Area: Exam_Sim

Question Number: 406

Question: An organization's risk appetite statement is the most relevant input to developing its overall risk profile, establishing acceptable levels of risk exposures.

Option 1: Risk register

Option 2: Loss event data

Option 3: Audit findings

Option 4: Threat intelligence

Correct Response: 1

Explanation: Risk appetite guides risk profiling.

Knowledge Area: Exam_Sim

Question Number: 407

Question: Realistic risk scenarios aligned to business objectives are critical in designing effective simulations to reveal relevant vulnerabilities requiring risk management focus.

Option 1: Recent threat trends

Option 2: Worst-case extrapolations

Option 3: Third-party assessments

Option 4: Leading practice templates

Correct Response: 2

Explanation: Scenario relevance provides targeted insights.

Knowledge Area: Exam_Sim

Question Number: 408

Question: Multi-factor authentication provides the best protection of online financial transactions by requiring additional credentials beyond usernames and passwords.

Option 1: Encryption

Option 2: Firewalls

Option 3: VPNs

Option 4: MFA

Correct Response: 4

Explanation: MFA best secures online transactions from improper access.

Knowledge Area: Exam_Sim

Question Number: 409

Question: Focusing discussions on how risks relate to strategy helps provide purpose and focus for risk conversations to drive meaningful decisions and actions.

Option 1: Reporting structures

Option 2: Monitoring metrics

Option 3: Historical losses

Option 4: Compliance impacts

Correct Response: 1

Explanation: Strategic relevance gives risk discussions purpose.

Knowledge Area: Exam_Sim

Question Number: 410

Question: Risks that may damage an organization's brand, reputation, or public image are categorized as strategic risks with impacts beyond just financials.

Option 1: Operational

Option 2: Cyber

Option 3: Financial

Option 4: Reputational

Correct Response: 4

Explanation: Reputational risks threaten public perception.

Knowledge Area: Exam_Sim

Question Number: 411

Question: Major changes in business strategy would significantly impact the standard information security governance model by requiring realignment to the new strategic objectives and risk conditions.

Option 1: Introduction of new technologies

Option 2: Results of a vulnerability assessment

Option 3: Audit recommendations

Option 4: Release of updated regulations

Correct Response: 1

Explanation: Strategy shifts drive information security model realignment.

Knowledge Area: Exam_Sim

Question Number: 412

Question: Natural disasters like floods, storms, or earthquakes pose physical and environmental risks that can damage assets and disrupt operations.

Option 1: Financial

Option 2: Regulatory

Option 3: Strategic

Option 4: External

Correct Response: 4

Explanation: Natural disasters are external environmental risks.

Knowledge Area: Exam_Sim

Question Number: 413

Question: Risk indicator trend reports tracking changes in key risk metrics over time best enable identifying increases or decreases in overall risk levels.

Option 1: Risk audits

Option 2: Loss event data

Option 3: Risk surveys

Option 4: Threat intelligence

Correct Response: 1

Explanation: Risk indicator trends identify changes in risk levels.

Knowledge Area: Exam_Sim

Question Number: 414

Question: In a decision tree analysis, the branches stemming from each decision node have defined probabilities attached to model the likelihood of each outcome scenario.

Option 1: End nodes

Option 2: Root nodes

Option 3: Leaf nodes

Option 4: Data nodes

Correct Response: 1

Explanation: Decision branches in a tree have set probability values.

Knowledge Area: Exam_Sim

Question Number: 415

Question: The data preparation process ensures extracted data sets are cleansed, formatted, and ready for input into risk analysis tools through activities like managing missing values and removing biases.

Option 1: Data modeling

Option 2: Quality assurance testing

Option 3: Regression analysis

Option 4: Blockchain transactions

Correct Response: 2

Explanation: Data preparation makes data analysis-ready.

Knowledge Area: Exam_Sim

Question Number: 416

Question: A strong ethical culture driven by executive commitment to integrity and accountability fosters a robust internal control environment.

Option 1: External audits

Option 2: Process automation

Option 3: Staff training

Option 4: System security controls

Correct Response: 1

Explanation: Culture and tone set by leadership enable controls.

Knowledge Area: Exam_Sim

Question Number: 417

Question: The primary reason for defining risk responses is to clarify accountability, steps, and timeframes for specific actions that will be taken to address intolerable risk exposures.

Option 1: Meet compliance mandates

Option 2: Enable qualitative analysis

Option 3: Secure budget for controls

Option 4: Limit audit findings

Correct Response: 1

Explanation: Responses define how unacceptable risks are handled.

Knowledge Area: Exam_Sim

Question Number: 418

Question: A disruption of operations that impacts the organization's ability to accomplish business objectives is considered a/an:

Option 1: Financial risk

Option 2: Strategic risk

Option 3: Compliance risk

Option 4: Operational risk

Correct Response: 4

Explanation: Business productivity loss is an operational risk.

Knowledge Area: Exam_Sim

Question Number: 419

Question: For large software projects, risk assessments are most effective when performed iteratively and continuously throughout the project lifecycle rather than just once at the start.

Option 1: At project closure

Option 2: During planning

Option 3: At design reviews

Option 4: After implementation

Correct Response: 2

Explanation: Continuous iterative assessments maximize risk insights.

Knowledge Area: Exam_Sim

Question Number: 420

Question: Lessons learned analyses of each risk management iteration gathered through techniques like retrospectives best enable continuous process improvements.

Option 1: Maturity model benchmarking

Option 2: Staff training

Option 3: Risk audits

Option 4: Adding reserve funds

Correct Response: 1

Explanation: Lessons learned drive refinements.

Knowledge Area: Exam_Sim

Question Number: 421

Question: Key risk indicators that closely correlate and rapidly respond to changes in risk levels provide early warnings of evolving conditions compared to lagging indicators.

Option 1: Loss event data

Option 2: Audit findings

Option 3: Threat intelligence

Option 4: Risk surveys

Correct Response: 1

Explanation: KRIs give early warning through correlation to risk.

Knowledge Area: Exam_Sim

Question Number: 422

Question: When developing key risk indicators, the most important focus is identifying metrics providing actionable, insightful data tied directly to strategic objectives and risk priorities.

Option 1: Using automated IT systems

Option 2: Having quantitative values

Option 3: Reducing manual processes

Option 4: Enabling tactical response

Correct Response: 1

Explanation: Relevant KRIs give insights into strategic risks.

Knowledge Area: Exam_Sim

Question Number: 423

Question: Which of the following BEST indicates the condition of a risk management program?

Option 1: Number of identified risks

Option 2: Frequency of risk assessments

Option 3: Compliance with risk management policies

Option 4: Cost of risk mitigation measures

Correct Response: 3

Explanation: The condition of a risk management program is best indicated by its compliance with risk management policies. Compliance ensures that the program follows established guidelines, procedures, and best practices in managing risks. It demonstrates that the program is implemented consistently and effectively, contributing to the overall success of risk management efforts.

Knowledge Area: Exam_Sim

Question Number: 424

Question: The purpose of requiring source code escrow in a contractual agreement is to:

Option 1: Protect intellectual property rights

Option 2: Ensure software functionality

Option 3: Facilitate software updates

Option 4: Secure access to source code for risk mitigation

Correct Response: 1

Explanation: The purpose of requiring source code escrow in a contractual agreement is to protect intellectual property rights. Source code escrow provides a mechanism for the licensee to access the source code if certain predefined conditions are met, such as the bankruptcy or non-performance of the software vendor. This ensures that the licensee can continue to use and maintain the software even if the vendor is unable to fulfill its obligations.

Knowledge Area: Exam_Sim

Question Number: 425

Question: What is the process for selecting and implementing measures to impact risk called?

Option 1: Risk identification

Option 2: Risk assessment

Option 3: Risk mitigation

Option 4: Risk monitoring

Correct Response: 3

Explanation: The process for selecting and implementing measures to impact risk is called risk mitigation. Risk mitigation involves identifying potential risks, assessing their likelihood and impact, and then selecting and implementing appropriate actions or measures to reduce the probability or impact of those risks. It aims to proactively manage risks and minimize their potential negative consequences.

Knowledge Area: Exam_Sim

Question Number: 426

Question: Which of the following controls do NOT come under the technical class of control?

Option 1: Firewalls

Option 2: Encryption algorithms

Option 3: Security awareness training

Option 4: Intrusion detection systems

Correct Response: 3

Explanation: Security awareness training does not fall under the technical class of control. It belongs to the administrative class of control as it focuses on educating and raising awareness among individuals to promote secure behaviors and practices. Technical controls, such as firewalls, encryption algorithms, and intrusion detection systems, are implemented through technology or automated mechanisms to safeguard systems and data.

Knowledge Area: Exam_Sim

Question Number: 427

Question: What is the value of the exposure factor if the asset is lost completely?

Option 1: 0%

Option 2: 25%

Option 3: 50%

Option 4: 100%

Correct Response: 4

Explanation: The value of the exposure factor is 100% if the asset is lost completely. Exposure factor represents the percentage of loss that would occur if a risk event materializes. In this scenario, the loss of the asset is total, resulting in a 100% exposure factor.

Knowledge Area: Exam_Sim

Question Number: 428

Question: Which of the following is an acceptable method for handling positive project risk?

Option 1: Risk avoidance

Option 2: Risk transference

Option 3: Risk acceptance

Option 4: Risk exploitation

Correct Response: 4

Explanation: Risk exploitation is an acceptable method for handling positive project risk. It involves identifying and taking advantage of opportunities that can bring positive outcomes or benefits to the project. By actively pursuing and exploiting these opportunities, organizations can enhance project success and achieve desired objectives.

Knowledge Area: Exam_Sim

Question Number: 429

Question: Which among the following is the MOST crucial part of the risk management process?

Option 1: Risk identification

Option 2: Risk assessment

Option 3: Risk monitoring

Option 4: Risk response planning

Correct Response: 2

Explanation: Risk assessment is the most crucial part of the risk management process. It involves evaluating the identified risks in terms of their likelihood, impact, and other relevant factors to determine their significance and prioritize them for further action. Risk assessment provides the foundation for making informed decisions and developing appropriate risk response strategies.

Knowledge Area: Exam_Sim

Question Number: 430

Question: What is the value of the exposure factor if the asset is lost completely?

Option 1: 0%

Option 2: 25%

Option 3: 50%

Option 4: 100%

Correct Response: 4

Explanation: The value of the exposure factor is 100% if the asset is lost completely. Exposure factor represents the percentage of loss that would occur if a risk event materializes. In this scenario, the loss of the asset is total, resulting in a 100% exposure factor.

Knowledge Area: Exam_Sim

Question Number: 431

Question: Which of the following approaches would BEST help to identify relevant risk scenarios?

Option 1: Brainstorming sessions

Option 2: Historical data analysis

Option 3: Expert judgment

Option 4: Scenario analysis

Correct Response: 1

Explanation: Brainstorming sessions would best help to identify relevant risk scenarios. By engaging project stakeholders and subject matter experts in a creative and open discussion, brainstorming sessions allow for the generation of a wide range of potential risk scenarios. This approach encourages diverse perspectives, stimulates innovative thinking, and helps uncover risks that may not be apparent through other methods.

Knowledge Area: Exam_Sim

Question Number: 432

Question: Which of the following would require updates to an organization's IT risk register?

Option 1: Changes in regulatory requirements

Option 2: Employee training programs

Option 3: Routine system maintenance

Option 4: Annual financial audits

Correct Response: 1

Explanation: Changes in regulatory requirements would require updates to an organization's IT risk register. RegulatoryApologies for the incomplete response.

Question Number: 433

Question: Which of the following is MOST helpful in developing key risk indicator thresholds?

Option 1: Historical data analysis

Option 2: Benchmarking with industry peers

Option 3: Expert judgment and experience

Option 4: Stakeholder feedback

Correct Response: 3

Explanation: Expert judgment and experience are most helpful in developing key risk indicator (KRI) thresholds. KRIs are specific metrics used to monitor and measure the performance and status of key risk factors. Expert judgment, based on experience and knowledge, enables the identification of relevant thresholds that align with the organization's risk appetite, industry standards, and best practices. Expertise in risk management provides valuable insights in setting effective KRIs and their associated thresholds.

Knowledge Area: Exam_Sim

Question Number: 434

Question: Which of the following would prompt changes in key risk indicator (KRI) thresholds?

Option 1: Annual financial audits

Option 2: Technology upgrades

Option 3: Compliance with regulatory requirements

Option 4: Employee training programs

Correct Response: 3

Explanation: Compliance with regulatory requirements would prompt changes in key risk indicator (KRI) thresholds. Regulatory changes can impact the risk landscape and may require adjustments to the organization's risk management approach. Adapting KRI thresholds ensures that they reflect the evolving regulatory environment and help monitor and assess risks in accordance with the updated requirements. Compliance with regulatory standards is crucial for effective risk management and governance.

Knowledge Area: Exam_Sim

Question Number: 435

Question: What is the main reason to continuously monitor IT risk?

Option 1: Validate control design

Option 2: Identify emerging issues

Option 3: Assess training needs

Option 4: Demonstrate diligence

Correct Response: 2

Explanation: Monitoring rapidly detects new risk issues.

Knowledge Area: Exam_Sim

Question Number: 436

Question: What should primarily guide IT control design?

Option 1: Industry standards

Option 2: Auditor recommendations

Option 3: Legal requirements

Option 4: Business needs

Correct Response: 4

Explanation: Controls should align to business needs and objectives.

Knowledge Area: Exam_Sim

Question Number: 437

Question: Quantifying a single asset's value helps determine the:

Option 1: Total risk exposure

Option 2: Control testing scope

Option 3: Policy exceptions needed

Option 4: Potential loss impact

Correct Response: 4

Explanation: Single asset value quantifies potential loss.

Knowledge Area: Exam_Sim

Question Number: 438

Question: An organization's policies should foremost reflect:

Option 1: Management risk appetite

Option 2: Industry best practices

Option 3: Regulator expectations

Option 4: Company values and objectives

Correct Response: 4

Explanation: Policies should align with organizational goals.

Knowledge Area: Exam_Sim

Question Number: 439

Question: Why perform ongoing risk assessments?

Option 1: Audit requirements

Option 2: Benchmark comparisons

Option 3: Issue validation

Option 4: Identify profile changes

Correct Response: 4

Explanation: Assessments identify risk profile shifts.

Knowledge Area: Exam_Sim

Question Number: 440

Question: When establishing enterprise risk management, the most important focus is:

Option 1: Funding

Option 2: Staffing

Option 3: Executive alignment

Option 4: Technology solutions

Correct Response: 3

Explanation: Executive alignment enables embedded ERM practices.

Knowledge Area: Exam_Sim

Question Number: 441

Question: What best determines software license compliance?

Option 1: Vendor attestations

Option 2: Purchase requisitions

Option 3: Installation tracking

Option 4: Automated discovery scans

Correct Response: 4

Explanation: Automated scans validate installed vs. purchased licenses.

Knowledge Area: Exam_Sim

Question Number: 442

Question: Why test new controls before deployment?

Option 1: Meet project deadlines

Option 2: Set implementation priority

Option 3: Demonstrate value

Option 4: Identify design issues

Correct Response: 4

Explanation: Testing uncovers control weaknesses to address pre-release.

Knowledge Area: Exam_Sim

Question Number: 443

Question: A teaming agreement exemplifies which risk response?

Option 1: Mitigation

Option 2: Exploitation

Option 3: Sharing

Option 4: Acceptance

Correct Response: 3

Explanation: Teaming shares risk with partners.

Knowledge Area: Exam_Sim

Question Number: 444

Question: Where are project risks and responses documented?

Option 1: Lessons learned

Option 2: Project management plan

Option 3: Risk register

Option 4: Status reports

Correct Response: 3

Explanation: The risk register centralizes risk details.

Knowledge Area: Exam_Sim

Question Number: 445

Question: Where are project risks and responses documented as the project progresses?

Option 1: Lessons learned

Option 2: Project management plan

Option 3: Risk register

Option 4: Status reports

Correct Response: 3

Explanation: The risk register tracks all project risk details.

Knowledge Area: Exam_Sim

Question Number: 446

Question: In which process are probability and impact matrices prepared?

Option 1: Qualitative analysis

Option 2: Risk identification

Option 3: Risk monitoring

Option 4: Quantitative analysis

Correct Response: 2

Explanation: Probability and impact matrices are prepared in qualitative analysis.

Knowledge Area: Exam_Sim

Question Number: 447

Question: Which of the following is NOT a method used in Qualitative risk analysis?

Option 1: Risk probability and impact assessment

Option 2: Risk categorization

Option 3: Risk scoring

Option 4: Monte Carlo simulation

Correct Response: 4

Explanation: Monte Carlo simulation is not a method used in Qualitative risk analysis. While it is a valuable technique for Quantitative risk analysis, it involves statistical modeling and simulation to analyze the impact of uncertainty on project objectives. In Qualitative risk analysis, the focus is on assessing risks qualitatively based on their probability and impact without involving complex simulations.

Knowledge Area: Exam_Sim

Question Number: 448

Question: Which of the following would BEST help an enterprise prioritize risk scenarios?

Option 1: Risk impact assessment

Option 2: Risk likelihood assessment

Option 3: Risk urgency assessment

Option 4: Risk tolerance assessment

Correct Response: 1

Explanation: Risk impact assessment would best help an enterprise prioritize risk scenarios. By assessing the potential impact of each risk scenario, the enterprise can understand the magnitude of the consequences and prioritize risks based on their potential impact on organizational objectives. This allows for the allocation of resources and efforts to address the most critical and impactful risks.

Knowledge Area: Exam_Sim

Question Number: 449

Question: Calculation of the recovery time objective (RTO) is necessary to determine the:

Option 1: Maximum tolerable downtime

Option 2: Recovery point objective (RPO)

Option 3: Mean time between failures (MTBF)

Option 4: Business impact analysis (BI

Correct Response: 1

Explanation: Calculation of the recovery time objective (RTO) is necessary to determine the maximum tolerable downtime. The RTO represents the duration within which a business process or system must be restored after an incident to avoid unacceptable consequences. It helps in setting recovery time targets and planning the necessary resources and strategies to minimize downtime and resume normal operations.

Knowledge Area: Exam_Sim

Question Number: 450

Question: Which of the following conditions presents the GREATEST risk to an application?

Option 1: Lack of access controls

Option 2: Inadequate backup procedures

Option 3: Weak encryption algorithms

Option 4: Limited system resources

Correct Response: 3

Explanation: Weak encryption algorithms present the greatest risk to an application. Encryption is crucial for protecting sensitive data and preventing unauthorized access. Weak encryption algorithms can be exploited by attackers, leading to data breaches and compromised security. It is crucial to use strong encryption algorithms to mitigate the risk of unauthorized access and ensure the confidentiality and integrity of data.

Knowledge Area: Exam_Sim

Question Number: 451

Question: The MAIN goal of the risk analysis process is to determine the:

Option 1: Probability of risks occurring

Option 2: Impact of risks on project objectives

Option 3: Root causes of risks

Option 4: Effectiveness of risk response strategies

Correct Response: 2

Explanation: The main goal of the risk analysis process is to determine the impact of risks on project objectives. By assessing the potential consequences of risks, organizations can understand the magnitude of the impact and make informed decisions regarding risk response strategies. The risk analysis process helps in identifying critical risks, evaluating their potential impact, and prioritizing actions to manage and mitigate them effectively.

Knowledge Area: Exam_Sim

Question Number: 452

Question: The MOST important reason for implementing change control procedures is to ensure:

Option 1: Stakeholder engagement

Option 2: Scope creep prevention

Option 3: Consistency in project deliverables

Option 4: Effective management of project changes

Correct Response: 4

Explanation: The most important reason for implementing change control procedures is to ensure effective management of project changes. Change control procedures provide a structured approach to evaluate, assess, and approve changes to project scope, objectives, and deliverables. By following change control procedures, organizations can assess the impact of proposed changes, evaluate their feasibility, and make informed decisions to approve or reject changes, ensuring that only authorized and beneficial changes are implemented.

Knowledge Area: Exam_Sim

Question Number: 453

Question: NIST SP 800-53 identifies controls in three primary classes. What are they?

Option 1: Administrative, physical, and technical

Option 2: Preventive, detective, and corrective

Option 3: Strategic, operational, and tactical

Option 4: Internal, external, and hybrid

Correct Response: 1

Explanation: NIST SP 800-53 identifies controls in three primary classes: administrative, physical, and technical. Administrative controls encompass policies, procedures, and guidelines that guide and govern the organization's security framework. Physical controls involve physical safeguards and measures to protect assets and facilities. Technical controls include technical safeguards, mechanisms, and configurations to secure IT systems and infrastructure.

Knowledge Area: Exam_Sim

Question Number: 454

Question: Which of the following is the BEST defense against successful phishing attacks?

Option 1: Regular security awareness training

Option 2: Strong password policies

Option 3: Multi-factor authentication

Option 4: Robust antivirus software

Correct Response: 3

Explanation: Multi-factor authentication is the best defense against successful phishing attacks. Phishing attacks often rely on stolen credentials to gain unauthorized access to sensitive information or systems. By implementing multi-factor authentication, which requires additional verification beyond a username and password, organizations can add an extra layer of security and significantly reduce the risk of successful phishing attacks.

Knowledge Area: Exam_Sim

Question Number: 455

Question: When developing a business continuity plan (BCP), it is MOST important to:

Option 1: Identify critical business functions and processes

Option 2: Define communication channels

Option 3: Establish recovery time objectives (RTOs)

Option 4: Conduct regular plan testing and maintenance

Correct Response: 1

Explanation: When developing a business continuity plan (BCP), it is most important to identify critical business functions and processes. This step ensures that the BCP focuses on the essential activities that must be maintained during and after a disruptive event. By identifying critical functions and processes, organizations can prioritize resources, establish recovery strategies, and develop appropriate response and recovery plans to minimize the impact of disruptions.

Knowledge Area: Exam_Sim

Question Number: 456

Question: The PRIMARY benefit associated with key risk indicators (KRIs) is that they:

Option 1: Identify emerging risks

Option 2: Quantify the financial impact of risks

Option 3: Prioritize risks based on likelihood and impact

Option 4: Assess the effectiveness of risk controls

Correct Response: 1

Explanation: The PRIMARY benefit associated with key risk indicators (KRIs) is that they identify emerging risks. KRIs are measurable metrics used to monitor and track conditions or events that indicate potential risks. By monitoring KRIs, organizations can detect early warning signs and emerging trends, allowing them to take proactive actions to manage and mitigate risks before they escalate. KRIs provide valuable insights into the evolving risk landscape and help organizations stay ahead of emerging risks.

Knowledge Area: Exam_Sim

Question Number: 457

Question: What is the PRIMARY reason to categorize risk scenarios by business process?

Option 1: To assess the financial impact of risks

Option 2: To prioritize risk response actions

Option 3: To identify the root causes of risks

Option 4: To understand the impact on critical operations and functions

Correct Response: 4

Explanation: The PRIMARY reason to categorize risk scenarios by business process is to understand the impact on critical operations and functions. Categorizing risks by business process helps organizations identify and evaluate the potential impact of risks on key operational areas. It allows for targeted risk assessment, response planning, and resource allocation to address risks that pose the greatest threat to critical operations and functions.

Knowledge Area: Exam_Sim

Question Number: 458

Question: What would trigger the need to execute a planned risk response?

Option 1: Reaching a milestone

Option 2: Quarterly risk meeting

Option 3: Exceeding defined risk tolerances

Option 4: Routine audit finding

Correct Response: 3

Explanation: Triggers like exceeding risk appetite signal the need for planned response.

Knowledge Area: Exam_Sim

Question Number: 459

Question: What compliance regulation mandates controls around patient healthcare information privacy and security?

Option 1: SOX

Option 2: GLBA

Option 3: FISMA

Option 4: HIPAA

Correct Response: 4

Explanation: HIPAA regulates protected health information privacy and security.

Knowledge Area: Exam_Sim

Question Number: 460

Question: When would an organization initiate a pre-defined risk response plan?

Option 1: After a schedule change

Option 2: When new risks are identified

Option 3: When risk appetite is exceeded

Option 4: During a project retrospective

Correct Response: 3

Explanation: Triggers like risk materialization require executing planned responses.

Knowledge Area: Exam_Sim

Question Number: 461

Question: A key benefit of an IT risk management framework is enabling centralized oversight and consistency through standardized processes across decentralized units.

Option 1: Optimizes budget allocation

Option 2: Provides quantitative modeling

Option 3: Satisfies certification requirements

Option 4: Reduces audit findings

Correct Response: 2

Explanation: Frameworks unify risk practices across siloed units.

Knowledge Area: Exam_Sim

Question Number: 462

Question: What technique helps identify unnecessary controls to remove?

Option 1: Internal audits

Option 2: Risk indicators

Option 3: Process modeling

Option 4: Gap/duplication analysis

Correct Response: 4

Explanation: Gap analysis exposes redundant or unnecessary controls.

Knowledge Area: Exam_Sim

Question Number: 463

Question: Why review key performance indicators periodically?

Option 1: Assess control quality

Option 2: Audit risk model accuracy

Option 3: Validate risk response effectiveness

Option 4: Ensure KPIs provide actionable insights

Correct Response: 4

Explanation: Regular reviews ensure KPIs remain relevant for risk insights.

Knowledge Area: Exam_Sim

Question Number: 464

Question: What effectively communicates risk summary data to executives?

Option 1: Total risks by department

Option 2: Qualitative analysis results

Option 3: Overdue risk lists

Option 4: Heat maps showing impact and likelihood

Correct Response: 4

Explanation: Heat maps concisely communicate risk profiles.

Knowledge Area: Exam_Sim

Question Number: 465

Question: How can you best measure operational control effectiveness?

Option 1: Risk surveys

Option 2: Audit deficiency trends

Option 3: Process impact analysis

Option 4: Residual risk metrics

Correct Response: 4

Explanation: Residual risk shows actual mitigation effectiveness.

Knowledge Area: Exam_Sim

Question Number: 466

Question: Why define controls during system design?

Option 1: Enables user access control

Option 2: Limits scope creep

Option 3: Lowers licensing costs

Option 4: Avoids costly rework later

Correct Response: 4

Explanation: Designing controls early prevents expensive fixes.

Knowledge Area: Exam_Sim

Question Number: 467

Question: Why analyze risk scenarios?

Option 1: Estimate inherent exposures

Option 2: Model hypothetical situations

Option 3: Calculate correlations

Option 4: Aggregate internal losses

Correct Response: 2

Explanation: Scenarios evaluate plausible risk situations.

Knowledge Area: Exam_Sim

Question Number: 468

Question: What indicates security awareness training effectiveness?

Option 1: Time between refreshers

Option 2: Training budget utilization

Option 3: Training materials created

Option 4: Test scores showing retention

Correct Response: 4

Explanation: Scores demonstrate improved behaviors.

Knowledge Area: Exam_Sim

Question Number: 469

Question: What is the first step in business continuity planning?

Option 1: Train staff on plans

Option 2: Acquire backup facilities

Option 3: Insure against losses

Option 4: Conduct impact analysis

Correct Response: 4

Explanation: Impact analysis identifies critical processes and needs.

Question Number: 470

Question: What helps validate that controls are functioning as intended?

Option 1: Vulnerability scans

Option 2: Compliance audits

Option 3: Penetration testing

Option 4: Control testing

Correct Response: 4

Explanation: Control testing specifically evaluates whether controls are operating effectively.

Knowledge Area: Exam_Sim

Question Number: 471

Question: What should be done if a critical vendor is deemed high risk?

Option 1: Terminate the contract

Option 2: Add contractual clauses

Option 3: Switch vendors

Option 4: Reduce spending

Correct Response: 2

Explanation: Adding security clauses helps mitigate third party risk contractually.

Knowledge Area: Exam_Sim

Question Number: 472

Question: Which threat actor often launches ransomware for financial gain?

Option 1: Script kiddies

Option 2: Hacktivists

Option 3: Nation states

Option 4: Organized crime

Correct Response: 4

Explanation: Ransomware's financial motives typically point to organized cybercrime.

Knowledge Area: Exam_Sim

Question Number: 473

Question: What helps assign accountability for managing a particular risk?

Option 1: Risk matrix

Option 2: Risk register

Option 3: Risk appetite

Option 4: Risk owner

Correct Response: 4

Explanation: The risk owner is responsible for managing the response to an assigned risk.

Knowledge Area: Exam_Sim

Question Number: 474

Question: Which risk analysis method models scenarios like disasters?

Option 1: Quantitative

Option 2: HRVA

Option 3: Qualitative

Option 4: Aleatory

Correct Response: 2

Explanation: HRVA analyzes risks using hypothetical disaster scenarios.

Knowledge Area: Exam_Sim

Question Number: 475

Question: What indicates a sound risk response decision?

Option 1: Low costs

Option 2: Fast implementation

Option 3: Risk owner approval

Option 4: High benefits

Correct Response: 3

Explanation: Risk owner approval ensures alignment on risk response.

Knowledge Area: Exam_Sim

Question Number: 476

Question: Which control would detect unauthorized changes to production data?

Option 1: Access logs

Option 2: IDS

Option 3: DLP

Option 4: File integrity monitoring

Correct Response: 4

Explanation: File integrity monitoring detects and alerts on unexpected data modifications.

Knowledge Area: Exam_Sim

Question Number: 477

Question: What should a risk manager do upon discovering a new regulatory requirement?

Option 1: Assess compliance gaps

Option 2: Update policies

Option 3: Assign ownership

Option 4: Purchase software

Correct Response: 1

Explanation: Gaps to compliance with new regulations should be promptly assessed.

Knowledge Area: Exam_Sim

Question Number: 478

Question: What helps avoid over-reporting insignificant risks?

Option 1: KRIs

Option 2: KPIs

Option 3: RTOs

Option 4: Risk appetite

Correct Response: 4

Explanation: Risk appetite distinguishes meaningful risks from minor nuisances.

Knowledge Area: Exam_Sim

Question Number: 479

Question: What provides continuous visibility into information security threats?

Option 1: VA scans

Option 2: Pen tests

Option 3: BCP reviews

Option 4: Threat intel

Correct Response: 4

Explanation: Threat intel provides real-time monitoring of emerging security threats.

Knowledge Area: Exam_Sim

Question Number: 480

Question: What would help gauge training effectiveness following a phishing exercise?

Option 1: Click rate

Option 2: Speed of reporting

Option 3: Quiz scores

Option 4: Simulation realism

Correct Response: 1

Explanation: Click rate measures susceptibility to phishing post-training.

Knowledge Area: Exam_Sim

Question Number: 481

Question: Where are the root causes of operational disruptions typically documented?

Option 1: Audit reports

Option 2: Risk register

Option 3: Incident reports

Option 4: RTOs

Correct Response: 3

Explanation: Incident reports contain details of root cause analysis.

Knowledge Area: Exam_Sim

Question Number: 482

Question: Most important for incident response is:

Option 1: Blocking attacks

Option 2: Timely recognition

Option 3: Data logging

Option 4: Tracing source

Correct Response: 2

Explanation: Quick recognition limits damage.

Knowledge Area: Exam_Sim

Question Number: 483

Question: Accountability for security controls belongs to:

Option 1: Risk owners

Option 2: IT management

Option 3: Security function

Option 4: Enterprise risk

Correct Response: 3

Explanation: Security owns control implementation.

Knowledge Area: Exam_Sim

Question Number: 484

Question: Anti-malware effectiveness is best indicated by:

Option 1: Staff hours lost

Option 2: Software patches

Option 3: Successful attacks

Option 4: Server downtime

Correct Response: 3

Explanation: Fewer successful attacks mean better protection.

Knowledge Area: Exam_Sim

Question Number: 485

Question: When evaluating IT risk management, most important is confirming:

Option 1: Risk appetite/tolerance

Option 2: New control processes

Option 3: Risk reporting

Option 4: Investment alignment

Correct Response: 1

Explanation: Appetite sets risk expectations.

Knowledge Area: Exam_Sim

Question Number: 486

Question: The primary KRI use is providing:

Option 1: Trend analysis

Option 2: Early warning

Option 3: Historical view

Option 4: Risk appetite indication

Correct Response: 2

Explanation: KRIs give early signals of emerging risk.

Knowledge Area: Exam_Sim

Question Number: 487

Question: An example of a non-technical control is:

Option 1: Encryption

Option 2: IDS

Option 3: Physical security

Option 4: Access control

Correct Response: 3

Explanation: Physical controls are non-technical.

Knowledge Area: Exam_Sim

Question Number: 488

Question: A risk assessment output is:

Option 1: Residual risk

Option 2: Control identification

Option 3: Risk identification

Option 4: Mitigated risk

Correct Response: 4

Explanation: Assessments reveal risks.

Knowledge Area: Exam_Sim

Question Number: 489

Question: The first security monitoring step is:

Option 1: Implement monitoring

Option 2: Prioritize risks

Option 3: Identify controls

Option 4: Report results

Correct Response: 3

Explanation: Monitoring depends on identified controls.

Knowledge Area: Exam_Sim

Question Number: 490

Question: Which is the BEST method to promote effective risk communication with the board?

Option 1: Detailed technical reports

Option 2: Dashboards with key risk indicators

Option 3: Risk register updates

Option 4: Heat maps illustrating severity

Correct Response: 2

Explanation: Dashboards with key risk/performance indicators effectively communicate with executives.

Knowledge Area: Exam_Sim

Question Number: 491

Question: Management has requested a routine information security risk report. Which format would BEST ensure the risks are understood by the audience?

Option 1: Detailed risk assessment

Option 2: Heat map of critical risks

Option 3: Technical vulnerability scan results

Option 4: Executive dashboard highlighting trends

Correct Response: 4

Explanation: Executive dashboards effectively communicate key risk information to management.

Knowledge Area: Exam_Sim

Question Number: 492

Question: Risk thresholds are specified in a:

Option 1: Impact matrix

Option 2: Probability matrix

Option 3: Risk indicator matrix

Option 4: Scenario matrix

Correct Response: 3

Explanation: A risk indicator matrix sets thresholds.

Knowledge Area: Exam_Sim

Question Number: 493

Question: The most important risk response factor is:

Option 1: Implementation capability

Option 2: Response efficiency

Option 3: Response cost

Option 4: Risk importance

Correct Response: 3

Explanation: Feasibility determines viability.

Knowledge Area: Exam_Sim

Question Number: 494

Question: A key outcome of risk ownership is:

Option 1: Communicating risk info

Option 2: Analyzing process risk

Option 3: Defining risk tasks

Option 4: Addressing responsibilities

Correct Response: 2

Explanation: Ownership ensures accountability.

Knowledge Area: Exam_Sim

Question Number: 495

Question: The main purpose of a risk profile is to:

Option 1: Prioritize investments

Option 2: Update the register

Option 3: Enable decisions

Option 4: Ensure compliance

Correct Response: 1

Explanation: It informs risk-based decisions.

Knowledge Area: Exam_Sim

Question Number: 496

Question: Maturity models primarily compare:

Option 1: Desired and current states

Option 2: Peers

Option 3: Best practices

Option 4: KPIs

Correct Response: 1

Explanation: The gap shows improvement opportunities.

Knowledge Area: Exam_Sim

Question Number: 497

Question: Effective risk analysis should:

Option 1: Limit scope

Option 2: Focus on likelihood

Option 3: Assume equal protection

Option 4: Address loss potential

Correct Response: 4

Explanation: Potential loss insight guides responses.

Knowledge Area: Exam_Sim

Question Number: 498

Question: The greatest reporting risk is to data:

Option 1: Availability

Option 2: Integrity

Option 3: Confidentiality

Option 4: Reliability

Correct Response: 2

Explanation: Integrity is critical for accurate reporting.

Knowledge Area: Exam_Sim

Question Number: 499

Question: Classifying assets is most important for:

Option 1: Access rights

Option 2: Risk ownership

Option 3: Security objectives

Option 4: Control identification

Correct Response: 4

Explanation: Classification guides required controls.

Knowledge Area: Exam_Sim

Question Number: 500

Question: An effective control environment is best indicated by controls that:

Option 1: Minimize risk tolerance

Option 2: Manage risk within appetite

Option 3: Are cost-effective

Option 4: Reduce KRI thresholds

Correct Response: 2

Explanation: Controls should align risk to appetite.

Question Number: 501

Question: What is most critical when designing controls?

Option 1: Process owner involvement

Option 2: Internal audit involvement

Option 3: KRI identification

Option 4: Risk impact

Correct Response: 1

Explanation: Involving the process owner is key.

Knowledge Area: Exam_Sim

Question Number: 502

Question: Whose risk tolerance matters most in decisions?

Option 1: Affected customers

Option 2: Information security manager

Option 3: Auditors and regulators

Option 4: Business process owner

Correct Response: 4

Explanation: The process owner's tolerance governs.

Knowledge Area: Exam_Sim

Question Number: 503

Question: The primary objective in selecting responses is to:

Option 1: Identify compensating controls

Option 2: Reduce risk factors

Option 3: Minimize residual risk

Option 4: Reduce risk to acceptable levels

Correct Response: 3

Explanation: The goal is to reach acceptable risk.

Knowledge Area: Exam_Sim

Question Number: 504

Question: The primary purpose of control reporting is to:

Option 1: Ensure governance compliance

Option 2: Benchmark with standards

Option 3: Support internal audit

Option 4: Compare current and desired states

Correct Response: 4

Explanation: It facilitates desired state comparison.

Knowledge Area: Exam_Sim

Question Number: 505

Question: Which is NOT true about risk governance?

Option 1: Seeks to fill risk gaps

Option 2: Requires annual reporting

Option 3: Enables risk management

Option 4: Is a systemic approach

Correct Response: 2

Explanation: Reporting is not necessarily annual.

Knowledge Area: Exam_Sim

Question Number: 506

Question: When developing scenarios, which role is critical to involve?

Option 1: IT managers

Option 2: Internal auditors

Option 3: Senior management

Option 4: Process owners

Correct Response: 4

Explanation: Involving process owners provides insights.

Knowledge Area: Exam_Sim

Question Number: 507

Question: A cloud provider contract must include:

Option 1: Financial statements

Option 2: Recovery plan

Option 3: Source code escrow

Option 4: Responsibility ownership

Correct Response: 2

Explanation: It should define accountability.

Knowledge Area: Exam_Sim

Question Number: 508

Question: The greatest concern with a risk register is:

Option 1: No executive reviews

Option 2: Excluding risk changes

Option 3: Unlinked IT risks

Option 4: Qualitative impacts

Correct Response: 2

Explanation: Excluding risk factor changes is most concerning.

Knowledge Area: Exam_Sim

Question Number: 509

Question: Accountability for a risk is best shown in a:

Option 1: Risk scenario

Option 2: Risk catalog

Option 3: RACI matrix

Option 4: Risk register

Correct Response: 3

Explanation: A RACI matrix clarifies accountability.

Knowledge Area: Exam_Sim

Question Number: 510

Question: For effective business support, a risk register must:

Option 1: Reflect assessments

Option 2: Support maturity models

Option 3: Be reviewed by IT steering

Option 4: Be available to risk groups

Correct Response: 1

Explanation: It must reflect current assessment results.

Knowledge Area: Exam_Sim

Question Number: 511

Question: The primary goal of risk management is to:

Option 1: Safeguard assets

Option 2: Prevent losses

Option 3: Ensure objectives are met

Option 4: Enable resources

Correct Response: 3

Explanation: The key goal is enabling objectives.

Knowledge Area: Exam_Sim

Question Number: 512

Question: The main purpose in designing risk programs is to:

Option 1: Reduce risk to an acceptable level

Option 2: Reduce risk until cost exceeds benefit

Option 3: Reduce risk to an immeasurable level

Option 4: Reduce risk to match cost of capital

Correct Response: 1

Explanation: The purpose is to reach acceptable risk levels.

Knowledge Area: Exam_Sim

Question Number: 513

Question: Who should implement security controls?

Option 1: Data custodian

Option 2: Internal auditor

Option 3: Data owner

Option 4: End user

Correct Response: 3

Explanation: The data owner is responsible.

Knowledge Area: Exam_Sim

Question Number: 514

Question: The most effective way to prioritize risks is by:

Option 1: Cost of response

Option 2: Input from experts

Option 3: Strategic alignment

Option 4: Industry best practices

Correct Response: 3

Explanation: Strategic plan alignment is optimal.

Knowledge Area: Exam_Sim

Question Number: 515

Question: The best criteria for selecting a risk response is:

Option 1: Capability to implement

Option 2: Effectiveness

Option 3: Industry alignment

Option 4: Response importance

Correct Response: 2

Explanation: Effectiveness should drive selection.

Knowledge Area: Exam_Sim

Question Number: 516

Question: The annualized loss expectancy (AL) method of risk analysis helps determine:

Option 1: Qualitative rankings

Option 2: Indirect impacts

Option 3: Expected control costs

Option 4: Cost-benefit analysis

Correct Response: 4

Explanation: ALE supports cost-benefit analysis.

Knowledge Area: Exam_Sim

Question Number: 517

Question: What is the primary need for assessing controls?

Option 1: Alignment with environment

Option 2: Objective achievement

Option 3: Design effectiveness

Option 4: Operating effectiveness

Correct Response: 4

Explanation: Operating effectiveness is most critical.

Knowledge Area: Exam_Sim

Question Number: 518

Question: Which statement about risk evaluation is true?

Option 1: Only after significant change

Option 2: Annually for all processes

Option 3: Annually or after change

Option 4: Every 4-6 months for critical

Correct Response: 3

Explanation: Evaluation should happen annually or after major change.

Knowledge Area: Exam_Sim

Question Number: 519

Question: Mapping open risk issues to the enterprise best facilitates:

Option 1: Risk identification

Option 2: Risk response

Option 3: Control monitoring

Option 4: Risk ownership

Correct Response: 4

Explanation: It clarifies risk accountability.

Knowledge Area: Exam_Sim

Question Number: 520

Question: Which negative response usually has a contract?

Option 1: Sharing

Option 2: Transference

Option 3: Mitigation

Option 4: Exploiting

Correct Response: 2

Explanation: Transference often involves a contract.

Knowledge Area: Exam_Sim

Question Number: 521

Question: Which statement best describes risk appetite?

Option 1: Acceptable variation in thresholds

Option 2: Amount of risk accepted

Option 3: Effective risk management

Option 4: Acceptable variation in objectives

Correct Response: 2

Explanation: Appetite reflects the amount of risk tolerated.

Knowledge Area: Exam_Sim

Question Number: 522

Question: IT risk assessments are best used by management:

Option 1: To show compliance

Option 2: As cost-benefit input

Option 3: To measure success

Option 4: To inform decisions

Correct Response: 4

Explanation: Assessments provide decision-making insights.

Knowledge Area: Exam_Sim

Question Number: 523

Question: A risk owner should be accountable for:

Option 1: Managing controls

Option 2: Implementing actions

Option 3: Risk management process

Option 4: Business process

Correct Response: 4

Explanation: The risk owner governs the business process.

Knowledge Area: Exam_Sim

Question Number: 524

Question: Which represents lack of adequate controls?

Option 1: Vulnerability

Option 2: Threat

Option 3: Asset

Option 4: Impact

Correct Response: 1

Explanation: Vulnerabilities indicate control gaps.

Knowledge Area: Exam_Sim

Question Number: 525

Question: Which would be considered a vulnerability?

Option 1: Delayed access removal

Option 2: Malware corruption

Option 3: Authorized access

Option 4: Downtime from DoS

Correct Response: 1

Explanation: Delayed access removal is a vulnerability.

Knowledge Area: Exam_Sim

Question Number: 526

Question: What can be determined from a risk scenario chart?

Option 1: Risk treatment options

Option 2: Capability to implement

Option 3: Relative risk map positions

Option 4: Risk factors addressed

Correct Response: 4

Explanation: It shows which factors a response addresses.

Knowledge Area: Exam_Sim

Question Number: 527

Question: Prudent practice requires risk appetite not exceed which level?

Option 1: Residual risk

Option 2: Inherent risk

Option 3: Risk tolerance

Option 4: Risk capacity

Correct Response: 4

Explanation: Appetite should not surpass capacity.

Knowledge Area: Exam_Sim

Question Number: 528

Question: What are the primary control objectives?

Option 1: Detect, recover, attack

Option 2: Prevent, respond, log

Option 3: Prevent, control, attack

Option 4: Prevent, recover, detect

Correct Response: 4

Explanation: Key goals are to prevent, recover and detect.

Knowledge Area: Exam_Sim

Question Number: 529

Question: Which is a detective control?

Option 1: Limit check

Option 2: Access software

Option 3: Periodic review

Option 4: Rerun procedures

Correct Response: 3

Explanation: Periodic reviews are detective controls.

Knowledge Area: Exam_Sim

Question Number: 530

Question: What is an administrative control?

Option 1: Water detection

Option 2: Reasonableness check

Option 3: Data loss prevention

Option 4: Session timeout

Correct Response: 4

Explanation: Session timeouts are administrative.

Knowledge Area: Exam_Sim

Question Number: 531

Question: Which statement describes policy?

Option 1: Minimum controls required

Option 2: Steps to ensure security

Option 3: Overall security direction

Option 4: Technology best practices

Correct Response: 3

Explanation: Policy sets overall security direction.

Question Number: 532

Question: What provides the most valuable input for assessing disaster recovery capabilities?

Option 1: Higher % systems meeting RTOs

Option 2: Fewer systems needing plans

Option 3: More systems tested annually

Option 4: Lower % systems with long RTOs

Correct Response: 4

Explanation: Fewer systems with lengthy recovery times indicates stronger DR readiness.

Knowledge Area: Exam_Sim

Question Number: 533

Question: Before adopting a new SaaS application, what activity provides the most risk insights?

Option 1: Review provider's uptime history

Option 2: Analyze provider's security architecture

Option 3: Assess provider's backup procedures

Option 4: Compare to industry standards

Correct Response: 3

Explanation: Assessing the provider's security controls is critical to manage SaaS risks.

Knowledge Area: Exam_Sim

Question Number: 534

Question: What is the main purpose of administrative controls like access reviews?

Option 1: Detect unauthorized access

Option 2: Recover from incidents

Option 3: Enforce password standards

Option 4: Prevent privileged access

Correct Response: 4

Explanation: Administrative controls aim to prevent unauthorized system and data access.

Knowledge Area: Exam_Sim

Question Number: 535

Question: How should management utilize IT risk assessment results?

Option 1: Demonstrate compliance

Option 2: Justify expenditures

Option 3: Measure success metrics

Option 4: Inform risk decisions

Correct Response: 4

Explanation: Risk assessments provide valuable insights to inform management decisions.

Knowledge Area: Exam_Sim

Question Number: 536

Question: To optimize risk management resource allocation, what should drive the focus areas?

Option 1: Regulatory requirements

Option 2: Senior management concerns

Option 3: Industry benchmarks

Option 4: Assessed risk appetite

Correct Response: 4

Explanation: Aligning efforts with the organization's risk appetite directs optimal focus.

Knowledge Area: Exam_Sim

Question Number: 537

Question: What is the most effective option to mitigate supply chain disruption risks?

Option 1: Increase inventory levels

Option 2: Improve demand forecasting

Option 3: Dual source critical components

Option 4: Negotiate volume discounts

Correct Response: 3

Explanation: Dual sourcing key items through alternate suppliers reduces risk.

Knowledge Area: Exam_Sim

Question Number: 538

Question: Per best practices, risk appetite should not surpass which level?

Option 1: Residual risk

Option 2: Inherent risk

Option 3: Risk tolerance

Option 4: Risk capacity

Correct Response: 4

Explanation: Risk appetite should not exceed the organization's overall risk capacity.

Knowledge Area: Exam_Sim

Question Number: 539

Question: What type of control is malicious code protection?

Option 1: Access control

Option 2: Integrity control

Option 3: Configuration management

Option 4: Recovery control

Correct Response: 2

Explanation: Malicious code protection is a system integrity control

Knowledge Area: Exam_Sim

Question Number: 540

Question: A vendor identified a new project risk. The risk register and responses were updated. What else should the project manager update?

Option 1: Project scope statement

Option 2: Project communications plan

Option 3: Project contractual agreements

Option 4: Project management plan

Correct Response: 4

Explanation: The project management plan should reflect new risk information.

Knowledge Area: Exam_Sim

Question Number: 541

Question: A director demands a late change to the project scope. What should the project manager do with the verbal change request?

Option 1: Implement the change immediately

Option 2: Direct the team to add it if possible

Option 3: Do not act without written request

Option 4: Report the director to the sponsor

Correct Response: 3

Explanation: Verbal direction should not dictate a change.

Knowledge Area: Exam_Sim

Question Number: 542

Question: A scope change request may impact cost, schedule, and other areas. What process evaluates the overall change impact?

Option 1: Risk analysis

Option 2: Configuration management

Option 3: Project change control

Option 4: Integrated change control

Correct Response: 4

Explanation: Integrated change control assesses all impacts.

Knowledge Area: Exam_Sim

Question Number: 543

Question: A machine will overheat and shutdown above 500 degrees. At 450 degrees it will pause to cool. What is 450 degrees called in this context?

Option 1: Risk identification

Option 2: Risk event

Option 3: Risk trigger

Option 4: Risk response

Correct Response: 3

Explanation: 450 degrees is the defined risk trigger point.

Knowledge Area: Exam_Sim

Question Number: 544

Question: A project is training on new materials to reduce costs though needing more time upfront. What is this risk approach called?

Option 1: Team development

Option 2: Cost conformance

Option 3: Cost-benefit analysis

Option 4: Benchmarking

Correct Response: 3

Explanation: It is a cost-benefit analysis of the new materials.

Knowledge Area: Exam_Sim

Question Number: 545

Question: Where should documented risk responses be included after project completion?

Option 1: Project management plan

Option 2: Risk management plan

Option 3: Lessons learned database

Option 4: Risk register

Correct Response: 3

Explanation: Captured responses belong in the lessons database.

Knowledge Area: Exam_Sim

Question Number: 546

Question: A project finds a cheaper way to complete work, saving $65,000 for a $25,000 cost. What response was used?

Option 1: Avoiding

Option 2: Accepting

Option 3: Exploiting

Option 4: Enhancing

Correct Response: 3

Explanation: The opportunity was exploited for project savings.

Knowledge Area: Exam_Sim

Question Number: 547

Question: A project manager assigns a resource to increase the probability of a positive risk event. What response is this?

Option 1: Transference

Option 2: Exploit

Option 3: Enhance

Option 4: Sharing

Correct Response: 3

Explanation: Enhancing seeks to increase positive risks.

Knowledge Area: Exam_Sim

Question Number: 548

Question: For a high-impact project, management wants early risk information to support avoidance. What determines avoidance preference?

Option 1: Mitigation-ready PM

Option 2: Risk-reward mentality

Option 3: Risk utility function

Option 4: Risk aversion

Correct Response: 4

Explanation: A risk utility function measures avoidance desire.

Knowledge Area: Exam_Sim

Question Number: 549

Question: A project manager wants anonymous risk identification. What method allows this?

Option 1: SWOT analysis

Option 2: Root cause analysis

Option 3: Isolated pilot groups

Option 4: Delphi technique

Correct Response: 4

Explanation: The Delphi technique maintains anonymity.

Knowledge Area: Exam_Sim

Question Number: 550

Question: For a high-profile project, what model assesses stakeholder power and interest?

Option 1: Stakeholder register

Option 2: Influence/impact grid

Option 3: Salience model

Option 4: Power/interest grid

Correct Response: 4

Explanation: The power/interest grid plots stakeholder influence.

Knowledge Area: Exam_Sim

Question Number: 551

Question: What communicates approval or denial of a proposed change request?

Option 1: Configuration management system

Option 2: Integrated change control

Option 3: Change log

Option 4: Scope change control

Correct Response: 2

Explanation: Integrated change control governs changes.

Knowledge Area: Exam_Sim

Question Number: 552

Question: Where should risks from new technology be documented for tracking?

Option 1: Project scope statement

Option 2: Project charter

Option 3: Watch list

Option 4: Risk register

Correct Response: 4

Explanation: The risk register tracks and manages risks.

Knowledge Area: Exam_Sim

Question Number: 553

Question: Why have recurring risk meetings throughout a project?

Option 1: Discuss past risks

Option 2: Communicate pending risks

Option 3: Allow stakeholder participation

Option 4: Identify new risks

Correct Response: 3

Explanation: It reveals new risks throughout the project.

Knowledge Area: Exam_Sim

Question Number: 554

Question: What process evaluates a change to reduce status reports from weekly to biweekly?

Option 1: Configuration management

Option 2: Communications management

Option 3: Integrated change control

Option 4: Project change control

Correct Response: 3

Explanation: Integrated change control governs changes.

Knowledge Area: Exam_Sim

Question Number: 555

Question: A project manager creates a contingent response to hire another vendor if the current vendor delivers late. This demonstrates:

Option 1: Risk acceptance

Option 2: Risk sharing

Option 3: Risk mitigation

Option 4: Risk avoidance

Correct Response: 2

Explanation: A contingent response involves risk sharing to reduce impact.

Knowledge Area: Exam_Sim

Question Number: 556

Question: The IRGC risk governance framework aims to:

Option 1: Evaluate secondary impacts

Option 2: Enhance organizational resilience

Option 3: Integrate risk disciplines

Option 4: Build robust models

Correct Response: 4

Explanation: IRGC integrates risk disciplines into robust governance models.

Knowledge Area: Exam_Sim

Question Number: 557

Question: During risk identification, all documents are used EXCEPT the:

Option 1: Requirements checklist

Option 2: Risk register

Option 3: Stakeholder analysis

Option 4: Cost baseline

Correct Response: 2

Explanation: The risk register tracks identified risks and is not an input.

Knowledge Area: Exam_Sim

Question Number: 558

Question: Redesigning overly complex systems to reduce cost and risk requires:

Option 1: Business case analysis

Option 2: Contagious risk management

Option 3: Quick risk mitigation

Option 4: Risk deferral

Correct Response: 1

Explanation: This strategic response needs a strong business case.

Knowledge Area: Exam_Sim

Question Number: 559

Question: Charting risk probability, impact, and cost supports:

Option 1: Qualitative analysis

Option 2: Risk acceptance

Option 3: Contingency planning

Option 4: Quantitative analysis

Correct Response: 4

Explanation: This analysis evaluates risk numerically and financially.

Knowledge Area: Exam_Sim

Question Number: 560

Question: When a vendor's costs increase, the change should pass through:

Option 1: Scope control

Option 2: Schedule control

Option 3: Cost control

Option 4: No control

Correct Response: 3

Explanation: Cost changes go through cost change control processes.

Knowledge Area: Exam_Sim

Question Number: 561

Question: Risk analysis can be improved by:

Option 1: Focusing on critical risks

Option 2: Involving select stakeholders

Option 3: Rushing qualitative assessments

Option 4: Using subject matter experts

Correct Response: 4

Explanation: Experts provide insights into risks and responses.

Knowledge Area: Exam_Sim

Question Number: 562

Question: To monitor network performance, packet loss is:

Option 1: A leading indicator

Option 2: A lagging indicator

Option 3: A key performance indicator

Option 4: A key risk indicator

Correct Response: 2

Explanation: Packet loss is a lagging indicator of problems.

Knowledge Area: Exam_Sim

Question Number: 563

Question: When a CIO introduces scope changes, the impact is reviewed through:

Option 1: Cost control

Option 2: Configuration control

Option 3: Scope control

Option 4: Integrated control

Correct Response: 3

Explanation: Scope changes go through scope change control.

Knowledge Area: Exam_Sim

Question Number: 564

Question: For risks from an approved change, mitigation responses are recorded in the:

Option 1: Risk register

Option 2: Project plan

Option 3: Risk management plan

Option 4: Risk log

Correct Response: 1

Explanation: The risk register tracks mitigation responses.

Knowledge Area: Exam_Sim

Question Number: 565

Question: A system not fulfilling needs and being unused reflects:

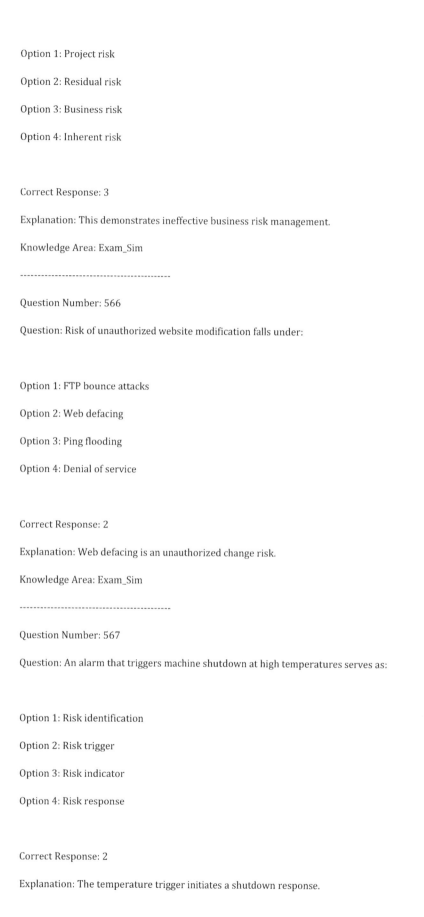

Option 1: Project risk

Option 2: Residual risk

Option 3: Business risk

Option 4: Inherent risk

Correct Response: 3

Explanation: This demonstrates ineffective business risk management.

Knowledge Area: Exam_Sim

Question Number: 566

Question: Risk of unauthorized website modification falls under:

Option 1: FTP bounce attacks

Option 2: Web defacing

Option 3: Ping flooding

Option 4: Denial of service

Correct Response: 2

Explanation: Web defacing is an unauthorized change risk.

Knowledge Area: Exam_Sim

Question Number: 567

Question: An alarm that triggers machine shutdown at high temperatures serves as:

Option 1: Risk identification

Option 2: Risk trigger

Option 3: Risk indicator

Option 4: Risk response

Correct Response: 2

Explanation: The temperature trigger initiates a shutdown response.

Knowledge Area: Exam_Sim

Question Number: 568

Question: A document defining risk identification, quantification, and contingencies is the:

Option 1: Resource plan

Option 2: Project plan

Option 3: Project management plan

Option 4: Risk management plan

Correct Response: 4

Explanation: This defines the risk management approach.

Knowledge Area: Exam_Sim

Question Number: 569

Question: To test disaster recovery, a project manager should review:

Option 1: Risk tolerance

Option 2: Incident response

Option 3: Recovery time

Option 4: Risk appetite

Correct Response: 3

Explanation: Recovery time shows disaster preparedness.

Knowledge Area: Exam_Sim

Question Number: 570

Question: When scope changes are approved in a project, what should the project manager update based on these changes?

Option 1: Risk assessment

Option 2: Communication plan

Option 3: Procurement strategy

Option 4: Quality management plan

Correct Response: 2

Explanation: When scope changes are approved in a project, the project manager should update the communication plan. Scope changes can affect project stakeholders and may require adjustments to the communication approach, channels, and frequency. By updating the communication plan, the project manager ensures effective and timely communication regarding the scope changes to relevant stakeholders.

Knowledge Area: Exam_Sim

Question Number: 571

Question: Which type of analysis examines the extent to which the uncertainty of each element affects the object under consideration when all other uncertain elements are held at their baseline values?

Option 1: Sensitivity analysis

Option 2: Monte Carlo simulation

Option 3: Root cause analysis

Option 4: Scenario analysis

Correct Response: 1

Explanation: The type of analysis described in this scenario is sensitivity analysis. Sensitivity analysis examines the impact of changing one variable while keeping all other variables at their baseline values. It helps identify which elements or factors have the highest potential to affect the object under consideration. By understanding these sensitivities, organizations can focus their risk management efforts on critical areas and make informed decisions.

Knowledge Area: Exam_Sim

Question Number: 572

Question: In rating project risks based on probability and impact, who is correct in the scenario where the project manager rates each risk separately, and a team member suggests creating an accumulative risk score?

Option 1: The project manager is correct

Option 2: The team member is correct

Option 3: Both approaches are valid

Option 4: Neither approach is valid

Correct Response: 1

Explanation: In this scenario, the project manager is correct. Rating each risk separately based on probability and impact allows for a more comprehensive understanding of the risks. It enables the project manager to prioritize risks and allocate resources accordingly. Creating an accumulative risk score may overlook specific risks that require specific attention and mitigation efforts.

Knowledge Area: Exam_Sim

Question Number: 573

Question: In response to a vendor delay, a project manager arranges for a local company to lease equipment until the ordered equipment arrives. This is an example of which risk response strategy?

Option 1: Avoidance

Option 2: Mitigation

Option 3: Transfer

Option 4: Acceptance

Correct Response: 3

Explanation: The example described represents the risk response strategy of transfer. By arranging for a local company to lease equipment, the project manager transfers the risk associated with the vendor delay to the local company. This strategy allows the project to continue without disruption and mitigates the potential impact of the vendor delay.

Knowledge Area: Exam_Sim

Question Number: 574

Question: Mary, a project manager, is using a facilitator to help generate ideas about project risks. What risk identification method is Mary likely using?

Option 1: Delphi technique

Option 2: Brainstorming

Option 3: SWOT analysis

Option 4: Checklist analysis

Correct Response: 2

Explanation: Mary is likely using the risk identification method of brainstorming. Brainstorming involves a facilitated session where project team members and stakeholders generate ideas and identify potential risks. It encourages open discussion and creativity, allowing for a wide range of risks to be identified. The involvement of a facilitator helps in guiding and managing the brainstorming session effectively.

Question Number: 575

Question: To configure a monitoring tool to report only when alerts are marked as "critical," what should be done?

Option 1: Adjust the alert thresholds

Option 2: Increase the monitoring frequency

Option 3: Modify the reporting format

Option 4: Define the alert severity levels

Correct Response: 1

Explanation: To configure a monitoring tool to report only when alerts are marked as "critical," the alert thresholds should be adjusted. By setting the thresholds specifically for critical alerts, the monitoring tool will generate reports only when the alerts meet the predefined criteria. This ensures that the focus is on critical events, allowing for efficient monitoring and response to significant risks.

Knowledge Area: Exam_Sim

Question Number: 576

Question: From a business perspective, what is the most important objective of a disaster recovery test?

Option 1: Validate the effectiveness of backup and recovery procedures

Option 2: Assess the performance of technical infrastructure components

Option 3: Identify gaps and areas for improvement in the recovery process

Option 4: Ensure minimal disruption and timely recovery of business operations

Correct Response: 4

Explanation: From a business perspective, the most important objective of a disaster recovery test is to ensure minimal disruption and timely recovery of business operations. The test aims to validate the organization's ability to recover critical processes and systems in the event of a disaster. By conducting the test, organizations can identify any gaps or areas for1 apologize for the incomplete response.

Knowledge Area: Exam_Sim

Question Number: 577

Question: You are managing a project to develop a new system interface. You've identified all possible risks. What is needed next to prioritize the risks?

Option 1: Mitigation strategies

Option 2: Qualitative analysis

Option 3: Probability and impact assessment

Option 4: Risk categorization

Correct Response: 3

Explanation: Prioritization requires probability and impact analysis of identified risks.

Knowledge Area: Exam_Sim

Question Number: 578

Question: You are managing a school network project. The school asks to add Wi-Fi, possibly impacting the project. After discussing with stakeholders, what is your next step?

Option 1: Refuse change as too risky

Option 2: Estimate time and cost to add Wi-Fi

Option 3: Add Wi-Fi without analysis

Option 4: Analyze change request impact

Correct Response: 4

Explanation: Analyze the change request's impact before acting on it.

Knowledge Area: Exam_Sim

Question Number: 579

Question: Your project's risk level exceeds tolerances. After applying responses, what should not be in the updated risk register?

Option 1: Risk owners

Option 2: Response strategies

Option 3: Trigger conditions

Option 4: Prior probabilities

Correct Response: 4

Explanation: Prior probabilities are not updated after applying risk responses.

Knowledge Area: Exam_Sim

Question Number: 580

Question: Your project has external stakeholders. What plan provides guidance on appropriately communicating risks?

Option 1: Risk management plan

Option 2: Communications management plan

Option 3: Stakeholder engagement plan

Option 4: Procurement management plan

Correct Response: 2

Explanation: The communications plan covers appropriate risk reporting.

Knowledge Area: Exam_Sim

Question Number: 581

Question: A risk could significantly reduce project costs if it occurs. Management may hire a vendor to assure realizing the savings. What is true of this risk?

Option 1: It should be avoided due to high impact.

Option 2: Its probability and impact should be reassessed.

Option 3: It presents an opportunity to the project.

Option 4: It should be mitigated to reduce costs.

Correct Response: 3

Explanation: The risk presents potential cost savings for the project.

Knowledge Area: Exam_Sim

Question Number: 582

Question: You are reassessing project risks. What should be done with events whose likelihood has passed?

Option 1: Update them as issues

Option 2: Keep them for historical records

Option 3: Delete them from register

Option 4: Archive them as unlikely

Correct Response: 3

Explanation: Risks that can no longer occur should be removed from the register.

Knowledge Area: Exam_Sim

Question Number: 583

Question: Identifying project risks requires inputs. Which is NOT an input to risk identification?

Option 1: Activity cost estimates

Option 2: Project documents

Option 3: Enterprise risk databases

Option 4: Lessons learned

Correct Response: 1

Explanation: Cost estimates are not an input to identifying risks.

Knowledge Area: Exam_Sim

Question Number: 584

Question: A new risk could significantly delay your project if it occurs. What should you do?

Option 1: Ignore the risk as impact is low

Option 2: Mitigate the risk to avoid the delay

Option 3: Reject the risk as outside project scope

Option 4: Accept the risk and monitor triggers

Correct Response: 4

Explanation: Accept the risk and monitor trigger conditions.

Question Number: 585

Question: A risk workshop brings together project team members and subject matter experts to brainstorm potential threats and opportunities.

Option 1: Schedule risk analysis

Option 2: Quantitative risk analysis

Option 3: Data gathering and representation

Option 4: Risk categorization

Correct Response: 1

Explanation: Risk workshops facilitate collaborative risk identification.

Knowledge Area: Exam_Sim

Question Number: 586

Question: You identified 47 project risks having low probability and impact. How should you manage these risks?

Option 1: Mitigate them

Option 2: Use risk tolerance

Option 3: Monitor trigger conditions

Option 4: Accept and monitor them

Correct Response: 4

Explanation: Accept and monitor lower priority risks.

Knowledge Area: Exam_Sim

Question Number: 587

Question: You are starting risk response planning for a 1-year, $350,000 project. What two inputs do you need?

Option 1: Risk register and budget

Option 2: Risk analysis and mitigation strategies

Option 3: Stakeholder register and procurement docs

Option 4: Risk register and risk appetite

Correct Response: 1

Explanation: The risk register and risk appetite guide response planning.

Knowledge Area: Exam_Sim

Question Number: 588

Question: A key permit for your project is delayed. How do you categorize this issue?

Option 1: Compliance risk

Option 2: Schedule risk

Option 3: Budget risk

Option 4: Scope creep

Correct Response: 2

Explanation: Permit delays present a project schedule risk.

Knowledge Area: Exam_Sim

Question Number: 589

Question: In qualitative analysis, you grouped risks by common causes. What is the primary advantage of this?

Option 1: Simplifies quantitative modeling

Option 2: Highlights correlation and impacts

Option 3: Satisfies governance requirements

Option 4: Aids risk monitoring

Correct Response: 2

Explanation: Grouping shows how risks interconnect.

Knowledge Area: Exam_Sim

Question Number: 590

Question: What input helps identify risks tied to activity time allowances?

Option 1: Risk categories

Option 2: Stakeholder register

Option 3: Scope statement

Option 4: Duration estimates

Correct Response: 4

Explanation: Duration estimates signal risks around activity timing.

Knowledge Area: Exam_Sim

Question Number: 591

Question: You refuse to accept risks threatening injury, so you hired vendors to remove the risk. What response is this?

Option 1: Mitigate

Option 2: Exploit

Option 3: Accept

Option 4: Avoid

Correct Response: 4

Explanation: Transferring the work avoids the risk fully.

Knowledge Area: Exam_Sim

Question Number: 592

Question: A team member's scope increase introduced new risks you removed by cutting added features. What is this called?

Option 1: Risk avoidance

Option 2: Risk sharing

Option 3: Risk mitigation

Option 4: Risk transference

Correct Response: 1

Explanation: Removing risky features avoids those risks.

Knowledge Area: Exam_Sim

Question Number: 593

Question: As a project manager, you must identify risks that could impact your project. What inputs help identify risks related to activity durations?

Option 1: Project budget

Option 2: Requirements docs

Option 3: Activity duration estimates

Option 4: Lessons learned

Correct Response: 3

Explanation: Duration estimates help highlight timing risks.

Knowledge Area: Exam_Sim

Question Number: 594

Question: Brainstorming with experts is an effective way to collaboratively identify potential project risks and opportunities.

Option 1: Quantitative analysis

Option 2: Data analysis

Option 3: Risk prioritization

Option 4: Risk categorization

Correct Response: 1

Explanation: Brainstorming facilitates risk identification.

Knowledge Area: Exam_Sim

Question Number: 595

Question: David, the project manager of the HRC project, decides not to engage in e-commerce to avoid the associated risks. What type of risk response has he adopted?

Option 1: Avoidance

Option 2: Mitigation

Option 3: Acceptance

Option 4: Transfer

Correct Response: 1

Explanation: David has adopted the risk response strategy of avoidance. By choosing not to engage in e-commerce, he is avoiding the risks associated with that line of business altogether. Avoidance is a risk response strategy where the project manager takes steps to eliminate the risk by avoiding the activities or situations that give rise to the risk.

Knowledge Area: Exam_Sim

Question Number: 596

Question: You are the project manager of the NHQ project in Bluewell Inc. The project has an asset valued at $200,000 and is subjected to an exposure factor of 45 percent. If the annual rate of occurrence of loss in this project is once a month, then what will be the Annual Loss Expectancy (ALE) of the project?

Option 1: US$90,000

Option 2: US$240,000

Option 3: US$2,400,000

Option 4: US$9,000

Correct Response: 2

Explanation: The Annual Loss Expectancy (ALE) can be calculated by multiplying the asset value by the exposure factor and the annual rate of occurrence. In this case, the ALE would be $200,000 * 45% * 12 months = $2,400,000. Therefore, the correct option is b) $2,400,000.

Knowledge Area: Exam_Sim

Question Number: 597

Question: You are working with a vendor on your project. A stakeholder has requested a change that will add value to the project deliverables. What system can help you introduce and execute the stakeholder change request with the vendor?

Option 1: Change request management system

Option 2: Vendor management system

Option 3: Risk management system

Option 4: Communication management system

Correct Response: 1

Explanation: The system that can help introduce and execute the stakeholder change request with the vendor is a change request management system. This system provides a structured approach to managing change requests, including capturing, evaluating, and implementing stakeholder change requests. It helps ensure that all requested changes are appropriately reviewed, approved, and communicated to the vendor for implementation.

Knowledge Area: Exam_Sim

Question Number: 598

Question: You are working in an enterprise where important files are stored on the computer. You have identified the risk of operational failure. To address this risk, you have required the system administrator to sign off on the daily backup. This scenario is an example of which of the following?

Option 1: Risk acceptance

Option 2: Risk avoidance

Option 3: Risk transfer

Option 4: Risk mitigation

Correct Response: 4

Explanation: The scenario described is an example of risk mitigation. By requiring the system administrator to sign off on the daily backup, the project manager is implementing a risk mitigation measure to reduce the likelihood and impact of operational failure. Risk mitigation involves taking proactive steps to minimize the risk or its consequences.

Knowledge Area: Exam_Sim

Question Number: 599

Question: You are the risk professional of your enterprise. You need to calculate the potential revenue loss if a specific risk occurs. Your enterprise has an e-commerce website that generates US $1 million of revenue each day. If a denial-of-service (DoS) attack occurs that lasts half a day, what is the potential loss?

Option 1: US $0.5 million

Option 2: US $0.25 million

Option 3: US $1 million

Option 4: US $2 million

Correct Response: 2

Explanation: The potential loss due to the DoS attack can be calculated by multiplying the revenue generated per day ($1 million) by the duration of the attack (half a day or 0.5). Therefore, the potential loss would be US $1 million * 0.5 = US $0.25 million. Hence, the correct option is b) US $0.25 million.

Knowledge Area: Exam_Sim

Question Number: 600

Question: Billy, the project manager of the HAR Project, is in month six of the project, which is scheduled to last for 18 months. Management asks Billy about the frequency of project team participation in risk reassessment. What should Billy tell management if he's following the best practices for risk management?

Option 1: Risk reassessment should be done monthly

Option 2: Risk reassessment should be done quarterly

Option 3: Risk reassessment should be done annually

Option 4: Risk reassessment should be done on an ad-hoc basis

Correct Response: 2

Explanation: Following the best practices for risk management, Billy should tell management that risk reassessment should be done quarterly. Regular risk reassessment helps ensure that risks are monitored and evaluated periodically, taking into account any changes in the project's context, risks, or risk responses. It allows for timely identification of emerging risks and reassessment of existing risks to ensure effective risk management.

Knowledge Area: Exam_Sim

HELP US IMPROVE!

WE WANT YOUR FEEDBACK

WalterEducation.com

Amazing!

You have been studying very hard to this stage.

How is your exam preparation so far? Can the practice test meet your needs and expectation? I desperately desire your voice.

Please kindly consider

1. Visiting my exam practice test books and consider purchasing them to assist you to pass your target exam, though the direct links provided at the beginning of this book
2. Visiting my exam practice test courses held at Udemy though the direct links provided at the beginning of this book
3. Leaving a positive review and feedback to me though the direct book review links provided at the next page.

Keep going! See you at the end of the book.

Warm regards,

Walter

Or the **Links at Amazon Book Store:**

CRISC 1200+ Practice Test, 2023 (Exam Simulation and Core & Advanced Knowledge)	
Paperback Review URL:	- https://www.amazon.com/review/create-review?&asin=B0CJ43R78T
Kindle eBook Review URL:	- https://www.amazon.com/review/create-review?&asin=B0CJ72JJLY

Direct URLs to visit all Walter's Practice Tests at Amazon

Visit Walter's author page:
http://WalterEducation.com

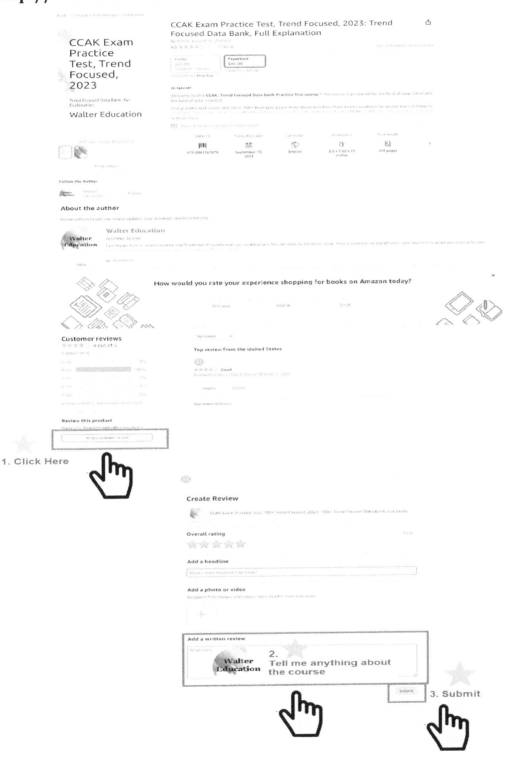

Question Number: 601

Question: A delay is hurting your project's schedule. With approval, you fast track work to finish faster. What will likely increase?

Option 1: Risk identification

Option 2: Project costs

Option 3: Schedule flexibility

Option 4: Project risks

Correct Response: 4

Explanation: Fast tracking compresses the schedule but increases risks.

Knowledge Area: Exam_Sim

Question Number: 602

Question: In a risk meeting, a stakeholder asks about discussing a current problem. What addresses when a risk becomes an issue?

Option 1: Issues reflect the absence of risks

Option 2: Risks are potential future events

Option 3: Issues are current project problems

Option 4: Risks and issues are identical

Correct Response: 3

Explanation: A risk is a problem when it moves from potential to current.

Knowledge Area: Exam_Sim

Question Number: 603

Question: You are completing quantitative risk analysis. Which is not a valid tool/technique?

Option 1: Interviewing

Option 2: Sensitivity analysis

Option 3: Cost estimation

Option 4: Decision tree analysis

Correct Response: 3

Explanation: Cost estimation is not used in quantitative risk analysis.

Knowledge Area: Exam_Sim

Question Number: 604

Question: By adding qualified resources you could reduce project duration. Seizing this opportunity exemplifies which response?

Option 1: Exploit

Option 2: Mitigate

Option 3: Accept

Option 4: Transfer

Correct Response: 1

Explanation: Exploit responses take advantage of positive risks.

Knowledge Area: Exam_Sim

Question Number: 605

Question: You are identifying stakeholders to communicate requirements and risks. Using a salience model involves which activity?

Option 1: Assessing reporting needs

Option 2: Grouping stakeholders by roles

Option 3: Mapping influence and impact

Option 4: Developing a communications matrix

Correct Response: 3

Explanation: Salience models map stakeholder influence/impact.

Knowledge Area: Exam_Sim

Question Number: 606

Question: In quantitative analysis, you identified unrecognized risks. What should you do with them?

Option 1: Reject and document the risks

Option 2: Plan responses to the risks

Option 3: Update the risk register

Option 4: Monitor the triggers

Correct Response: 3

Explanation: Previously unidentified risks get added to the risk register.

Knowledge Area: Exam_Sim

Question Number: 607

Question: You are communicating analysis results, reporting risk activities, and identifying opportunities. What process are you in?

Option 1: Risk identification

Option 2: Qualitative risk analysis

Option 3: Risk response planning

Option 4: Risk monitoring and control

Correct Response: 4

Explanation: These activities are part of risk monitoring and control.

Knowledge Area: Exam_Sim

Question Number: 608

Question: To gain a bonus, you elect to crash the project schedule. This exemplifies which response?

Option 1: Mitigate

Option 2: Avoid

Option 3: Exploit

Option 4: Accept

Correct Response: 3

Explanation: Crashing accepts increased risk to pursue an opportunity.

Knowledge Area: Exam_Sim

Question Number: 609

Question: To determine risk probability and impacts, you could conduct an expected monetary value (EMV) analysis of potential costs.

Option 1: Decision tree analysis

Option 2: Risk urgency assessment

Option 3: RBS development

Option 4: Stakeholder analysis

Correct Response: 1

Explanation: EMV analysis evaluates risk impacts and likelihood.

Knowledge Area: Exam_Sim

Question Number: 610

Question: What tool will help you measure the probability, impact, and risk exposure?

Option 1: Risk probability and impact assessment matrix

Option 2: Risk breakdown structure

Option 3: Risk register

Option 4: Risk assessment questionnaire

Correct Response: 1

Explanation: The tool that will help you measure the probability, impact, and risk exposure is the risk probability and impact assessment matrix. This tool allows you to assess the likelihood and consequences of identified risks and calculate their overall risk exposure. By using the matrix, you can prioritize risks based on their probability and impact, helping you focus on those with higher risk exposure.

Knowledge Area: Exam_Sim

Question Number: 611

Question: John wants the project team to work together on establishing risk thresholds. What is the purpose of establishing risk thresholds?

Option 1: To determine the acceptable level of risk for the project

Option 2: To identify potential risks and their impacts

Option 3: To develop risk response plans

Option 4: To monitor and control risks

Correct Response: 1

Explanation: The purpose of establishing risk thresholds is to determine the acceptable level of risk for the project. By setting risk thresholds, the project team can define the boundaries within which risks are considered acceptable or unacceptable. This helps in decision-making, risk prioritization, and determining appropriate risk response actions. Risk thresholds provide guidance for monitoring and controlling risks throughout the project lifecycle.

Knowledge Area: Exam_Sim

Question Number: 612

Question: You are the project manager for your organization and are preparing for the quantitative risk analysis. as a project team member, you wants to know why you need to do quantitative risk analysis when you just completed qualitative risk analysis. What statement best defines quantitative risk analysis?

Option 1: Quantitative risk analysis involves assessing the numerical values of risks to determine their impact on project objectives.

Option 2: Quantitative risk analysis focuses on categorizing risks based on their severity and likelihood.

Option 3: Quantitative risk analysis identifies risks and their potential impacts qualitatively.

Option 4: Quantitative risk analysis involves evaluating the overall project risk tolerance.

Correct Response: 1

Explanation: Quantitative risk analysis involves assessing the numerical values of risks to determine their impact on project objectives. It involves assigning values to risks based on probability and impact, calculating expected monetary value (EMV), and conducting quantitative modeling to analyze the potential outcomes. This analysis provides a more precise understanding of the project's overall risk exposure and helps in prioritizing risk response actions.

Knowledge Area: Exam_Sim

Question Number: 613

Question: In which project management process group will you implement risk response plans for the ABC project?

Option 1: Initiating

Option 2: Planning

Option 3: Executing

Option 4: Monitoring and controlling

Correct Response: 2

Explanation: The project management process group in which risk response plans will be implemented for the GHY project is the planning process group. During the planning phase, the project manager identifies risks, assesses their impacts and likelihood, and develops risk response plans to address them. Implementing risk response plans involves executing the planned risk mitigation and contingency actions to reduce the impact or likelihood of identified risks.

Knowledge Area: Exam_Sim

Question Number: 614

Question: As an experienced Project Manager working on a project to develop a machine for producing auto components, you schedule meetings with the project team and key stakeholders to identify risks. What is a key output of this process?

Option 1: Risk management plan

Option 2: Risk register

Option 3: Risk breakdown structure

Option 4: Risk identification checklist

Correct Response: 2

Explanation: A key output of the risk identification process is the risk register. The risk register is a comprehensive document that captures all identified risks, their descriptions, potential impacts, and initial assessments. It serves as a central repository of project risks and provides a foundation for further risk analysis, response planning, and monitoring.

Knowledge Area: Exam_Sim

Question Number: 615

Question: The hardware vendor for your ABC project has left you a voicemail stating that the delivery of the ordered equipment will not arrive on time. Which statement is TRUE?

Option 1: The risk event has occurred

Option 2: The risk event is imminent

Option 3: The risk event has not occurred yet

Option 4: The risk event is in progress

Correct Response: 3

Explanation: In this scenario, the risk event of the delayed delivery has not occurred yet. The vendor's voicemail serves as a notification or early warning of a potential risk event. While the delivery delay is expected, it has not yet happened at the time of receiving the voicemail.

Knowledge Area: Exam_Sim

Question Number: 616

Question: During the qualitative risk analysis process, you discover that the risk categories have not been created. When should the risk categories have been created?

Option 1: During the project initiation phase

Option 2: During the project planning phase

Option 3: During the project execution phase

Option 4: During the project closure phase

Correct Response: 2

Explanation: The risk categories should have been created during the project planning phase. Establishing risk categories is an essential step in the qualitative risk analysis process. It involves grouping risks into common categories based on their nature, source, or impact. The risk categories provide a structured approach to identify, assess, and manage risks throughout the project.

Knowledge Area: Exam_Sim

Question Number: 617

Question: Executives feel IT should own IT risks in an IT scenario review. How should you address this?

Option 1: Agree that IT owns the risks

Option 2: Explain all stakeholders own a share of risk

Option 3: Let executives delegate all IT risks to IT

Option 4: Focus only on non-IT risks

Correct Response: 2

Explanation: Explain that all stakeholders share responsibility for mitigating risks.

Question Number: 618

Question: Managing stakeholder expectations creates an output that can generate new project risks. What output is this?

Option 1: Risk register updates

Option 2: Change requests

Option 3: Issue log

Option 4: Lessons learned

Correct Response: 2

Explanation: Changes in expectations lead stakeholders to initiate changes, causing risks.

Knowledge Area: Exam_Sim

Question Number: 619

Question: You want to remove a requirement to eliminate an associated high probability, high impact risk. What response is this?

Option 1: Mitigate

Option 2: Transfer

Option 3: Exploit

Option 4: Avoid

Correct Response: 4

Explanation: Removing the requirement avoids the risk entirely.

Knowledge Area: Exam_Sim

Question Number: 620

Question: Why include the cost management plan in quantitative risk analysis?

Option 1: It calculates the project ROI

Option 2: It estimates activity costs for impacts

Option 3: It outlines the risk budget

Option 4: It defines risk reporting formats

Correct Response: 2

Explanation: Cost estimates support quantifying risk impacts.

Knowledge Area: Exam_Sim

Question Number: 621

Question: After monitoring occurred risks, what is the next risk management step?

Option 1: Risk identification

Option 2: Qualitative analysis

Option 3: Risk response

Option 4: Control enhancements

Correct Response: 4

Explanation: Improve controls through learned lessons.

Knowledge Area: Exam_Sim

Question Number: 622

Question: To add a change, what must the project manager do?

Option 1: Consult the project sponsor

Option 2: Update risk register

Option 3: Conduct impact analysis

Option 4: Submit a change request

Correct Response: 4

Explanation: Changes require a formal change request and analysis.

Knowledge Area: Exam_Sim

Question Number: 623

Question: You will create procedures to address regulatory noncompliance risk. What response priority fits this?

Option 1: Exploit

Option 2: Transfer

Option 3: Mitigate

Option 4: Avoid

Correct Response: 3

Explanation: Creating controls to address noncompliance mitigates the risk.

Knowledge Area: Exam_Sim

Question Number: 624

Question: Disabled employee accounts weren't deleted promptly. You will monitor the situation for 3 months. This risk is now:

Option 1: Transferred

Option 2: Avoided

Option 3: Accepted

Option 4: Mitigated

Correct Response: 3

Explanation: Monitoring accepts the risk to gather more information.

Knowledge Area: Exam_Sim

Question Number: 625

Question: To identify potential schedule delay risks, you compare planned and actual progress to date. What technique is this?

Option 1: Risk urgency assessment

Option 2: Schedule analysis

Option 3: Cost-benefit analysis

Option 4: Risk categorization

Correct Response: 2

Explanation: Schedule analysis exposes risks around activity timelines.

Knowledge Area: Exam_Sim

Question Number: 626

Question: Which technique helps identify risks posed by changes to an IT system?

Option 1: Regression testing

Option 2: Impact analysis

Option 3: User acceptance testing

Option 4: Load testing

Correct Response: 2

Explanation: Impact analysis studies how changes affect related processes and technologies to identify potential risks.

Knowledge Area: Exam_Sim

Question Number: 627

Question: What is an advantage of the bow tie risk analysis method?

Option 1: It quantifies risk

Option 2: It estimates financial impact

Option 3: It visualizes cause and effect

Option 4: It models scenarios

Correct Response: 3

Explanation: The bow tie diagram shows causes leading to a risk event and effects stemming from the event.

Knowledge Area: Exam_Sim

Question Number: 628

Question: An employee lost a laptop containing sensitive data. What should be done FIRST?

Option 1: Locate the laptop

Option 2: Identify the data lost

Option 3: Suspend the employee

Option 4: Invoke incident response

Correct Response: 4

Explanation: Following incident response ensures an orderly and effective response to the data loss event.

Knowledge Area: Exam_Sim

Question Number: 629

Question: Which threat actor typically launches ransomware attacks?

Option 1: Script kiddies

Option 2: Hacktivists

Option 3: Organized crime

Option 4: Nation states

Correct Response: 3

Explanation: Ransomware attacks are often financially motivated, making organized crime the most likely actor.

Knowledge Area: Exam_Sim

Question Number: 630

Question: What helps assign accountability for responding to a particular risk?

Option 1: Risk register

Option 2: Risk matrix

Option 3: Risk appetite

Option 4: Risk owner

Correct Response: 4

Explanation: The risk owner is responsible for managing the response to a given risk.

Knowledge Area: Exam_Sim

Question Number: 631

Question: Which control helps detect unauthorized changes to production environments?

Option 1: Change requests

Option 2: Access controls

Option 3: Vulnerability scans

Option 4: File integrity monitoring

Correct Response: 4

Explanation: File integrity monitoring detects and alerts on unexpected modifications to files.

Knowledge Area: Exam_Sim

Question Number: 632

Question: What metric helps evaluate patching effectiveness?

Option 1: Time to patch

Option 2: Patch coverage

Option 3: Patch errors

Option 4: Exploitation rate

Correct Response: 4

Explanation: The exploitation rate measures if patched systems are still being compromised.

Knowledge Area: Exam_Sim

Question Number: 633

Question: Where should root causes of operational disruptions be documented?

Option 1: Risk register

Option 2: Incident reports

Option 3: Audit reports

Option 4: Business impact assessments

Correct Response: 2

Explanation: Incident reports detail the root causes found during an investigation of operational events.

Knowledge Area: Exam_Sim

Question Number: 634

Question: Many policy exceptions indicate:

Option 1: Risk owners want efficiency

Option 2: Risk approaches tolerance

Option 3: Policies need reviewing

Option 4: Vulnerabilities persist

Correct Response: 2

Explanation: Exceptions increase aggregate risk exposure.

Knowledge Area: Exam_Sim

Question Number: 635

Question: To augment ransomware awareness, the next priority is:

Option 1: Multifactor authentication

Option 2: Encryption in motion

Option 3: Encryption at rest

Option 4: Continuous backup

Correct Response: 4

Explanation: Backups enable recovery after an attack.

Knowledge Area: Exam_Sim

Question Number: 636

Question: To augment ransomware awareness, the next priority is:

Option 1: Inclusion of all resources

Option 2: External log sources

Option 3: Time synchronization

Option 4: Access permissions

Correct Response: 2

Explanation: Time sync enables event correlation.

Knowledge Area: Exam_Sim

Question Number: 637

Question: When a provider says hacking risk is low, you should:

Option 1: Accept the risk assessment

Option 2: Perform your own assessment

Option 3: Implement more controls

Option 4: Audit the provider

Correct Response: 4

Explanation: An independent assessment is needed.

Knowledge Area: Exam_Sim

Question Number: 638

Question: To reduce residual risk, the best step is to:

Option 1: Develop new actions

Option 2: Recommend risk acceptance

Option 3: Prioritize remediation

Option 4: Add controls

Correct Response: 3

Explanation: Focusing on remediation is most effective.

Knowledge Area: Exam_Sim

Question Number: 639

Question: New website payments will likely increase:

Option 1: Inherent risk

Option 2: Risk tolerance

Option 3: Residual risk

Option 4: Risk appetite

Correct Response: 3

Explanation: More activity creates more residual risk exposure.

Knowledge Area: Exam_Sim

Question Number: 640

Question: With a computer center on an earthquake fault, most important is:

Option 1: Hot site readiness

Option 2: Offsite backup media

Option 3: Avoiding shared sites

Option 4: Remote location

Correct Response: 4

Explanation: Immediate processing resumption is critical.

Knowledge Area: Exam_Sim

Question Number: 641

Question: For a new CRM system, who should own data leakage risk?

Option 1: CRO

Option 2: Controls manager

Option 3: CISO

Option 4: Business owner

Correct Response: 4

Explanation: The business process owner is accountable.

Knowledge Area: Exam_Sim

Question Number: 642

Question: A software vulnerability scan identified several high risk flaws in an internet-facing web application. Due to the criticality of the application, the flaws must be addressed quickly. Which response is appropriate to remediate this risk?

Option 1: Report findings to developers and monitor for fixes

Option 2: Disable the web application until patches are complete

Option 3: Overhaul security architecture to prevent future issues

Option 4: Engage auditors to assess all systems for similar exposures

Correct Response: 1

Explanation: Reporting high priority flaws to developers to implement fixes is the most direct response to address the discovered risk.

Knowledge Area: Exam_Sim

Question Number: 643

Question: A spike in detected malware downloads was observed following rollout of a new remote work platform. Additional security controls may be needed to manage the risk of infection. What should trigger implementation of a response?

Option 1: Excessive false positives from antivirus software

Option 2: Independent validation of actual malware incidents

Option 3: Concerns expressed on social media about security

Option 4: Comparison to historic malware infection rates

Correct Response: 2

Explanation: The observed increase should be validated before initiating a disproportionate response.

Knowledge Area: Exam_Sim

Question Number: 644

Question: A company is implementing a new cloud-based ERP system. What approach would BEST protect business objectives?

Option 1: Perform real-time transaction monitoring

Option 2: Utilize the cloud provider's security controls

Option 3: Implement redundant ERP instances

Option 4: Negotiate comprehensive SLA terms

Correct Response: 4

Explanation: Strong SLAs help ensure ERP availability and performance.

Knowledge Area: Exam_Sim

Question Number: 645

Question: A hospital is deploying a new MRI machine. What should the risk practitioner recommend to support objectives?

Option 1: Conduct mandatory staff training

Option 2: Perform scans in a Faraday cage

Option 3: Follow manufacturer maintenance procedures

Option 4: Activate built-in authentication controls

Correct Response: 3

Explanation: Proper maintenance protects availability and reduces downtime.

Knowledge Area: Exam_Sim

Question Number: 646

Question: A change management process has recently been updated with new testing procedures. The NEXT step is to:

Option 1: Conduct training sessions for all employees

Option 2: Immediately implement the new process across all changes

Option 3: Gradually rollout the updated process to pilot groups first

Option 4: Delay implementation until after current projects complete

Correct Response: 3

Explanation: Gradually rolling out the updated process to pilot groups allows testing it prior to full implementation. This helps identify potential issues before a major organizational impact.

Knowledge Area: Exam_Sim

Question Number: 647

Question: A risk assessment of a customer database supporting a critical business application identified several high severity vulnerabilities. The FIRST course of action should be to:

Option 1: Implement monitoring for suspicious database activity

Option 2: Migrate the database to a cloud provider

Option 3: Apply database patches on a weekly basis

Option 4: Remediate the high severity findings immediately

Correct Response: 4

Explanation: Remediating high severity vulnerabilities protects the production database's confidentiality, integrity and availability.

Knowledge Area: Exam_Sim

Question Number: 648

Question: A risk assessment of an accounting system determined the Oracle database is out of support. The BEST response would be to:

Option 1: Migrate to a supported version after testing

Option 2: Implement additional database monitoring

Option 3: Rely on the application vendor for support

Option 4: Accept the risk until next year's budget

Correct Response: 1

Explanation: Migrating to a supported version after thorough testing protects the accounting system while minimizing disruptions.

Knowledge Area: Exam_Sim

Question Number: 649

Question: A healthcare organization is concerned about potential HIPAA data leakage. Which control would BEST manage this risk?

Option 1: Annual cybersecurity training

Option 2: Encrypted email communications

Option 3: Access controls for medical records

Option 4: Deep packet inspection firewall

Correct Response: 3

Explanation: Tight access controls prevents unauthorized exposure of protected health information.

Knowledge Area: Exam_Sim

Question Number: 650

Question: An accounting firm wants to reduce the risk of client data theft. Which approach would be MOST effective?

Option 1: Block USB drives via group policy

Option 2: Implement DLP scanning on email attachments

Option 3: Enable remote wipe on mobile devices

Option 4: Prohibit use of personal cloud storage

Correct Response: 2

Explanation: DLP scanning would identify confidential data transmitted via email.

Knowledge Area: Exam_Sim

Question Number: 651

Question: An organization faces regulatory compliance risk from an outdated legacy system. Which risk treatment option would be BEST?

Option 1: Accept the risk

Option 2: Implement controls to protect legacy system

Option 3: Migrate applications to a supported platform

Option 4: Insure compliance-related losses

Correct Response: 3

Explanation: Migrating to supported platforms reduces inherent risk.

Knowledge Area: Exam_Sim

Question Number: 652

Question: A hospital faces the risk of medical device malfunctions during surgeries. Which option would be optimal for managing this risk?

Option 1: Increase staff training on devices

Option 2: Purchase additional spare parts inventory

Option 3: Implement preventive maintenance procedures

Option 4: Outsource surgeries to external facilities

Correct Response: 3

Explanation: Preventive maintenance reduces probability of medical device failures.

Knowledge Area: Exam_Sim

Question Number: 653

Question: Which practice indicates a HIGH degree of risk management maturity?

Option 1: Ad-hoc assessments when issues arise

Option 2: Quarterly risk reporting to executives

Option 3: Continuous control monitoring and testing

Option 4: Annual GRC program reviews

Correct Response: 3

Explanation: Continuous control monitoring demonstrates sustainable risk practices.

Knowledge Area: Exam_Sim

Question Number: 654

Question: A risk manager seeks to enhance the program's maturity. Which action would help achieve this?

Option 1: Purchase integrated GRC software

Option 2: Present findings to senior management

Option 3: Shift from qualitative to quantitative methods

Option 4: Update risk management policies annually

Correct Response: 2

Explanation: Regular reporting to executives gains visibility and buy-in.

Knowledge Area: Exam_Sim

Question Number: 655

Question: An organization is concerned about intellectual property theft and wants to implement a data loss prevention program to better protect sensitive information. Which approach would provide the MOST value?

Option 1: Conduct periodic user security awareness training

Option 2: Disable external storage devices via group policy

Option 3: Implement network monitoring to detect abnormal data transfers

Option 4: Install endpoint DLP agents to scan and block confidential data exfiltration

Correct Response: 4

Explanation: Installing DLP agents provides automated scanning and blocking of confidential data extraction, preventing exploitation of authorized access for IP theft.

Knowledge Area: Exam_Sim

Question Number: 656

Question: A hospital is deploying automated medication dispensing cabinets to improve drug inventory controls. What would BEST manage risks and support related objectives?

Option 1: Utilize default system credentials to minimize administrative overhead

Option 2: Rely on general physical access restrictions for dispensing cabinets

Option 3: Ensure cabinets integrate with pharmacy inventory management system

Option 4: Accept risk of dispensing errors to maximize clinician productivity

Correct Response: 3

Explanation: Integration with the pharmacy system provides necessary drug inventory visibility and control for the automated dispensing process.

Knowledge Area: Exam_Sim

Question Number: 657

Question: An organization wants to improve its ability to anticipate emerging risks and exposures. Which approach would add the MOST value?

Option 1: Conduct annual risk assessments

Option 2: Monitor industry threat reports

Option 3: Analyze internal incident data trends

Option 4: Perform quarterly vulnerability scans

Correct Response: 3

Explanation: Analyzing internal incident data can reveal risk trends and systemic issues.

Knowledge Area: Exam_Sim

Question Number: 658

Question: A hospital is concerned about patient readmission rates. Which technique would BEST identify contributing risk factors?

Option 1: Regression analysis of readmission data

Option 2: Interviews with care providers

Option 3: Root cause analysis of sample cases

Option 4: Comparison to industry readmission benchmarks

Correct Response: 1

Explanation: Regression analysis of readmission data could expose correlations with risk factors.

Knowledge Area: Exam_Sim

Question Number: 659

Question: An organization wants to identify potential causes leading to missed customer delivery dates. Which approach would be MOST useful?

Option 1: Fault tree analysis

Option 2: Regression testing

Option 3: Fishbone diagram

Option 4: Failure modes analysis

Correct Response: 3

Explanation: A fishbone diagram can map out causes of an effect like missed deliveries.

Knowledge Area: Exam_Sim

Question Number: 660

Question: A hospital is trying to reduce surgery delays. Which technique would effectively analyze contributing factors?

Option 1: Control charts

Option 2: Pareto analysis

Option 3: Ishikawa diagram

Option 4: Decision tree

Correct Response: 3

Explanation: A fishbone diagram can trace surgery delays back to root causes for analysis.

Knowledge Area: Exam_Sim

Question Number: 661

Question: An organization wants to evaluate risks associated with a new product launch. Which technique would be MOST helpful for analyzing potential scenarios and impacts?

Option 1: Decision tree analysis

Option 2: Monte Carlo simulations

Option 3: Fault tree mapping

Option 4: Bowtie diagramming

Correct Response: 2

Explanation: Monte Carlo simulations allow modeling of multiple possible scenarios and sensitivity analysis.

Knowledge Area: Exam_Sim

Question Number: 662

Question: A company is assessing risks related to delays in new software releases. Which approach would BEST analyze the sensitivity of the project schedule to task uncertainties?

Option 1: Probabilistic network modeling

Option 2: Failure modes and effects analysis

Option 3: Bayesian network diagramming

Option 4: Ishikawa fishbone diagram

Correct Response: 1

Explanation: Probabilistic modeling evaluates the likelihood of overall delays based on task uncertainties.

Knowledge Area: Exam_Sim

Question Number: 663

Question: A financial organization wants to assess operational risks of a new blockchain-based transaction system. Which technique would be MOST effective?

Option 1: Threat modeling

Option 2: Petri net simulations

Option 3: Vulnerability scanning

Option 4: Cost-benefit analysis

Correct Response: 2

Explanation: Petri net simulations can model complex system dependencies and workflows.

Knowledge Area: Exam_Sim

Question Number: 664

Question: A retailer is concerned about cyber risks to a new e-commerce platform. Which approach would allow modeling different attack scenarios?

Option 1: Bowtie diagram

Option 2: Failure tree analysis

Option 3: Actuarial data modeling

Option 4: Bayesian network analysis

Correct Response: 4

Explanation: Bayesian networks can probabilistically model cyber attack scenarios and effects.

Knowledge Area: Exam_Sim

Question Number: 665

Question: An organization is adopting a BYOD policy and wants to evaluate the likelihood and impact of security risks associated with employee-owned devices accessing corporate resources. Which quantitative risk analysis method would provide the MOST accurate assessment?

Option 1: Threat surveys

Option 2: Vulnerability scans

Option 3: Annualized loss expectancies

Option 4: Monte Carlo simulations

Correct Response: 4

Explanation: Monte Carlo simulations using probability distributions for threat frequency and statistical loss data provides a quantitative risk estimate.

Knowledge Area: Exam_Sim

Question Number: 666

Question: A hospital is upgrading its EHR system and wants to assess the likelihood and impact of patient record availability and integrity risks during the transition. Which technique would enable statistically modeling this risk scenario?

Option 1: Key risk indicators

Option 2: Failure modes analysis

Option 3: Sensitivity analysis

Option 4: Bayesian network diagrams

Correct Response: 4

Explanation: Bayesian network analysis incorporates probabilities for risk event likelihoods and statistical impact distributions.

Knowledge Area: Exam_Sim

Question Number: 667

Question: After a risk assessment, the NEXT step is to:

Option 1: Implement all identified risk responses

Option 2: Present findings to senior management

Option 3: Update the risk register with new identified risks

Option 4: Re-assess accepted risks for any changes

Correct Response: 3

Explanation: The risk register should be updated with new risks identified in the assessment.

Knowledge Area: Exam_Sim

Question Number: 668

Question: Following a project risk assessment, what should the risk manager update FIRST?

Option 1: Risk treatment plans

Option 2: Risk reporting dashboards

Option 3: The organizational risk register

Option 4: Risk assessment methodology

Correct Response: 3

Explanation: The risk register is updated first with new identified risks from the assessment.

Knowledge Area: Exam_Sim

Question Number: 669

Question: An audit identified multiple weaknesses in an organization's change management controls. Which risk analysis method would BEST prioritize the most significant deficiencies to address?

Option 1: COSO framework review

Option 2: Control testing sample size

Option 3: Risk likelihood determinations

Option 4: Risk impact estimations

Correct Response: 4

Explanation: Estimating risk impact of deficiencies can determine which pose the greatest significance.

Knowledge Area: Exam_Sim

Question Number: 670

Question: An assessment of a manufacturing plant's safety controls revealed several gaps. Which approach would help identify the MOST critical areas needing improvement?

Option 1: Threat likelihood rating

Option 2: Industry benchmarking

Option 3: Risk register integration

Option 4: Risk exposure calculations

Correct Response: 4

Explanation: Risk exposure from safety control gaps provides priority for remediation efforts.

Knowledge Area: Exam_Sim

Question Number: 671

Question: An organization conducted an audit of GDPR compliance controls and identified multiple gaps that could lead to regulatory noncompliance and data breaches. Which risk analysis technique would provide the MOST value in prioritizing the most significant deficiencies needing remediation?

Option 1: Process flow mapping

Option 2: Industry benchmarking

Option 3: Likelihood determinations

Option 4: Risk exposure calculations through estimating potential impact

Correct Response: 4

Explanation: Estimating risk exposure from potential regulatory fines and data breach impacts helps prioritize addressing deficiencies posing the greatest significance.

Knowledge Area: Exam_Sim

Question Number: 672

Question: A hospital assessed its controls for hazardous chemical management and found several vulnerabilities that could result in improper handling and environmental discharges. Which approach would enable focusing risk treatment plans on the MOST critical gaps?

Option 1: Fishbone diagram of causes

Option 2: Industry best practice reviews

Option 3: Risk register integration

Option 4: Risk analysis quantifying environmental and safety impacts

Correct Response: 4

Explanation: Quantitatively estimating potential safety and environmental impacts from control gaps guides priority for risk treatment.

Knowledge Area: Exam_Sim

Question Number: 673

Question: An organization wants a visualized risk rating method. Which tool would be MOST effective?

Option 1: Risk likelihood/impact matrix

Option 2: Bowtie analysis diagrams

Option 3: RACI responsibility chart

Option 4: Risk control maturity model

Correct Response: 1

Explanation: A risk heat map plots risks by likelihood and impact in a color-coded matrix.

Knowledge Area: Exam_Sim

Question Number: 674

Question: A company needs to prioritize information security risks for remediation. Which technique would provide the MOST value?

Option 1: Threat trend analysis

Option 2: Vulnerability scan results

Option 3: Risk register scoring

Option 4: Risk heat map visualization

Correct Response: 4

Explanation: A risk heat map graphically identifies high priority risks based on likelihood and impact.

Knowledge Area: Exam_Sim

Question Number: 675

Question: An organization wants to visually represent key cybersecurity risks for the board of directors to provide clear risk rankings and priorities for treatment. Which risk analysis output would provide the MOST effective visualization of significant risks requiring remediation?

Option 1: Risk likelihood and impact matrix

Option 2: Threat trend analysis

Option 3: Vulnerability scan results

Option 4: Risk heat map with color-coded severity indicators

Correct Response: 4

Explanation: A risk heat map provides graphical color-coded visualization of risk likelihood vs impact comparisons to identify high priority risks for treatment.

Knowledge Area: Exam_Sim

Question Number: 676

Question: A hospital is conducting an enterprise risk assessment of patient safety hazards and desires a technique to effectively communicate key risks to executive leadership for risk treatment prioritization. Which approach would provide the BEST visualization of the most critical patient safety risks?

Option 1: Bowtie analysis diagrams

Option 2: Failure modes analysis

Option 3: Risk register scoring

Option 4: Risk heat map illustrating color-coded criticality levels

Correct Response: 4

Explanation: A risk heat map vividly highlights patient safety risks requiring priority attention through color-coded criticality indicators.

Knowledge Area: Exam_Sim

Question Number: 677

Question: An organization wants to be notified when operational risks exceed acceptable levels and require intervention. Which risk management technique would be MOST effective for setting thresholds and identifying exceeded risk appetite conditions?

Option 1: Annual risk assessments

Option 2: Industry benchmarking

Option 3: Key risk indicators with triggers

Option 4: Risk register reporting

Correct Response: 3

Explanation: Implementing key risk indicators with defined thresholds identifies when risks exceed accepted levels per risk appetite.

Knowledge Area: Exam_Sim

Question Number: 678

Question: A retailer desires to promptly identify cybersecurity incidents likely to cause significant business disruption and financial impacts. Which risk management method would provide the BEST means of defining thresholds and alerting when unacceptable risk levels are reached?

Option 1: Risk heat mapping

Option 2: Threat intelligence monitoring

Option 3: Key risk indicators tied to risk tolerance

Option 4: Penetration test results

Correct Response: 3

Explanation: Configuring key risk indicators with thresholds based on risk tolerance facilitates automated identification of unacceptable risks.

Knowledge Area: Exam_Sim

Question Number: 679

Question: Which group is responsible for establishing and implementing risk management policies and controls as the SECOND line of defense?

Option 1: External auditors

Option 2: The board of directors

Option 3: Business unit managers

Option 4: The risk management function

Correct Response: 4

Explanation: The risk management function is the second line of defense for managing policies and controls.

Knowledge Area: Exam_Sim

Question Number: 680

Question: What is the role of business unit leaders regarding risk management under the Three Lines of Defense model?

Option 1: Identifying emerging risks

Option 2: Conducting risk assessments

Option 3: Implementing risk responses

Option 4: Monitoring risk practices

Correct Response: 3

Explanation: Business units implement risk responses under the first line of defense.

Knowledge Area: Exam_Sim

Question Number: 681

Question: What is the FIRST step when developing a new business continuity plan?

Option 1: Documenting procedures and processes

Option 2: Training staff on procedures

Option 3: Performing a business impact analysis

Option 4: Implementing risk reduction measures

Correct Response: 3

Explanation: The initial step is a BIA to identify critical processes and recovery priorities.

Knowledge Area: Exam_Sim

Question Number: 682

Question: An organization is implementing a business continuity management program. What should be the FIRST activity performed?

Option 1: Developing the continuity plan

Option 2: Training employees on procedures

Option 3: Selecting alternate facilities

Option 4: Conducting a business impact analysis

Correct Response: 4

Explanation: The BIA is the initial step to identify critical operations, RPOs/RTOs.

Knowledge Area: Exam_Sim

Question Number: 683

Question: An organization needs to determine whether its security awareness training is effectively improving employee behavior and reducing related risks like phishing and social engineering. Which approach would provide the BEST evaluation?

Option 1: Conduct surveys on training satisfaction

Option 2: Assess training completion rates

Option 3: Measure phishing click rates before and after training

Option 4: Compare to industry security training benchmarks

Correct Response: 3

Explanation: Measuring changes in phishing click rates through simulated tests before and after training evaluates its effectiveness in improving security behavior.

Knowledge Area: Exam_Sim

Question Number: 684

Question: To evaluate if new security awareness training is successfully impacting employee mindset and actions, an information security manager wants quantitative data on training results. Which method would give the MOST direct assessment of whether the training improved resilience to phishing and other social engineering attacks?

Option 1: User satisfaction surveys

Option 2: Training comprehension quizzes

Option 3: Phishing click rate comparisons before and after training

Option 4: Industry training benchmark comparisons

Correct Response: 3

Explanation: Comparing phishing click rates through simulated phishing tests before and after training provides measurable results on improved resilience.

Knowledge Area: Exam_Sim

Question Number: 685

Question: An organization wants to model different cyber attack scenarios against a new system. Which technique would provide the MOST thorough analysis?

Option 1: Threat modeling

Option 2: Vulnerability scanning

Option 3: Penetration testing

Option 4: Attack tree analysis

Correct Response: 4

Explanation: Attack trees trace paths through different attack steps enabling thorough scenario analysis.

Knowledge Area: Exam_Sim

Question Number: 686

Question: A company is developing a new online transaction system and wants to analyze risk exposure from web application threats. Which approach would enable quantitatively evaluating attack scenarios?

Option 1: COST methodology

Option 2: Failure Mode and Effect Analysis

Option 3: Threat intelligence monitoring

Option 4: Threat modeling with STRIDE

Correct Response: 4

Explanation: The STRIDE threat modeling approach allows systematically evaluating attack scenarios.

Knowledge Area: Exam_Sim

Question Number: 687

Question: When is the BEST point in the systems development life cycle (SDLC) to design security and risk controls?

Option 1: During requirements gathering

Option 2: After user acceptance testing

Option 3: During implementation and deployment

Option 4: During technical design and architecture

Correct Response: 4

Explanation: Controls should be designed into the technical architecture during design phases.

Knowledge Area: Exam_Sim

Question Number: 688

Question: At what phase of the SDLC should an application's security controls and protections be identified?

Option 1: Project initiation

Option 2: Production deployment

Option 3: Technical design specification

Option 4: User acceptance testing

Correct Response: 3

Explanation: Controls should be designed during technical design before build phases.

Knowledge Area: Exam_Sim

Question Number: 689

Question: What method enables real-time monitoring of controls and alerts when results exceed defined risk tolerances?

Option 1: Ad hoc reporting

Option 2: Control self-assessment

Option 3: Continuous monitoring

Option 4: Predictive analytics

Correct Response: 3

Explanation: Continuous monitoring provides real-time tracking of controls against risk thresholds.

Knowledge Area: Exam_Sim

Question Number: 690

Question: Which technique uses data modeling and statistical methods to forecast future risk likelihood and impacts?

Option 1: Control self-assessment

Option 2: Process flow analysis

Option 3: Predictive analytics

Option 4: Benchmarking

Correct Response: 3

Explanation: Predictive analytics leverages data modeling to predict future risks.

Knowledge Area: Exam_Sim

Question Number: 691

Question: What technique involves personnel performing evaluations of the existence and effectiveness of controls within their business unit?

Option 1: Key risk indicators

Option 2: Continuous auditing

Option 3: Control self-assessment

Option 4: Regression analysis

Correct Response: 3

Explanation: Control self-assessment engages staff in evaluating controls.

Knowledge Area: Exam_Sim

Question Number: 692

Question: A risk practitioner is conducting an initial assessment of a company's business environment. Which of the following represents the BEST source of information?

Option 1: Financial statements and budgets

Option 2: Policies and procedures manuals

Option 3: Prior risk assessments

Option 4: Interviews with business process owners

Correct Response: 4

Explanation: Interviews provide direct insights into operations, risks, and priorities from business process owners.

Knowledge Area: SUPPORTING TASKS

Question Number: 693

Question: A risk practitioner needs to review technical controls and system configurations. Which artifact would provide the MOST relevant information?

Option 1: Data flow diagrams

Option 2: Network architecture diagrams

Option 3: System security plans

Option 4: Business process maps

Correct Response: 2

Explanation: Network architecture diagrams outline IT systems and technical controls at a level relevant for risk analysis.

Knowledge Area: SUPPORTING TASKS

Question Number: 694

Question: An organization wants to understand the regulatory environment it operates in. Which of the following would provide the BEST source for identifying applicable laws and regulations?

Option 1: Interviews with business management

Option 2: Review of contracts with customers

Option 3: Examination of HR policies

Option 4: Analysis of legal and compliance department materials

Correct Response: 4

Explanation: Legal/compliance materials outline relevant regulatory requirements the organization must adhere to.

Knowledge Area: SUPPORTING TASKS

Question Number: 695

Question: A risk practitioner is reviewing a new client's internal audit reports. What is the PRIMARY reason for doing so?

Option 1: To identify control issues already reported

Option 2: To evaluate auditing standards and procedures

Option 3: To analyze internal audit's risk approach

Option 4: To understand the business's risk culture

Correct Response: 1

Explanation: Reviewing past audit findings provides visibility into known control gaps and risk issues.

Knowledge Area: SUPPORTING TASKS

Question Number: 696

Question: Which of the following techniques would BEST identify impacts of IT risks on business objectives?

Option 1: Reviewing security logs

Option 2: Conducting breach simulations

Option 3: Surveying business management

Option 4: Analyzing vulnerability scan results

Correct Response: 2

Explanation: Breach simulations model realistic threat scenarios to assess potential business impacts.

Knowledge Area: SUPPORTING TASKS

Question Number: 697

Question: A new CIO has been hired and wants to understand how IT risks could affect business goals. What artifact should be reviewed?

Option 1: IT policies

Option 2: Risk register

Option 3: Asset inventory

Option 4: Threat intelligence reports

Correct Response: 2

Explanation: The risk register outlines identified IT risks and their potential effects on business operations.

Knowledge Area: SUPPORTING TASKS

Question Number: 698

Question: Which of the following risks could prevent an organization from meeting customer SLAs?

Option 1: Increased security events

Option 2: Failed change request

Option 3: System unavailability

Option 4: Malware infection

Correct Response: 3

Explanation: Prolonged system outages directly prevent meeting SLAs.

Knowledge Area: SUPPORTING TASKS

Question Number: 699

Question: A cloud migration project is underway. What should the risk practitioner assess?

Option 1: Vendor management practices

Option 2: Security control gaps

Option 3: Cost overruns

Option 4: Business process disruption

Correct Response: 4

Explanation: A risk practitioner should focus on potential business impacts like process disruption from the cloud migration.

Knowledge Area: SUPPORTING TASKS

Question Number: 700

Question: An organization is adopting a BYOD policy. Which of the following represents the GREATEST vulnerability introduced by this change?

Option 1: Unpatched devices

Option 2: Insecure networks

Option 3: Weak passwords

Option 4: Unsecured sensitive data

Correct Response: 4

Explanation: Personal devices are more likely to have unsecured sensitive corporate data.

Knowledge Area: SUPPORTING TASKS

Question Number: 701

Question: Which technique would help identify vulnerabilities in an organization's public cloud environment?

Option 1: Review security logs

Option 2: Conduct penetration testing

Option 3: Analyze threat intelligence

Option 4: Interview staff

Correct Response: 2

Explanation: Penetration testing attempts to actually exploit cloud vulnerabilities.

Knowledge Area: SUPPORTING TASKS

Question Number: 702

Question: A new video conferencing platform has been implemented. What is the GREATEST threat to assess?

Option 1: Malware infection

Option 2: DDoS attacks

Option 3: Data leakage

Option 4: Password cracking

Correct Response: 3

Explanation: Video conferencing introduces risks of accidental data leakage.

Knowledge Area: SUPPORTING TASKS

Question Number: 703

Question: What technique can reveal vulnerabilities in an organization's web application security?

Option 1: Architecture analysis

Option 2: Backup testing

Option 3: Log correlation

Option 4: Fuzz testing

Correct Response: 4

Explanation: Fuzz testing inputs malformed data into web apps to identify weaknesses.

Knowledge Area: SUPPORTING TASKS

Question Number: 704

Question: An organization has identified a threat of DDoS attacks and a vulnerability of limited network bandwidth. What is the resulting risk scenario?

Option 1: Excessive ping requests saturate available bandwidth

Option 2: Attackers gain access to sensitive data

Option 3: New malware bypasses antivirus software

Option 4: Users fall for phishing emails

Correct Response: 1

Explanation: The threat and vulnerability combine to create a DDoS bandwidth saturation risk.

Knowledge Area: SUPPORTING TASKS

Question Number: 705

Question: A hospital has an aging MRI machine still running Windows XP. What is the greatest risk scenario?

Option 1: Ransomware infection

Option 2: DDoS attack

Option 3: Insider data theft

Option 4: Password compromise

Correct Response: 1

Explanation: The outdated OS is vulnerable to ransomware which could impact patient care.

Knowledge Area: SUPPORTING TASKS

Question Number: 706

Question: Which threat-vulnerability pair could result in data theft by rogue employees?

Option 1: Weak access controls - Disgruntled employee

Option 2: SQL injection - Poor input validation

Option 3: DDoS attack - Underprovisioned network

Option 4: Password reuse - Phishing attack

Correct Response: 1

Explanation: Weak access controls and rogue employees pose an insider data theft risk.

Knowledge Area: SUPPORTING TASKS

Question Number: 707

Question: A retailer's website lacks input sanitization. An increase in SQL injection attacks has been reported. What is the resulting risk scenario?

Option 1: Large-scale data theft via SQLi

Option 2: Site defacement by hackers

Option 3: Unplanned website outages

Option 4: POS malware infections

Correct Response: 1

Explanation: The SQLi threat and web vulnerability may enable large-scale data theft.

Knowledge Area: SUPPORTING TASKS

Question Number: 708

Question: Which role would be BEST to assign as the risk owner for cloud security threats?

Option 1: CIO

Option 2: CISO

Option 3: Cloud provider

Option 4: Business manager

Correct Response: 2

Explanation: The CISO has relevant cloud security expertise to manage this risk.

Knowledge Area: SUPPORTING TASKS

Question Number: 709

Question: A new online payment system is being implemented. Who should own the related data security risk?

Option 1: IT manager

Option 2: CFO

Option 3: COO

Option 4: Payment processor

Correct Response: 3

Explanation: The COO oversees payment operations and should own associated data risks.

Knowledge Area: SUPPORTING TASKS

Question Number: 710

Question: Which scenario indicates ineffective risk ownership assignment?

Option 1: Excessive delays in risk response

Option 2: Unclear risk tolerance

Option 3: Duplicative risk registers

Option 4: Inconsistent metrics

Correct Response: 1

Explanation: Delays point to poor accountability from misaligned or absent risk owners.

Knowledge Area: SUPPORTING TASKS

Question Number: 711

Question: A key regulatory compliance risk was supposed to be addressed. However, the work was never started. What is the MOST likely reason?

Option 1: Insufficient budget

Option 2: Lack of skills

Option 3: Poor risk analysis

Option 4: Unassigned risk ownership

Correct Response: 4

Explanation: Unassigned ownership allowed accountability gaps for managing the risk.

Knowledge Area: SUPPORTING TASKS

Question Number: 712

Question: Why is it important to incorporate the IT risk register into the enterprise-wide risk profile?

Option 1: Alignment between IT risks and overall organizational risks

Option 2: Prioritizing IT risks over other business risks

Option 3: Separating IT risks from other business risks

Option 4: Minimizing visibility of IT risks to senior management

Correct Response: 1

Explanation: Incorporating the IT risk register into the enterprise-wide risk profile ensures alignment between IT risks and overall organizational risks. This allows for a comprehensive view of risks, enabling effective resource allocation, decision-making, and risk mitigation efforts.

Knowledge Area: SUPPORTING TASKS

Question Number: 713

Question: What action should be taken to incorporate identified risks into the IT risk register?

Option 1: Assigning risk owners and developing response strategies

Option 2: Conducting cost-benefit analysis of the risks

Option 3: Transferring risks to external parties through insurance

Option 4: Accepting risks without proactive measures

Correct Response: 1

Explanation: To incorporate identified risks into the IT risk register, the appropriate action is assigning risk owners and developing response strategies. This ensures accountability, proactive risk management, and the implementation of measures to mitigate or respond to identified risks.

Knowledge Area: SUPPORTING TASKS

Question Number: 714

Question: Which technique helps guide discussions to establish risk tolerance with business leaders?

Option 1: Control testing

Option 2: Process flow analysis

Option 3: Risk assessment workshops

Option 4: Cost-benefit analysis

Correct Response: 3

Explanation: Interactive workshops facilitate risk dialogues with stakeholders.

Knowledge Area: SUPPORTING TASKS

Question Number: 715

Question: A risk practitioner is meeting with system owners to define risk appetite. What metric would be MOST useful?

Option 1: Residual risk ratings

Option 2: Threat levels

Option 3: Inherent risk scores

Option 4: Loss expectancy

Correct Response: 4

Explanation: Loss expectancy metrics quantify risk appetite in financial terms.

Knowledge Area: SUPPORTING TASKS

Question Number: 716

Question: Which scenario reflects ineffective facilitation of risk appetite dialogues?

Option 1: Exceeding risk tolerance

Option 2: Universal risk avoidance

Option 3: Perfectly quantified appetite

Option 4: Differing assumptions

Correct Response: 4

Explanation: Misaligned assumptions lead to inconsistent or conflicting risk appetites.

Knowledge Area: SUPPORTING TASKS

Question Number: 717

Question: Interviews with business managers reveal varying levels of acceptable brand reputation risk. What should the risk practitioner do?

Option 1: Default to the most conservative view

Option 2: Report the differences to the board

Option 3: Consolidate the input and average

Option 4: Lead further discussions to align

Correct Response: 4

Explanation: The practitioner should drive consensus on a unified appetite.

Knowledge Area: SUPPORTING TASKS

Question Number: 718

Question: Which approach is MOST effective for sustaining user engagement during security awareness training?

Option 1: Long lectures

Option 2: Frequent phishing tests

Option 3: Gamification techniques

Option 4: Thorough quizzes

Correct Response: 3

Explanation: Gamification applies game elements to maintain learner interest.

Knowledge Area: SUPPORTING TASKS

Question Number: 719

Question: A company wants to improve security awareness. Which training topic would be LEAST impactful?

Option 1: Password hygiene

Option 2: Social engineering

Option 3: VPN protocols

Option 4: Data handling

Correct Response: 3

Explanation: Technical VPN concepts have low relevance to most staff.

Knowledge Area: SUPPORTING TASKS

Question Number: 720

Question: Which metric indicates the greatest success in improving security awareness?

Option 1: Training attendance

Option 2: Phishing click rate

Option 3: Training satisfaction

Option 4: Test scores

Correct Response: 2

Explanation: Reduced phishing susceptibility shows improved awareness.

Knowledge Area: SUPPORTING TASKS

Question Number: 721

Question: How should training effectiveness be evaluated?

Option 1: Trainee feedback surveys

Option 2: Testing comprehension

Option 3: Measuring behavioral change

Option 4: Training expense

Correct Response: 2

Explanation: Testing measures actual improvements in security behaviors

Knowledge Area: SUPPORTING TASKS

Question Number: 722

Question: A risk practitioner is assessing a scenario of disrupted online services due to a DDoS attack. Which would help determine likelihood?

Option 1: Vendor contracts

Option 2: Network traffic patterns

Option 3: Profit margins

Option 4: Incident reports

Correct Response: 2

Explanation: Analyzing network traffic would reveal DDoS vulnerability.

Knowledge Area: SUPPORTING TASKS

Question Number: 723

Question: When analyzing the business impact of a risk scenario, which data point is LESS relevant?

Option 1: RTO

Option 2: Revenue loss

Option 3: Staff hours

Option 4: Incident response costs

Correct Response: 4

Explanation: Incident response costs have lower business impact than disruption.

Knowledge Area: SUPPORTING TASKS

Question Number: 724

Question: An organization experiences frequent security incidents. What does this suggest about their risk assessments?

Option 1: Threats are overestimated

Option 2: Impacts are underestimated

Option 3: Likelihoods are underestimated

Option 4: Vulnerabilities are overlooked

Correct Response: 3

Explanation: The incidents show threat likelihood is higher than initially assessed.

Knowledge Area: SUPPORTING TASKS

Question Number: 725

Question: Which technique helps quantify annualized loss expectancy (ALE) for a risk?

Option 1: Surveys

Option 2: Interviews

Option 3: Cost analysis

Option 4: Loss forecasting

Correct Response: 3

Explanation: ALE uses cost analysis to quantify potential annual losses.

Knowledge Area: SUPPORTING TASKS

Question Number: 726

Question: An organization implements a new cloud access security broker (CASB) to prevent unauthorized SaaS usage. Which action would allow the risk practitioner to MOST accurately evaluate the control?

Option 1: Review CASB training completion

Option 2: Analyze blocked SaaS access attempts

Option 3: Survey employee CASB satisfaction

Option 4: Assess documentation of security features

Correct Response: 2

Explanation: Analyzing instances of blocked unauthorized access evaluates CASB effectiveness.

Knowledge Area: SUPPORTING TASKS

Question Number: 727

Question: A company installs a new database activity monitoring solution to detect suspicious transactions. How should the risk practitioner initially assess the control?

Option 1: Wait 3 months then measure incidents detected

Option 2: Review architecture and configuration against best practices

Option 3: Verify it is running smoothly with no errors or downtime

Option 4: Survey database administrators to get their feedback

Correct Response: 2

Explanation: Reviewing proper implementation per best practices evaluates effectiveness.

Knowledge Area: SUPPORTING TASKS

Question Number: 728

Question: To reduce data exfiltration threats, DLP software has been deployed on endpoint devices. What indicates the control is operating as intended?

Option 1: Number of devices with DLP installed

Option 2: Decrease in policy violations

Option 3: Encryption of removable media

Option 4: Blocking of unauthorized email attachments

Correct Response: 2

Explanation: Decline in DLP policy violations demonstrates effectiveness.

Knowledge Area: SUPPORTING TASKS

Question Number: 729

Question: An organization implements MFA to reduce unauthorized account access. What would determine if the control is working properly?

Option 1: Compliance with security standards

Option 2: Complexity of MFA policies

Option 3: Number of accounts requiring MFA

Option 4: Decrease in successful account takeovers

Correct Response: 4

Explanation: A decline in unauthorized access proves MFA is effective.

Knowledge Area: SUPPORTING TASKS

Question Number: 730

Question: A risk analysis identified data theft via unauthorized access as a critical risk. A control analysis shows access management controls are inadequately designed and implemented. What is this an example of?

Option 1: Accepted risk

Option 2: Residual risk

Option 3: Control gap

Option 4: Non-compliance

Correct Response: 3

Explanation: The poor controls represent a gap compared to the desired state of strong access controls.

Knowledge Area: SUPPORTING TASKS

Question Number: 731

Question: An organization has a goal of zero malware infections on endpoints. Last year there were 200 infections. What does this indicate?

Option 1: Insufficient anti-malware controls

Option 2: Inaccurate risk analysis

Option 3: Excessive risk appetite

Option 4: A risk-control gap

Correct Response: 4

Explanation: The gap between the goal and infections indicates a risk-control gap.

Knowledge Area: SUPPORTING TASKS

Question Number: 732

Question: A recent DDoS attack caused a 4-hour outage. The RTO is 2 hours. What does this exemplify?

Option 1: Realized risk

Option 2: Residual risk

Option 3: Inherent risk

Option 4: Risk-control gap

Correct Response: 4

Explanation: The longer outage than targeted RTO shows a risk-control gap.

Question Number: 733

Question: Risk analysis identified data leakage via email as high-likelihood with high business impact. However, no DLP controls are implemented for email. What does this signify?

Option 1: Non-compliance

Option 2: Mitigated risk

Option 3: An accepted risk

Option 4: A risk-control gap

Correct Response: 4

Explanation: The lack of email DLP indicates a gap versus desired control state.

Knowledge Area: SUPPORTING TASKS

Question Number: 734

Question: A risk scenario has been assessed as above risk tolerance. Which technique would BEST facilitate selecting an appropriate response with stakeholders?

Option 1: Surveys

Option 2: Cost-benefit analysis

Option 3: Decision trees

Option 4: Focus groups

Correct Response: 2

Explanation: Cost-benefit analysis quantifies response options for decision making.

Knowledge Area: SUPPORTING TASKS

Question Number: 735

Question: When evaluating risk response options, what is the BEST criteria for selection?

Option 1: Cost

Option 2: Speed

Option 3: Risk owner preference

Option 4: Effectiveness

Correct Response: 4

Explanation: Effectiveness in mitigating risk is the most important criteria.

Knowledge Area: SUPPORTING TASKS

Question Number: 736

Question: A risk practitioner is meeting with system owners to discuss response options for a regulatory compliance risk above tolerance. What should be the MAIN focus?

Option 1: Internal audit recommendations

Option 2: Costs of remediation

Option 3: Alignment to risk appetite

Option 4: Solution offered by technology vendors

Correct Response: 3

Explanation: Ensuring alignment to risk appetite drives stakeholder decisions.

Knowledge Area: SUPPORTING TASKS

Question Number: 737

Question: Which response is preferable if a risk is being knowingly accepted?

Option 1: Reduce

Option 2: Transfer

Option 3: Enhance controls

Option 4: Increase monitoring

Correct Response: 4

Explanation: Accepted risks warrant enhanced monitoring and oversight.

Knowledge Area: SUPPORTING TASKS

Question Number: 738

Question: A risk owner is developing a treatment plan for a high priority risk scenario. What should the risk practitioner recommend focusing on first?

Option 1: Budget

Option 2: Vendors

Option 3: Timing

Option 4: Scope

Correct Response: 4

Explanation: The scope of risk treatment must be defined before other details.

Knowledge Area: SUPPORTING TASKS

Question Number: 739

Question: During creation of a risk treatment plan, which topic would the risk practitioner be LEAST involved in?

Option 1: Cost analysis

Option 2: Control selection

Option 3: Implementation roles

Option 4: Training development

Correct Response: 2

Explanation: Control selection is driven primarily by the risk and process owners.

Knowledge Area: SUPPORTING TASKS

Question Number: 740

Question: A risk treatment plan includes procurement of new DLP software. What MUST the risk practitioner validate before finalizing the plan?

Option 1: Pricing

Option 2: Stakeholder consensus

Option 3: Compliance impact

Option 4: Implementation timeline

Correct Response: 2

Explanation: Stakeholders must align on the control solution selected.

Knowledge Area: SUPPORTING TASKS

Question Number: 741

Question: The CISO drafted a risk treatment plan and sent it to the risk practitioner for review. What would be the BEST course of action?

Option 1: Revise the plan as needed

Option 2: Notify executive leadership of gaps

Option 3: Reject the plan and start over

Option 4: Provide input and recommend changes

Correct Response: 4

Explanation: The practitioner should collaborate with the CISO to enhance the draft plan.

Knowledge Area: SUPPORTING TASKS

Question Number: 742

Question: A risk treatment plan calls for implementation of a new firewall by Q3. It is now Q4, but no firewall is in place. What should the risk practitioner do?

Option 1: Update the risk register

Option 2: Inform executive management

Option 3: Confirm the vendor contract

Option 4: Revise the implementation timeline

Correct Response: 2

Explanation: Leadership should be notified that the planned response was not executed.

Knowledge Area: SUPPORTING TASKS

Question Number: 743

Question: MFA was implemented to mitigate unauthorized cloud access risks. What should occur to validate proper execution?

Option 1: Request user feedback

Option 2: Review security policies

Option 3: Confirm reduction in access breaches

Option 4: Perform an architecture review

Correct Response: 3

Explanation: Validating decreased unauthorized access proves planned MFA controls were implemented.

Knowledge Area: SUPPORTING TASKS

Question Number: 744

Question: A plan specifies replacing legacy AV software by December. December has passed but the legacy AV is still installed. What action should the risk practitioner take?

Option 1: Mark the risk as accepted

Option 2: Update the treatment plan

Option 3: Perform a tool assessment

Option 4: Notify the risk owner

Correct Response: 4

Explanation: The owner should address why the response was not executed as planned.

Knowledge Area: SUPPORTING TASKS

Question Number: 745

Question: DLP tools were implemented per a risk treatment plan. What validates execution per the plan?

Option 1: Decrease in policy violations

Option 2: Number of endpoints with DLP

Option 3: Measuring mean time to detect

Option 4: Reviewing tool procurement paperwork

Correct Response: 1

Explanation: Seeing fewer DLP violations proves planned implementation and effectiveness.

Knowledge Area: SUPPORTING TASKS

Question Number: 746

Question: Which metric could serve as a KRI to provide early warning of emerging insider data theft risks?

Option 1: Authorized failed logins

Option 2: Database scan results

Option 3: Policy violation trends

Option 4: IDS alert volume

Correct Response: 3

Explanation: Increasing policy violations may reflect potential insider issues.

Knowledge Area: SUPPORTING TASKS

Question Number: 747

Question: What is an advantage of leveraging KRIs for risk monitoring?

Option 1: Faster response

Option 2: Lower costs

Option 3: Higher accuracy

Option 4: Improved reporting

Correct Response: 1

Explanation: KRIs enable quicker responses by providing early signals of increasing risk.

Knowledge Area: SUPPORTING TASKS

Question Number: 748

Question: An organization implements daily malware scan failures as a KRI. What does a spike in failures indicate?

Option 1: Increased likelihood of infection

Option 2: Antivirus software is outdated

Option 3: Scans are being skipped or manipulated

Option 4: More devices are being scanned

Correct Response: 1

Explanation: More failures indicates increased infection risk.

Knowledge Area: SUPPORTING TASKS

Question Number: 749

Question: Which metric could serve as a useful KRI for application security risks?

Option 1: Logins during non-business hours

Option 2: PHP errors in web logs

Option 3: Cloud storage consumption

Option 4: BYOD policy exemptions

Correct Response: 2

Explanation: Increasing PHP errors may reflect emerging web app vulnerabilities.

Knowledge Area: SUPPORTING TASKS

Question Number: 750

Question: The number of critical vulnerabilities detected serves as a KRI. A spike over the threshold is observed. What should occur first?

Option 1: Tune the KRI metrics

Option 2: Perform vulnerability scanning

Option 3: Update the risk register

Option 4: Notify security operations

Correct Response: 4

Explanation: Notifying ops facilitates immediate response to the emerging risk.

Knowledge Area: SUPPORTING TASKS

Question Number: 751

Question: A KRI tracking unauthorized WiFi access points detects an upwards trend. What should the risk practitioner do?

Option 1: Report a risk control failure

Option 2: Conduct security awareness training

Option 3: Tune the indicator threshold

Option 4: Perform a wireless survey

Correct Response: 3

Explanation: The threshold may need adjustment if too sensitive to normal fluctuations.

Knowledge Area: SUPPORTING TASKS

Question Number: 752

Question: The risk practitioner notices a KRI for privileged account access exceeding its threshold. What is the BEST next step?

Option 1: Update access control policies

Option 2: Perform an account audit

Option 3: Lower the defined threshold

Option 4: Request added monitoring

Correct Response: 2

Explanation: Analyze and investigate the underlying cause of the spike.

Knowledge Area: SUPPORTING TASKS

Question Number: 753

Question: A KRI measuring firewall CPU utilization spikes over threshold. How should the risk practitioner respond?

Option 1: Report an increasing risk trend

Option 2: Add firewall capacity immediately

Option 3: Validate the KRI's formula

Option 4: Determine if utilization has stabilized

Correct Response: 4

Explanation: First confirm it reflects a sustained significant increase in load.

Knowledge Area: SUPPORTING TASKS

Question Number: 754

Question: An organization implements a new web application firewall (WAF). Which metric would be the BEST key control indicators (KCIs for it?

Option 1: Network latency

Option 2: Blocked SQL injections

Option 3: Up-time percentage

Option 4: HTML errors in web logs

Correct Response: 2

Explanation: Blocked attacks indicates WAF is performing as intended.

Knowledge Area: SUPPORTING TASKS

Question Number: 755

Question: A new secure email gateway is deployed. Which would be the BEST KPI for it?

Option 1: Template-based phishing reporting rate

Option 2: Policy exception requests

Option 3: Total spam emails stopped

Option 4: Percentage of encrypted emails

Correct Response: 3

Explanation: Total spam blocked measures effectiveness of the control.

Question Number: 756

Question: Which metric could serve as a useful key control indicators (KCIs) for multi-factor authentication controls?

Option 1: Accounts enrolled in MFA

Option 2: Successful remote logins

Option 3: Rejected authentication attempts

Option 4: Password reset tickets

Correct Response: 2

Explanation: Successful logins shows MFA is operating effectively.

Knowledge Area: SUPPORTING TASKS

Question Number: 757

Question: An organization deploys new antivirus software. What provides meaningful data as a KPI?

Option 1: Threat definitions updated

Option 2: Scan frequency and coverage

Option 3: Malware infections quarantined

Option 4: Signature update failures

Correct Response: 3

Explanation: Infections caught proves AV effectiveness.

Knowledge Area: SUPPORTING TASKS

Question Number: 758

Question: An assessment reveals a web application firewall is inconsistently blocking SQL injection attacks. What does this indicate about the control environment?

Option 1: Non-compliance issues exist

Option 2: The environment lacks maturity

Option 3: Risks are being accepted

Option 4: Threats are being underestimated

Correct Response: 2

Explanation: The inconsistent blocking reflects immaturity of the WAF control.

Knowledge Area: SUPPORTING TASKS

Question Number: 759

Question: An assessment reveals antivirus only scans critical servers, missing endpoints. What does this indicate?

Option 1: Insufficient skills and resources

Option 2: Lack of execution

Option 3: Overconfidence in controls

Option 4: Control environment immaturity

Correct Response: 4

Explanation: The limited inconsistent AV indicates immaturity.

Knowledge Area: SUPPORTING TASKS

Question Number: 760

Question: A phishing test shows a slight decline in clicks over last year. What does this show about the environment?

Option 1: Improved end user behavior

Option 2: Increased training effectiveness

Option 3: Control degradation

Option 4: Complacent leadership

Correct Response: 1

Explanation: The small decline indicates minor behavioral improvements.

Knowledge Area: SUPPORTING TASKS

Question Number: 761

Question: A recent assessment identified several high severity vulnerabilities in customer facing web applications. What should the risk practitioner report to leadership?

Option 1: Underlying threat sources

Option 2: Timelines for remediation

Option 3: Effort required for patching

Option 4: Potential business impact

Correct Response: 4

Explanation: Business impact reporting facilitates risk-based decisions.

Knowledge Area: SUPPORTING TASKS

Question Number: 762

Question: The CTO has requested a risk management report before approving funding for new controls. What should be the focus of the report?

Option 1: Compliance status

Option 2: Description of controls

Option 3: Summary of risks

Option 4: Metrics on control effectiveness

Correct Response: 3

Explanation: Current risks drive decisions on funding new controls.

Knowledge Area: SUPPORTING TASKS

Question Number: 763

Question: A new cloud access security broker (CASB) tool was recently implemented. What reporting would LEAST influence stakeholder risk decisions?

Option 1: User satisfaction results

Option 2: Threats blocked by CASB

Option 3: Reduction in data exposure events

Option 4: Policy compliance improvement

Correct Response: 1

Explanation: Reporting user feedback has little risk management value.

Knowledge Area: SUPPORTING TASKS

Question Number: 764

Question: What is an advantage of using risk dashboard reporting?

Option 1: Increased thoroughness

Option 2: Enhanced presentation formats

Option 3: Improved context for metrics

Option 4: Faster identification of issues

Correct Response: 4

Explanation: Dashboards allow quicker recognition of risk issues through visuals.

Knowledge Area: SUPPORTING TASKS

Question Number: 765

Question: An organization wants to implement the NIST Cybersecurity Framework (CSF). What is the FIRST step the risk practitioner should take?

Option 1: Assess current state using CSF profiles

Option 2: Train staff on CSF components

Option 3: Purchase a GRC tool for automation

Option 4: Obtain leadership approval and sponsorship

Correct Response: 4

Explanation: Gaining leadership buy-in is critical before adopting a new framework.

Knowledge Area: SUPPORTING TASKS

Question Number: 766

Question: A risk practitioner is assessing alignment with ISO 27001 controls. Which documentation would provide the LEAST value?

Option 1: Information security policies

Option 2: Risk assessment results

Option 3: Inventory of assets

Option 4: SLAs with vendors

Correct Response: 3

Explanation: An asset inventory provides limited visibility into actual control implementation.

Knowledge Area: SUPPORTING TASKS

Question Number: 767

Question: When evaluating alignment with the CIS Critical Security Controls, which activities provide the MOST value?

Option 1: Surveys to staff

Option 2: Review of network diagrams

Option 3: Control validation testing

Option 4: Comparison of security budgets

Correct Response: 3

Explanation: Testing provides empirical evidence of real-world implementation.

Knowledge Area: SUPPORTING TASKS

Question Number: 768

Question: What practice is MOST important when mapping controls to frameworks?

Option 1: Using automated tools

Option 2: Reviewing multiple sources

Option 3: Interviewing control owners

Option 4: Verifying documentation

Correct Response: 3

Explanation: Discussions with owners will reveal actual realities more than documentation.

Knowledge Area: SUPPORTING TASKS

----------------------------------- ----------

Question Number: 769

Question: An organization is reviewing its IT architecture to improve resilience against emerging threats. As the Chief Risk Officer, which of the following alternatives should receive PRIMARY consideration to strengthen the overall security posture in a cost effective manner?

Option 1: Deploying additional firewalls and network segmentation

Option 2: Investing in regular employee security awareness

Option 3: Outsourcing the entire network infrastructure

Option 4: Centrally monitoring all systems and applications for anomalies

Correct Response: 2

Explanation: , Employee training programs help identify and address human vulnerabi

Knowledge Area: IT Enterprise Architecture in Risk Management

----

Question Number: 770

Question: A retailer experienced lengthy website outages during peak holiday shopping seasons due to infrastructure limitations. As a risk consultant, the BEST first step recommendation is to:

Option 1: Seek cloud migration proposals to facilitate scalability

Option 2: Hire additional in-house IT support staff

Option 3: Benchmark uptime indices of rival companies

Option 4: Partition the website across multiple redundant data centers

Correct Response: 4

Explanation: , Distributing digital properties across diverse locations employing redundancy techniques fortifies availability during high demand periods.

Knowledge Area: IT Enterprise Architecture in Risk Management

----

Question Number: 771

Question: A government agency requires its constituent departments standardize on core technologies. As the IT Risk Manager, your priority should be to:

Option 1: Assess interoperability across proposed solutions

Option 2: Socialize change management plans to impacted teams

Option 3: Justify additional budgets to the Finance department

Option 4: Waive procurement policies temporarily for faster deployment

Correct Response: 1

Explanation: , Vetting solution coherence reduces integration vulnerabilities prior to rollout at scale.

Knowledge Area: IT Enterprise Architecture in Risk Management

----

Question Number: 772

Question: An internal audit found applications lacked consistency in access controls, patching and configurations. The Chief Information Security Officer should FIRST:

Option 1: Mandate quarterly vulnerability assessments

Option 2: Centralize configuration management

Option 3: Outsource application management

Option 4: Enforce standardized baselines across all software

Correct Response: 3

Explanation: , Instituting configuration governance stabilizes individual weaknesses bringing coherence to the overall risk profile.

Knowledge Area: IT Enterprise Architecture in Risk Management

----

Question Number: 773

Question: A system outage impacted customers for over 3 hours and exposed a weakness in change management processes. The CISO should FIRST implement:

Option 1: Regular risk assessments

Option 2: Documentation standards

Option 3: Testing for all changes

Option 4: Change advisory board reviews,

Correct Response: 3

Explanation: , Testing mitigates unintended impacts from modifications.

Knowledge Area: IT Operations Management (e.g., change management, IT assets, problems, incidents) in Risk Management

----

Question Number: 774

Question: To improve problem resolution oversight, the IT director is evaluating tracking systems. The BEST selection criterion is one that provides:

Option 1: Automated workflows

Option 2: Audit logs

Option 3: Performance dashboards

Option 4: Capacity planning,

Correct Response: 2

Explanation: , Audit trails maintain transparency and accountability in issue handling.

Knowledge Area: IT Operations Management (e.g., change management, IT assets, problems, incidents) in Risk Management

----

Question Number: 775

Question: The CRO must report key risk indicators to the Board. The BEST metric related to availability is:

Option 1: Number of assets

Option 2: Mean time to resolution

Option 3: System uptime percentage

Option 4: Service alerts,

Correct Response: 3

Explanation: , Uptime encapsulates overall digital service delivery.

Knowledge Area: IT Operations Management (e.g., change management, IT assets, problems, incidents) in Risk Management

----

Question Number: 776

Question: Legacy systems hamper incident response capabilities. The MOST effective way to modernize is through:

Option 1: Virtualization

Option 2: Integration

Option 3: Containerization

Option 4: Outsourcing

Correct Response: 1

Explanation: , Virtualization streamlines systems for faster management and fault isolation.

Knowledge Area: IT Operations Management (e.g., change management, IT assets, problems, incidents) in Risk Management

----

Question Number: 777

Question: An IT project manager is conducting risk management planning for a new software development project. What should be the FIRST step performed?

Option 1: Brainstorm risk sources

Option 2: Review risk management policies

Option 3: Identify risk response strategies

Option 4: Define risk assessment methodologies

Correct Response: 2

Explanation: Policies/standards should first be reviewed when planning project risk management.

Knowledge Area: Project Management in Risk Management

Question Number: 778

Question: An IT project manager is implementing risk responses during a project to address identified risks. Which response would be the LEAST effective for high priority risks?

Option 1: Risk acceptance

Option 2: Risk mitigation

Option 3: Risk avoidance

Option 4: Risk transference

Correct Response: 1

Explanation: High priority project risks warrant active responses like mitigation or transfer.

Knowledge Area: Project Management in Risk Management

Question Number: 779

Question: A complex IT system implementation has several uncertain requirements. What risk management strategy would BEST address this uncertainty?

Option 1: Detailed project planning

Option 2: Progress monitoring

Option 3: Contingency budgeting

Option 4: Flexible scope management

Correct Response: 4

Explanation: An agile, flexible scope approach manages uncertain requirements.

Knowledge Area: Project Management in Risk Management

Question Number: 780

Question: An IT project risk has occurred, causing delays and budget overruns. What is the BEST immediate response?

Option 1: Lessons learned review

Option 2: Status report to sponsor

Option 3: Re-baselining schedule/budget

Option 4: Assess impact and response plans

Correct Response: 4

Explanation: First assess risk impact and response options when a risk occurs.

Knowledge Area: Project Management in Risk Management

Question Number: 781

Question: An organization is developing a disaster recovery plan. What is the FIRST step of the process?

Option 1: Document recovery procedures

Option 2: Implement resilience controls

Option 3: Test the plan

Option 4: Conduct a business impact analysis

Correct Response: 4

Explanation: A BIA identifying critical systems is the first DRM step.

Knowledge Area: Disaster Recovery Management (DRM) in Risk Management

----

Question Number: 782

Question: A company is assessing disaster recovery strategies for an enterprise system. Which option would provide the FASTEST recovery time?

Option 1: Cold site contract

Option 2: Warm site contract

Option 3: Hot site contract

Option 4: Multiple data center redundancy

Correct Response: 3

Explanation: A hot site provides the fastest recovery time.

Knowledge Area: Disaster Recovery Management (DRM) in Risk Management

----

Question Number: 783

Question: During a disruption event, what should the disaster recovery team do FIRST?

Option 1: Activate crisis communications plans

Option 2: Declare a disaster event

Option 3: Conduct salvage and restoration

Option 4: Determine impact and invoke recovery plans

Correct Response: 4

Explanation: First assess incident impact and response decisions.

Knowledge Area: Disaster Recovery Management (DRM) in Risk Management

----

Question Number: 784

Question: A company has encountered a cyberattack disrupting operations. What is the HIGHEST priority when invoking disaster recovery plans?

Option 1: Restoring compromised systems

Option 2: Analyzing the attack

Option 3: Communicating with stakeholders

Option 4: Activating critical business processes

Correct Response: 4

Explanation: Recovering critical business operations is the top priority.

Knowledge Area: Disaster Recovery Management (DRM) in Risk Management

----

Question Number: 785

Question: What is the first step in implementing Data Lifecycle Management in risk management?

Option 1: Data classification and categorization

Option 2: Data backup and storage

Option 3: Data disposal and destruction

Option 4: Data encryption and access control

Correct Response: 1

Explanation: The first step in implementing Data Lifecycle Management in risk management is data classification and categorization. This step involves identifying and classifying data based on its sensitivity, criticality, and regulatory requirements. It helps organizations understand the types of data they have and prioritize their risk management efforts accordingly.

Knowledge Area: Data Lifecycle Management in Risk Management

Question Number: 786

Question: What is a key benefit of implementing Data Lifecycle Management in risk management?

Option 1: Enhanced data security and protection

Option 2: Increased data storage capacity

Option 3: Streamlined data processing

Option 4: Reduced data backup requirements

Correct Response: 1

Explanation: A key benefit of implementing Data Lifecycle Management in risk management is enhanced data security and protection. By implementing proper controls, organizations can ensure data confidentiality, integrity, and availability, reducing the risk of data breaches, unauthorized access, and data loss.

Knowledge Area: Data Lifecycle Management in Risk Management

Question Number: 787

Question: Which phase of the data lifecycle involves securely disposing of data at the end of its usefulness?

Option 1: Data disposal and destruction

Option 2: Data backup and storage

Option 3: Data processing and utilization

Option 4: Data classification and categorization

Correct Response: 1

Explanation: The phase of the data lifecycle that involves securely disposing of data at the end of its usefulness is the data disposal and destruction phase. This phase ensures that data is properly and securely disposed of to prevent unauthorized access or retrieval, reducing the risk of data breaches or privacy violations.

Knowledge Area: Data Lifecycle Management in Risk Management

Question Number: 788

Question: What is a primary objective of data lifecycle management in risk management?

Option 1: Mitigate data-related risks throughout its lifecycle

Option 2: Optimize data storage and retrieval processes

Option 3: Ensure data compliance with industry regulations

Option 4: Minimize data backup and retention costs

Correct Response: 1

Explanation: The primary objective of data lifecycle management in risk management is to mitigate data-related risks throughout its lifecycle. This involves implementing appropriate controls, processes, and strategies to identify, assess, and manage risks associated with data collection, storage, processing, and disposal.

Knowledge Area: Data Lifecycle Management in Risk Management

Question Number: 789

Question: Which phase of the System Development Life Cycle (SDLC) is focused on identifying and assessing risks associated with the proposed system?

Option 1: Requirements gathering and analysis

Option 2: Design and development

Option 3: Implementation and testing

Option 4: Maintenance and evaluation

Correct Response: 1

Explanation: The requirements gathering and analysis phase of the SDLC is focused on identifying and assessing risks associated with the proposed system. This phase involves gathering user requirements, analyzing business processes, and identifying potential risks and vulnerabilities that need to be addressed in the system design.

Knowledge Area: System Development Life Cycle (SDLC) in Risk Management

----

Question Number: 790

Question: What is the primary goal of integrating risk management into the System Development Life Cycle (SDLC)?

Option 1: To ensure that risks are identified, assessed, and mitigated throughout the development process

Option 2: To eliminate all risks associated with the system development

Option 3: To transfer risks to external parties through insurance or contracts

Option 4: To accept risks without taking any proactive measures

Correct Response: 1

Explanation: The primary goal of integrating risk management into the SDLC is to ensure that risks are identified, assessed, and mitigated throughout the development process. By incorporating risk management practices at each stage of the SDLC, organizations can proactively address potential risks, reduce vulnerabilities, and enhance the overall security and quality of the developed system.

Knowledge Area: System Development Life Cycle (SDLC) in Risk Management

----

Question Number: 791

Question: What is the first step in integrating risk management into the System Development Life Cycle (SDLC)?

Option 1: Identifying and analyzing potential risks and vulnerabilities

Option 2: Developing a risk management plan

Option 3: Implementing risk mitigation measures

Option 4: Testing and evaluating the system for potential risks

Correct Response: 1

Explanation: The first step in integrating risk management into the SDLC is to identify and analyze potential risks and vulnerabilities. This involves conducting a comprehensive assessment of potential risks associated with the system development, considering both internal and external factors that could impact the project's success.

Knowledge Area: System Development Life Cycle (SDLC) in Risk Management

----

Question Number: 792

Question: What is the role of risk management in the System Development Life Cycle (SDLC)?

Option 1: To identify, assess, and mitigate risks throughout the development process

Option 2: To ignore risks and focus solely on system functionality

Option 3: To transfer risks to external parties through contracts

Option 4: To accept all risks without taking any proactive measures

Correct Response: 1

Explanation: The role of risk management in the SDLC is to identify, assess, and mitigate risks throughout the development process. This includes conducting risk assessments, implementing risk mitigation measures, and continuously monitoring and managing risks to ensure the successful delivery of the developed system while minimizing potential negative impacts.

Knowledge Area: System Development Life Cycle (SDLC) in Risk Management

----

Question Number: 793

Question: Which of the following is an example of an emerging technology that can be used in risk management?

Option 1: Artificial Intelligence (AI)

Option 2: Traditional spreadsheet software

Option 3: Legacy mainframe systems

Option 4: Paper-based documentation

Correct Response: 1

Explanation: Artificial Intelligence (AI) is an example of an emerging technology that can be used in risk management. AI can analyze large volumes of data, identify patterns and trends, and provide insights to support risk assessment and decision-making processes.

Knowledge Area: Emerging Technologies in Risk Management

Question Number: 794

Question: What advantage does blockchain technology offer in risk management?

Option 1: Increased transparency and immutability of data

Option 2: Slower processing speed compared to traditional systems

Option 3: Limited scalability and storage capacity

Option 4: Inability to track and trace data transactions

Correct Response: 1

Explanation: Blockchain technology offers increased transparency and immutability of data, which can be advantageous in risk management. The decentralized nature of blockchain ensures that transactions are securely recorded and cannot be altered, providing a reliable and transparent audit trail for risk analysis and management.

Knowledge Area: Emerging Technologies in Risk Management

Question Number: 795

Question: Which of the following is a potential risk associated with the adoption of emerging technologies in risk management?

Option 1: Cybersecurity vulnerabilities

Option 2: Compatibility with legacy systems

Option 3: Limited functionality and capabilities

Option 4: Decreased efficiency and productivity

Correct Response: 1

Explanation: A potential risk associated with the adoption of emerging technologies in risk management is cybersecurity vulnerabilities. As new technologies are implemented, organizations face the challenge of protecting their systems and data from potential cyber threats, such as hacking, data breaches, and malware attacks.

Knowledge Area: Emerging Technologies in Risk Management

Question Number: 796

Question: How can data analytics contribute to risk management?

Option 1: By analyzing large volumes of data to identify patterns and trends

Option 2: By relying solely on subjective assessments and opinions

Option 3: By avoiding the need for risk assessment and mitigation

Option 4: By eliminating the need for risk management processes

Correct Response: 1

Explanation: Data analytics can contribute to risk management by analyzing large volumes of data to identify patterns and trends. By leveraging data analytics techniques and tools, organizations can gain insights into potential risks, assess their likelihood and impact, and make informed decisions regarding risk mitigation and management strategies.

Knowledge Area: Emerging Technologies in Risk Management

Question Number: 797

Question: Which of the following is a widely recognized information security framework used in risk management?

Option 1: ISO/IEC 27001

Option 2: Six Sigma

Option 3: ITIL (Information Technology Infrastructure Library)

Option 4: COSO (Committee of Sponsoring Organizations of the Treadway Commission)

Correct Response: 1

Explanation: ISO/IEC 27001 is a widely recognized information security framework used in risk management. It provides a systematic approach for establishing, implementing, maintaining, and continually improving an information security management system (ISMS) based on risk management principles and best practices.

Knowledge Area: Information Security Concepts, Frameworks and Standards in Risk Management

----

Question Number: 798

Question: What is the primary goal of implementing information security frameworks, standards, and concepts in risk management?

Option 1: To protect information assets and minimize risks

Option 2: To increase operational efficiency and reduce costs

Option 3: To comply with legal and regulatory requirements

Option 4: To improve customer satisfaction and loyalty

Correct Response: 1

Explanation: The primary goal of implementing information security frameworks, standards, and concepts in risk management is to protect information assets and minimize risks. By adopting best practices and applying appropriate controls, organizations can safeguard their sensitive information, reduce the likelihood and impact of security incidents, and ensure the confidentiality, integrity, and availability of data.

Knowledge Area: Information Security Concepts, Frameworks and Standards in Risk Management

----

Question Number: 799

Question: Which of the following is an international standard for information security management?

Option 1: ISO/IEC 20000

Option 2: ITIL (Information Technology Infrastructure Library)

Option 3: ISO/IEC 27001

Option 4: COBIT (Control Objectives for Information and Related Technologies)

Correct Response: 3

Explanation: ISO/IEC 27001 is an international standard for information security management. It provides a framework for establishing, implementing, maintaining, and continually improving an information security management system (ISMS) within the context of the organization's overall business risks.

Knowledge Area: Information Security Concepts, Frameworks and Standards in Risk Management

----

Question Number: 800

Question: What role do information security frameworks, standards, and concepts play in risk management?

Option 1: They provide guidance and best practices for managing information security risks.

Option 2: They eliminate all risks associated with information security.

Option 3: They transfer risks to external parties through contracts.

Option 4: They increase complexity and hinder risk management efforts.

Correct Response: 1

Explanation: Information security frameworks, standards, and concepts play a crucial role in risk management by providing guidance and best practices for managing information security risks. They help organizations identify, assess, and mitigate information security risks, establish appropriate controls, and ensure the confidentiality, integrity, and availability of sensitive information.

Knowledge Area: Information Security Concepts, Frameworks and Standards in Risk Management

----

WHAT'S YOUR

FEEDBACK?

TELL US WHAT YOU THINK

Amazing!

You have been studying very hard to this stage.

How is your exam preparation so far? Can the practice test meet your needs and expectation? I desperately desire your voice.

Please kindly consider

1. Visiting my exam practice test books and consider purchasing them to assist you to pass your target exam, though the direct links provided at the beginning of this book
2. Visiting my exam practice test courses held at Udemy though the direct links provided at the beginning of this book
3. Leaving a positive review and feedback to me though the direct book review links provided at the next page.

Keep going! See you at the end of the book.

Warm regards,

Walter

Or the **Links at Amazon Book Store:**

CRISC 1200+ Practice Test, 2023 (Exam Simulation and Core & Advanced Knowledge)	
Paperback Review URL:	- https://www.amazon.com/review/create-review?&asin=B0CJ43R78T
Kindle eBook Review URL:	- https://www.amazon.com/review/create-review?&asin=B0CJ72JJLY

Direct URLs to visit all Walter's Practice Tests at Amazon

Visit Walter's author page:
http://WalterEducation.com

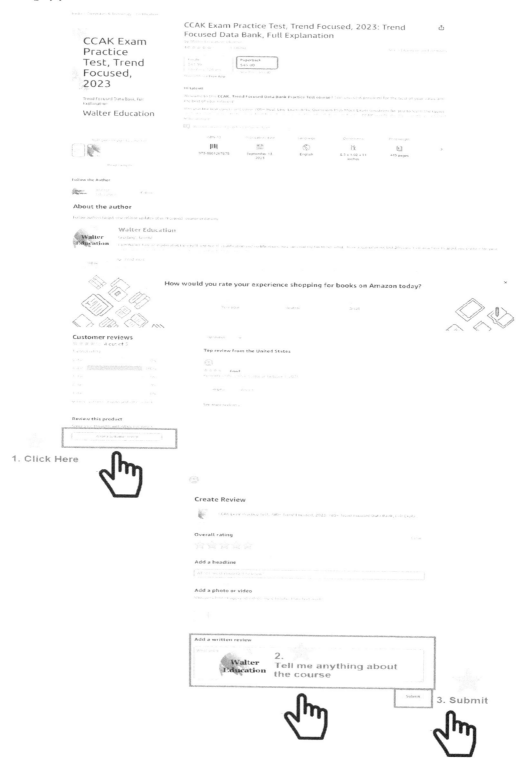

1. Click Here

Create Review

Overall rating

Add a headline

Add a photo or video

Add a written review

2. Tell me anything about the course

3. Submit

Question Number: 801

Question: What is the primary goal of information security awareness training in risk management?

Option 1: To ensure employees are aware of potential risks and their responsibilities in protecting information

Option 2: To enhance technical security controls and measures

Option 3: To transfer risks to external parties through contracts

Option 4: To eliminate all risks associated with information security

Correct Response: 1

Explanation: The primary goal of information security awareness training in risk management is to ensure employees are aware of potential risks and their responsibilities in protecting information. By providing training and education, organizations can empower employees to identify and respond to security threats, follow best practices, and contribute to a culture of security awareness and risk mitigation.

Knowledge Area: Information Security Awareness Training in Risk Management

----

Question Number: 802

Question: What is the first step in implementing an effective information security awareness training program?

Option 1: Assessing training needs and identifying target audience

Option 2: Developing training materials and content

Option 3: Delivering training sessions to employees

Option 4: Evaluating the effectiveness of the training program

Correct Response: 1

Explanation: The first step in implementing an effective information security awareness training program is assessing training needs and identifying the target audience. This involves understanding the organization's specific security risks, identifying the roles and responsibilities of different employees, and determining the knowledge and skills required to address those risks.

Knowledge Area: Information Security Awareness Training in Risk Management

----

Question Number: 803

Question: Which of the following is a potential benefit of information security awareness training in risk management?

Option 1: Reduced likelihood of security incidents caused by human error

Option 2: Increased complexity in managing security controls

Option 3: Decreased need for technical security measures

Option 4: Enhanced scalability and performance of IT systems

Correct Response: 1

Explanation: A potential benefit of information security awareness training in risk management is a reduced likelihood of security incidents caused by human error. By educating employees about security best practices, organizations can minimize the risk of unintentional actions that could compromise information security, such as falling for phishing scams or mishandling sensitive data.

Knowledge Area: Information Security Awareness Training in Risk Management

----

Question Number: 804

Question: How can information security awareness training contribute to risk management efforts?

Option 1: By promoting a culture of security awareness and responsibility

Option 2: By eliminating all risks associated with information security

Option 3: By transferring risks to external parties through contracts

Option 4: By reducing the need for technical security controls

Correct Response: 1

Explanation: Information security awareness training can contribute to risk management efforts by promoting a culture of security awareness and responsibility. By educating employees about their role in safeguarding information and fostering a security-conscious mindset, organizations can enhance their overall risk management efforts and create a more resilient security posture.

Knowledge Area: Information Security Awareness Training in Risk Management

----

Question Number: 805

Question: What is the primary goal of Business Continuity Management (BCM) in risk management?

Option 1: To ensure the continuity of critical business operations during disruptions

Option 2: To eliminate all risks associated with business operations

Option 3: To transfer risks to external parties through contracts

Option 4: To accept risks without taking any proactive measures

Correct Response: 1

Explanation: The primary goal of Business Continuity Management (BCM) in risk management is to ensure the continuity of critical business operations during disruptions. BCM involves developing strategies, plans, and procedures to enable the organization to respond effectively to incidents and restore operations to an acceptable level within a defined timeframe.

Knowledge Area: Business Continuity Management in Risk Management

----

Question Number: 806

Question: Which of the following is a key component of Business Continuity Management (BCM)?

Option 1: Risk assessment and analysis

Option 2: Budgeting and financial planning

Option 3: Employee performance evaluations

Option 4: Marketing and advertising strategies

Correct Response: 1

Explanation: Risk assessment and analysis is a key component of Business Continuity Management (BCM). It involves identifying potential risks and vulnerabilities to critical business operations, assessing their likelihood and impact, and developing appropriate strategies and plans for mitigating those risks.

Knowledge Area: Business Continuity Management in Risk Management

----

Question Number: 807

Question: What is the purpose of conducting business impact analysis in Business Continuity Management (BCM)?

Option 1: To identify critical business functions and their dependencies

Option 2: To eliminate all risks associated with critical business operations

Option 3: To transfer risks to external parties through contracts

Option 4: To accept risks without taking any proactive measures

Correct Response: 1

Explanation: The purpose of conducting business impact analysis in Business Continuity Management (BCM) is to identify critical business functions and their dependencies. This analysis helps organizations understand the potential impacts of disruptions on these functions, prioritize recovery efforts, and allocate resources effectively to ensure the continuity of essential operations.

Knowledge Area: Business Continuity Management in Risk Management

----

Question Number: 808

Question: How does Business Continuity Management (BCM) contribute to risk management efforts?

Option 1: By ensuring the continuity of critical business operations during disruptions

Option 2: By eliminating all risks associated with business operations

Option 3: By transferring risks to external parties through contracts

Option 4: By accepting risks without taking any proactive measures

Correct Response: 1

Explanation: Business Continuity Management (BCM) contributes to risk management efforts by ensuring the continuity of critical business operations during disruptions. By developing strategies, plans, and procedures for effective response and recovery, organizations can minimize the impact of disruptions, mitigate risks to business operations, and enhance resilience.

Knowledge Area: Business Continuity Management in Risk Management

----

Question Number: 809

Question: What is the primary goal of incorporating data privacy and data protection principles in risk management?

Option 1: To ensure the confidentiality and integrity of sensitive data

Option 2: To eliminate all risks associated with data privacy and protection

Option 3: To transfer risks to external parties through contracts

Option 4: To accept risks without taking any proactive measures

Correct Response: 1

Explanation: The primary goal of incorporating data privacy and data protection principles in risk management is to ensure the confidentiality and integrity of sensitive data. By implementing appropriate controls and practices, organizations can safeguard personal and sensitive information, mitigate the risk of data breaches, and ensure compliance with data protection regulations.

Knowledge Area: Data Privacy and Data Protection Principles in Risk Management

----

Question Number: 810

Question: Which of the following is a fundamental principle of data privacy and data protection?

Option 1: Data minimization and purpose limitation

Option 2: Data monetization and commercialization

Option 3: Data obfuscation and manipulation

Option 4: Data deletion and destruction

Correct Response: 1

Explanation: Data minimization and purpose limitation is a fundamental principle of data privacy and data protection. It involves collecting and retaining only the necessary data for a specific purpose and ensuring that the data is not used beyond the intended scope. By applying this principle, organizations can reduce the risk of unauthorized access and misuse of personal information.

Knowledge Area: Data Privacy and Data Protection Principles in Risk Management

----

Question Number: 811

Question: What is the significance of conducting data protection impact assessments (DPIAs) in risk management?

Option 1: To identify and assess privacy risks associated with data processing activities

Option 2: To eliminate all risks associated with data protection

Option 3: To transfer risks to external parties through contracts

Option 4: To accept risks without taking any proactive measures

Correct Response: 1

Explanation: The significance of conducting data protection impact assessments (DPIAs) in risk management is to identify and assess privacy risks associated with data processing activities. DPIAs help organizations evaluate the potential impact of data processing on individual privacy rights, identify potential risks and vulnerabilities, and implement appropriate controls and measures to mitigate these risks.

Knowledge Area: Data Privacy and Data Protection Principles in Risk Management

----

Question Number: 812

Question: How does data privacy and data protection contribute to overall risk management efforts?

Option 1: By mitigating the risk of data breaches and regulatory non-compliance

Option 2: By eliminating all risks associated with data processing

Option 3: By transferring risks to external parties through contracts

Option 4: By accepting risks without taking any proactive measures

Correct Response: 1

Explanation: Data privacy and data protection contribute to overall risk management efforts by mitigating the risk of data breaches and regulatory non-compliance. By implementing appropriate safeguards, organizations can protect sensitive data, reduce the likelihood of security incidents, and ensure compliance with applicable data protection laws and regulations.

Knowledge Area: Data Privacy and Data Protection Principles in Risk Management

----

Amazing!

You have worked very hard to this stage.

How is your exam preparation so far? Can the practice test meet your needs and expectation? I desperately desire your voice.

Please kindly consider leaving a review and feedback to me and I have prepared a free gift as a token of gratitude. For details, please refer to the first Three pages at the beginning of this book.

Keep going! See you at the end of the book.

Warm regards,

Walter

DOMAIN 3 – RISK RESPONSE AND REPORTING

Question Number: 813

Question: A company is evaluating risk response options for a high priority threat. Which strategy would be the LEAST effective?

Option 1: Risk avoidance

Option 2: Risk sharing

Option 3: Risk acceptance

Option 4: Risk mitigation

Correct Response: 3

Explanation: High risks warrant active responses like mitigation rather than acceptance.

Knowledge Area: Risk Treatment / Risk Response Options in Risk Management

----

Question Number: 814

Question: An organization wants to address a recurring operational risk. Which risk response would reduce future impacts?

Option 1: Enhanced controls

Option 2: Incident response plan

Option 3: Disaster recovery setup

Option 4: Insurance policy

Correct Response: 1

Explanation: Enhancing controls addresses the root cause to reduce likelihood.

Knowledge Area: Risk Treatment / Risk Response Options in Risk Management

----

Question Number: 815

Question: A supply chain disruption poses major risk to product delivery times. What is the BEST risk treatment option?

Option 1: Accept the risk

Option 2: Transfer to vendors

Option 3: Add redundancy suppliers

Option 4: Outsource shipping

Correct Response: 3

Explanation: Redundant suppliers mitigate supply chain risk impact.

Knowledge Area: Risk Treatment / Risk Response Options in Risk Management

----

Question Number: 816

Question: A new regulation necessitates improved client data security. Which risk response would BEST address compliance?

Option 1: Insurance purchase

Option 2: Process audits

Option 3: Control implementation

Option 4: Fines budgeting

Correct Response: 3

Explanation: Implementing controls reduces compliance risk exposure.

Knowledge Area: Risk Treatment / Risk Response Options in Risk Management

----

Question Number: 817

Question: An organization is implementing a centralized governance model for IT risk management. Which role should have primary RESPONSIBILITY for managing risks?

Option 1: Individual business units

Option 2: The compliance department

Option 3: The risk management function

Option 4: Senior management

Correct Response: 1

Explanation: Business units have primary responsibility for managing risks under decentralized models.

Knowledge Area: Risk and Control Ownership in Risk Management

----

Question Number: 818

Question: A company wants to clarify roles for risk management activities. Which position should have authority and accountability for implementing risk responses?

Option 1: Chief Risk Officer

Option 2: Internal Audit

Option 3: Business process owners

Option 4: Risk Management Committee

Correct Response: 3

Explanation: Business process owners are directly responsible for managing risk responses.

Knowledge Area: Risk and Control Ownership in Risk Management

----

Question Number: 819

Question: Which role is BEST positioned to oversee day-to-day operation of security controls within their department?

Option 1: Data owners

Option 2: Internal auditors

Option 3: Risk managers

Option 4: Department managers

Correct Response: 4

Explanation: Department managers are directly responsible for controls within their area.

Knowledge Area: Risk and Control Ownership in Risk Management

----

Question Number: 820

Question: An IT project is implementing a new system with security requirements. Who should be MOST involved in defining controls?

Option 1: Internal audit

Option 2: Project manager

Option 3: Project sponsor

Option 4: System end users

Correct Response: 4

Explanation: End users know processes and requirements to define appropriate controls.

Knowledge Area: Risk and Control Ownership in Risk Management

----

Question Number: 821

Question: What is the primary goal of third-party risk management in risk management?

Option 1: To identify and mitigate risks associated with third-party vendors and suppliers

Option 2: To eliminate all risks associated with third-party relationships

Option 3: To transfer risks to external parties through contracts

Option 4: To accept risks without taking any proactive measures

Correct Response: 1

Explanation: The primary goal of third-party risk management in risk management is to identify and mitigate risks associated with third-party vendors and suppliers. By assessing the risks posed by third-party relationships, organizations can implement appropriate controls, monitor performance, and ensure compliance to reduce potential threats and vulnerabilities.

Knowledge Area: Third-Party Risk Management in Risk Management

----

Question Number: 822

Question: Which of the following is a key component of third-party risk management?

Option 1: Due diligence and vendor selection process

Option 2: Internal employee performance evaluation

Option 3: Product development and innovation

Option 4: Marketing and advertising strategies

Correct Response: 1

Explanation: Due diligence and vendor selection process is a key component of third-party risk management. It involves conducting thorough assessments of potential vendors or suppliers, evaluating their security controls, conducting background checks, and verifying their compliance with relevant regulations. This process helps organizations make informed decisions and choose reliable and secure third-party partners.

Knowledge Area: Third-Party Risk Management in Risk Management

----

Question Number: 823

Question: Why is third-party risk management important in risk management efforts?

Option 1: Third-party relationships can introduce additional risks to an organization

Option 2: Third-party risk management eliminates all risks associated with third-party relationships

Option 3: Third-party risk management hinders business operations and growth

Option 4: Third-party risk management is not relevant for effective risk management

Correct Response: 1

Explanation: Third-party risk management is important in risk management efforts because third-party relationships can introduce additional risks to an organization. By properly managing these risks, organizations can protect their assets, sensitive information, and reputation while ensuring the continuity of business operations.

Knowledge Area: Third-Party Risk Management in Risk Management

----

Question Number: 824

Question: How does third-party risk management contribute to overall risk management efforts?

Option 1: By identifying and mitigating risks associated with third-party relationships

Option 2: By accepting risks without taking any proactive measures

Option 3: By transferring risks to external parties through contracts

Option 4: By eliminating all risks associated with third-party relationships

Correct Response: 1

Explanation: Third-party risk management contributes to overall risk management efforts by identifying and mitigating risks associated with third-party relationships. By assessing and managing risks related to vendors, suppliers, and business partners, organizations can protect themselves from potential vulnerabilities and disruptions caused by third-party activities.

Knowledge Area: Third-Party Risk Management in Risk Management

----

Question Number: 825

Question: During a risk assessment, a major control gap is identified. What should be the FIRST step?

Option 1: Implement a new control

Option 2: Report finding to management

Option 3: Log issue in tracking system

Option 4: Update risk register

Correct Response: 3

Explanation: The first step is to log the finding in the issue tracking system.

Knowledge Area: Issue, Finding and Exception Management in Risk Management

----

Question Number: 826

Question: An audit identifies multiple high severity findings related to user access controls. What should the audit team do FIRST?

Option 1: Report findings to management

Option 2: Assign finding owners

Option 3: Prioritize remediation timeframes

Option 4: Verify the scope of issues

Correct Response: 2

Explanation: Audit findings should first be assigned owners responsible for remediation.

Knowledge Area: Issue, Finding and Exception Management in Risk Management

----

Question Number: 827

Question: A data analytics dashboard shows a spike in rejected transactions. What is the BEST first response?

Option 1: Tune detection algorithms

Option 2: Report finding to managers

Option 3: Log issue and assign ownership

Option 4: Request more data

Correct Response: 3

Explanation: The first step is to log the exception and assign an owner.

Knowledge Area: Issue, Finding and Exception Management in Risk Management

----

Question Number: 828

Question: What is the MOST important action when remediating a non-compliant issue?

Option 1: Implement tactical fix

Option 2: Report on remediation

Option 3: Diagnose the root cause

Option 4: Verify resolution effectiveness

Correct Response: 3

Explanation: Focus on diagnosing and resolving the root cause first.

Knowledge Area: Issue, Finding and Exception Management in Risk Management

----

Question Number: 829

Question: Scenario: An organization is facing new technological advancements in its industry. What is the primary step in managing emerging risks in risk management?

Option 1: Conducting a thorough assessment of the potential impact of new technologies

Option 2: Implementing appropriate controls to mitigate emerging risks

Option 3: Continuously monitoring industry trends and technological developments

Option 4: Developing a risk mitigation strategy to address emerging risks

Correct Response: 3

Explanation: The primary step in managing emerging risks in risk management is continuously monitoring industry trends and technological developments. By staying updated on new advancements, organizations can identify potential emerging risks and respond effectively to mitigate their potential impact.

Knowledge Area: Management of Emerging Risk in Risk Management

----

Question Number: 830

Question: Scenario: A company is expanding its operations into a new market where regulatory requirements are constantly evolving. What is the recommended approach in managing emerging risks in this situation?

Option 1: Stay informed about the changing regulatory landscape and adapt compliance practices accordingly

Option 2: Transfer all risks to external parties through contracts and agreements

Option 3: Ignore emerging risks and rely on existing risk management practices

Option 4: Accept risks without taking any proactive measures

Correct Response: 1

Explanation: The recommended approach in managing emerging risks in a situation with evolving regulatory requirements is to stay informed about the changing regulatory landscape and adapt compliance practices accordingly. By staying updated on regulatory changes, organizations can identify emerging risks, ensure compliance, and mitigate potential legal and compliance-related consequences.

Knowledge Area: Management of Emerging Risk in Risk Management

----

Question Number: 831

Question: Scenario: A company is considering adopting a new technology that has recently emerged in the market. What is the primary consideration in managing the risks associated with the new technology?

Option 1: Conducting a thorough risk assessment to identify potential risks and vulnerabilities

Option 2: Eliminating all risks associated with the new technology through proactive measures

Option 3: Transferring all risks to external parties through contracts and agreements

Option 4: Accepting risks without taking any proactive measures

Correct Response: 1

Explanation: The primary consideration in managing risks associated with a new technology is conducting a thorough risk assessment to identify potential risks and vulnerabilities. By assessing the risks, organizations can develop appropriate risk mitigation strategies, implement necessary controls, and ensure a proactive approach to managing technology-related risks.

Knowledge Area: Management of Emerging Risk in Risk Management

----

Question Number: 832

Question: Scenario: An organization is entering into a strategic partnership with a third-party vendor to outsource certain operations. What is the primary step in managing the risks associated with the partnership?

Option 1: Conducting due diligence and performing a comprehensive vendor assessment

Option 2: Eliminating all risks associated with the partnership through proactive measures

Option 3: Transferring all risks to the third-party vendor through contractual agreements

Option 4: Accepting risks without taking any proactive measures

Correct Response: 1

Explanation: The primary step in managing the risks associated with a strategic partnership with a third-party vendor is conducting due diligence and performing a comprehensive vendor assessment. By thoroughly evaluating the vendor's capabilities, security practices, and compliance with regulations, organizations can mitigate potential risks and ensure a trusted and secure partnership.

Knowledge Area: Management of Emerging Risk in Risk Management

----

Question Number: 833

Question: An organization wants to ensure confidential data remains protected. Which control type would BEST meet this objective?

Option 1: Corrective

Option 2: Detective

Option 3: Compensating

Option 4: Preventive

Correct Response: 4

Explanation: Preventive controls protect confidentiality by preventing exposure.

Knowledge Area: Control Types, Standards and Frameworks in Risk Management

----

Question Number: 834

Question: A company is implementing a new system and wants to align security controls with industry best practices. Which framework would be BEST to follow?

Option 1: COBIT

Option 2: ISO 27001

Option 3: NIST Cybersecurity Framework

Option 4: COSO

Correct Response: 3

Explanation: The NIST Cybersecurity Framework provides industry standard security controls.

Knowledge Area: Control Types, Standards and Frameworks in Risk Management

----

Question Number: 835

Question: Regulators have mandated a financial organization implement stricter access controls. Which control standard should they look to first?

Option 1: COBIT

Option 2: PCI DSS

Option 3: ISO 27001

Option 4: NIST SP 800-53

Correct Response: 4

Explanation: NIST SP 800-53 provides guidance on access control standards.

Knowledge Area: Control Types, Standards and Frameworks in Risk Management

----

Question Number: 836

Question: What is the BEST control model for ensuring financial data integrity?

Option 1: COSO

Option 2: CMMI

Option 3: ITIL

Option 4: COBIT

Correct Response: 1

Explanation: COSO provides control principles for financial reporting integrity.

Knowledge Area: Control Types, Standards and Frameworks in Risk Management

----

Question Number: 837

Question: An organization wants to improve identity and access controls. Which factor is MOST important when selecting a new single sign-on system?

Option 1: Total cost of ownership

Option 2: Ease of use

Option 3: Integration with applications

Option 4: Vendor reputation

Correct Response: 3

Explanation: Focus on how well it integrates with existing apps.

Knowledge Area: Control Design, Selection and Analysis in Risk Management

----

Question Number: 838

Question: A company is implementing a new cloud-based payroll system. What is the BEST way to evaluate controls before adoption?

Option 1: Review vendor audit report

Option 2: Conduct onsite assessment

Option 3: Examine certification compliance

Option 4: Request test account to validate controls

Correct Response: 4

Explanation: Validating controls with a test account provides best assurance.

Knowledge Area: Control Design, Selection and Analysis in Risk Management

----

Question Number: 839

Question: New software is being deployed that will collect sensitive customer data. What is the PRIMARY consideration when selecting controls?

Option 1: Total cost of ownership

Option 2: Ease of implementation

Option 3: Security risks and regulations

Option 4: Analyst recommendations

Correct Response: 3

Explanation: Align controls to risks and compliance obligations.

Knowledge Area: Control Design, Selection and Analysis in Risk Management

----

Question Number: 840

Question: An application audit shows input validation controls are deficient. What is the BEST remediation?

Option 1: Validate all inputs on server

Option 2: Implement client-side validation also

Option 3: Rely more on output encoding

Option 4: Use length check constraints on inputs

Correct Response: 2

Explanation: Implement validation at multiple levels for defense in depth.

Knowledge Area: Control Design, Selection and Analysis in Risk Management

----

Question Number: 841

Question: An organization is rolling out new endpoint security controls. What is the BEST way to drive adoption?

Option 1: Mandate usage in policy

Option 2: Provide frequent training

Option 3: Send compliance notifications

Option 4: Publish security metrics

Correct Response: 2

Explanation: Hands-on training drives engagement and usage.

Knowledge Area: Control Implementation in Risk Management

Question Number: 842

Question: A company wants to improve security over customer data. Which approach would BEST ensure controls stay effective over time?

Option 1: One-time implementation

Option 2: Monthly control testing

Option 3: Continuous monitoring

Option 4: Annual control audits

Correct Response: 3

Explanation: Continuous monitoring maintains control effectiveness.

Knowledge Area: Control Implementation in Risk Management

Question Number: 843

Question: A new cloud solution did not meet security requirements during testing. What should happen NEXT before deployment?

Option 1: Grant exception

Option 2: Reassess after launch

Option 3: Develop remediation plan

Option 4: Terminate initiative

Correct Response: 3

Explanation: Develop a plan to remediate deficiencies first.

Knowledge Area: Control Implementation in Risk Management

Question Number: 844

Question: Before closing an audit finding, what should be validated FIRST?

Option 1: Remediation plan approved

Option 2: Fix implemented and working

Option 3: Root cause analyzed

Option 4: Management sign-off obtained

Correct Response: 2

Explanation: Confirm the control fix is operating as intended.

Knowledge Area: Control Implementation in Risk Management

Question Number: 845

Question: An organization wants to evaluate the effectiveness of firewall rules. Which testing approach would BEST meet this objective?

Option 1: Policy review

Option 2: Control self-assessment

Option 3: Penetration testing

Option 4: Vulnerability scanning

Correct Response: 3

Explanation: Penetration testing is best to validate firewall rule effectiveness.

Knowledge Area: Control Testing and Effectiveness Evaluation in Risk Management

----

Question Number: 846

Question: A new access management system was implemented. What is the BEST way to evaluate operational effectiveness?

Option 1: Compliance audit

Option 2: Control self-assessment

Option 3: User acceptance testing

Option 4: Monitor usage and violations trends

Correct Response: 4

Explanation: Monitor usage and violations to assess operational effectiveness.

Knowledge Area: Control Testing and Effectiveness Evaluation in Risk Management

----

Question Number: 847

Question: Which technique would provide the MOST accurate assessment of a control's design effectiveness?

Option 1: Process walkthrough

Option 2: Control configuration review

Option 3: Simulation testing

Option 4: Policy review

Correct Response: 3

Explanation: Simulating the control in action assesses design effectiveness.

Knowledge Area: Control Testing and Effectiveness Evaluation in Risk Management

----

Question Number: 848

Question: An application audit identified input validation weaknesses. What should be done FIRST before closing findings?

Option 1: Re-test application post-fix

Option 2: Review remediation plan

Option 3: Inspect code changes

Option 4: Confirm stakeholder sign-off

Correct Response: 1

Explanation: Retest to verify control effectiveness before closure.

Knowledge Area: Control Testing and Effectiveness Evaluation in Risk Management

----

Question Number: 849

Question: What is the primary goal of managing emerging risks in risk management?

Option 1: To identify and assess new and evolving risks

Option 2: To eliminate all risks associated with emerging risks

Option 3: To transfer risks to external parties through contracts

Option 4: To accept risks without taking any proactive measures

Correct Response: 1

Explanation: The primary goal of managing emerging risks in risk management is to identify and assess new and evolving risks. By proactively identifying and assessing emerging risks, organizations can develop appropriate strategies and plans to mitigate their potential impact.

Knowledge Area: Risk Treatment Plans in Risk Management

Question Number: 850

Question: Which of the following is a key component of managing emerging risks?

Option 1: Continuous monitoring and surveillance

Option 2: Risk avoidance and elimination

Option 3: Risk transfer to external parties through contracts

Option 4: Risk acceptance and mitigation

Correct Response: 1

Explanation: Continuous monitoring and surveillance is a key component of managing emerging risks. By continuously monitoring the environment, staying updated on new trends and developments, and conducting proactive surveillance, organizations can identify emerging risks in a timely manner and respond effectively to mitigate their potential impact.

Knowledge Area: Risk Treatment Plans in Risk Management

Question Number: 851

Question: An organization wants to build a risk analytics dashboard for management. What data would provide the MOST meaningful insights?

Option 1: Audit findings

Option 2: Policy and procedure review

Option 3: Key risk and performance indicators

Option 4: Risk assessment surveys

Correct Response: 3

Explanation: Key risk/performance indicators provide actionable insights.

Knowledge Area: Data Collection, Aggregation, Analysis and Validation in Risk Management

----

Question Number: 852

Question: A risk manager needs to prepare a quarterly risk report for the board. What is the BEST approach for aggregating data?

Option 1: Take sum or average across periods

Option 2: Highlight peak values from datasets

Option 3: Use data as of last month end

Option 4: Normalize data into standard units first

Correct Response: 4

Explanation: Normalizing data (common scales/units) enables meaningful aggregation.

Knowledge Area: Data Collection, Aggregation, Analysis and Validation in Risk Management

----

Question Number: 853

Question: When analyzing security event log data, what technique would BEST detect anomalies?

Option 1: Mean and standard deviation

Option 2: Linear regression

Option 3: Machine learning

Option 4: Multivariate clustering

Correct Response: 3

Explanation: Machine learning models can detect complex anomalies.

Knowledge Area: Data Collection, Aggregation, Analysis and Validation in Risk Management

----

Question Number: 854

Question: How should the accuracy of risk data be validated before using in reporting?

Option 1: Compare totals to last year

Option 2: Review for reasonableness

Option 3: Spot check source system

Option 4: All of the above

Correct Response: 4

Explanation: Use reasonability checks, spot checks, trending to validate accuracy.

Knowledge Area: Data Collection, Aggregation, Analysis and Validation in Risk Management

----

Question Number: 855

Question: An organization wants to monitor endpoint security controls. Which technique would provide CONTINUOUS monitoring?

Option 1: Annual audits

Option 2: Daily log reviews

Option 3: Periodic testing

Option 4: Automatedensors and analytics

Correct Response: 4

Explanation: Automated sensors and analytics enable continuous monitoring.

Knowledge Area: Risk and Control Monitoring Techniques in Risk Management

----

Question Number: 856

Question: A retailer needs to improve monitoring of POS system controls. Which technique would BEST detect suspicious activity?

Option 1: Code review

Option 2: Penetration testing

Option 3: Transaction analytics

Option 4: Vulnerability scanning

Correct Response: 3

Explanation: Transaction analytics can identify anomalies and misuse.

Knowledge Area: Risk and Control Monitoring Techniques in Risk Management

----

Question Number: 857

Question: A hospital wants to identify potential PHI exposure risks. Which technique would provide the BROADEST monitoring coverage?

Option 1: user access review

Option 2: network penetration test

Option 3: physical walkthroughs

Option 4: automated scan of systems

Correct Response: 4

Explanation: Automated scanning monitors entire IT environment for risks

Knowledge Area: Risk and Control Monitoring Techniques in Risk Management

----

Question Number: 858

Question: What technique would BEST assess operational resilience of a critical system?

Option 1: Review recovery documentation

Option 2: Walkthrough failover processes

Option 3: Execute simulated crisis scenario

Option 4: Audit failover infrastructure

Correct Response: 3

Explanation: Simulating failover provides best test of resilience.

Knowledge Area: Risk and Control Monitoring Techniques in Risk Management

----

Question Number: 859

Question: An organization wants a snapshot of top operational risks for the board. Which report format would be BEST?

Option 1: Detailed risk descriptions

Option 2: Risk maturity scorecard

Option 3: Heatmap of top risks

Option 4: Risk trend dashboard

Correct Response: 3

Explanation: A heatmap visually summarizes high priority risks.

Knowledge Area: Risk and Control Reporting Techniques (heatmap, scorecards, dashboards) in Risk Management

----

Question Number: 860

Question: The CIO has asked for a routine report on security posture. Which report would provide the MOST meaningful view?

Option 1: Latest penetration test results

Option 2: Compliance audit status

Option 3: Dashboard of key risk metrics

Option 4: Inventory of security controls

Correct Response: 3

Explanation: Key risk metrics quickly communicate security posture.

Knowledge Area: Risk and Control Reporting Techniques (heatmap, scorecards, dashboards) in Risk Management

----

Question Number: 861

Question: What visualization would BEST show improvement in risk exposure over time?

Option 1: Heatmap

Option 2: Pie chart

Option 3: Bar graph

Option 4: Risk trend dashboard

Correct Response: 4

Explanation: A risk dashboard shows exposure trends.

Knowledge Area: Risk and Control Reporting Techniques (heatmap, scorecards, dashboards) in Risk Management

----

Question Number: 862

Question: A risk committee has asked for a report on resilience. What would be MOST relevant?

Option 1: Recovery procedures

Option 2: Incident response plans

Option 3: Dashboard of resilience KRIs

Option 4: Failover test results

Correct Response: 3

Explanation: Key resilience indicators quickly communicate posture.

Knowledge Area: Risk and Control Reporting Techniques (heatmap, scorecards, dashboards) in Risk Management

----

Question Number: 863

Question: A CIO wants to monitor user access control effectiveness. Which metric would be MOST relevant?

Option 1: Password reset rate

Option 2: Failed login attempts

Option 3: User access certification rate

Option 4: Account lockout rate

Correct Response: 3

Explanation: Certification rate measures access control oversight.

Knowledge Area: Key Performance Indicators in Risk Management

----

Question Number: 864

Question: A security team needs to report on malware defense effectiveness. Which metric would be BEST?

Option 1: Anti-virus definition age

Option 2: Malware detection rate

Option 3: Firewall ruleset size

Option 4: Intrusion detection alerts

Correct Response: 2

Explanation: Malware detection rate measures defenses working.

Knowledge Area: Key Performance Indicators in Risk Management

----

Question Number: 865

Question: What metric BEST indicates phishing defense maturity?

Option 1: Email spam rate

Option 2: Reported phishing attacks

Option 3: Phishing click-through rate

Option 4: User security training attendance

Correct Response: 3

Explanation: Click-through measures success deceiving users.

Knowledge Area: Key Performance Indicators in Risk Management

----

Question Number: 866

Question: Which metric would BEST demonstrate security incident response capabilities?

Option 1: Time to isolate compromised systems

Option 2: Length of system outages

Option 3: Time to reimage affected endpoints

Option 4: Time to notify impacted customers

Correct Response: 1

Explanation: Speed isolating systems shows response ability.

Knowledge Area: Key Performance Indicators in Risk Management

----

Question Number: 867

Question: An organization wants to monitor cybersecurity posture. Which risk indicator would provide the MOST predictive view?

Option 1: Vulnerability scan results

Option 2: Penetration test findings

Option 3: Threat intel alerts correlated

Option 4: Malware infections detected

Correct Response: 3

Explanation: Threat intel alerts signal emerging risks.

Knowledge Area: Key Risk Indicators (KRIs) in Risk Management

----

Question Number: 868

Question: A bank wants early warning of fraud risks. Which indicator would be MOST useful to monitor?

Option 1: Decline rates of transactions

Option 2: High risk transactions flagged

Option 3: Fraud losses over time

Option 4: Number of fraud alerts

Correct Response: 2

Explanation: High risk transactions flagged predict fraud trends.

Knowledge Area: Key Risk Indicators (KRIs) in Risk Management

----

Question Number: 869

Question: A hospital needs to minimize PHI exposure risk. Which indicator would be MOST helpful?

Option 1: Policy attestations completed

Option 2: Audit findings related to PHI

Option 3: PHI records accessed per user

Option 4: PHI access complaints

Correct Response: 3

Explanation: Unusual access patterns signal PHI exposure.

Knowledge Area: Key Risk Indicators (KRIs) in Risk Management

----

Question Number: 870

Question: What metric indicates business continuity program maturity?

Option 1: Recovery time objective

Option 2: Recovery point objective

Option 3: Failed disaster recovery tests

Option 4: Unplanned downtime

Correct Response: 4

Explanation: Unplanned downtime measures resilience.

Knowledge Area: Key Risk Indicators (KRIs) in Risk Management

----

Question Number: 871

Question: An organization wants to monitor firewall effectiveness. Which metric would be MOST relevant?

Option 1: Firewall uptime

Option 2: Number of violations logged

Option 3: Time since last configuration change

Option 4: Percentage of traffic blocked

Correct Response: 2

Explanation: Violations logged show firewall is detecting threats.

Knowledge Area: Key Control Indicators (KCIs) in Risk Management

----

Question Number: 872

Question: A compliance team needs to report on user access controls. Which metric is MOST meaningful?

Option 1: Password complexity enabled

Option 2: Access certification completion rate

Option 3: Privilege entitlement approvals

Option 4: User accounts recertified annually

Correct Response: 2

Explanation: Completion rate shows access oversight.

Knowledge Area: Key Control Indicators (KCIs) in Risk Management

----

Question Number: 873

Question: What metric BEST measures effectiveness of input validation controls?

Option 1: Cross-site scripting flaws remediated

Option 2: Input fields restricted by type

Option 3: Automated scanning alerts

Option 4: Rejected invalid submissions

Correct Response: 4

Explanation: Rejected invalid input shows controls working.

Knowledge Area: Key Control Indicators (KCIs) in Risk Management

----

Question Number: 874

Question: Which indicator would BEST demonstrate security patching performance?

Option 1: Time between patch release and deployment

Option 2: Number of endpoints patched

Option 3: Percentage of systems patched

Option 4: Number of exploitation attempts blocked

Correct Response: 3

Explanation: Percentage patched measures program effectiveness.

Knowledge Area: Key Control Indicators (KCIs) in Risk Management

----

DOMAIN 2 – IT RISK ASSESSMENT

Question Number: 875

Question: Scenario: An organization experiences a data breach resulting in the exposure of customer information. What is the primary contributing condition to this risk event?

Option 1: Inadequate cybersecurity controls and vulnerabilities

Option 2: External hacking attempts and malicious activities

Option 3: Insider threat and unauthorized access by employees

Option 4: Natural disasters and physical damage to infrastructure

Correct Response: 1

Explanation: The primary contributing condition to the data breach risk event is inadequate cybersecurity controls and vulnerabilities. Weaknesses in the organization's security measures and systems can expose customer information to unauthorized access and potential data breaches.

Knowledge Area: Risk Events (e.g., contributing conditions, loss result) in Risk Management

----

Question Number: 876

Question: Scenario: An organization faces a significant financial loss due to a major operational disruption. What is the primary result of this risk event?

Option 1: Financial losses and decreased revenue

Option 2: Reputational damage and loss of customer trust

Option 3: Legal and regulatory consequences

Option 4: Disruption of business operations and productivity

Correct Response: 1

Explanation: The primary result of the risk event, major operational disruption, is financial losses and decreased revenue. The organization may face additional costs for recovery and remediation, while the disruption to business operations can impact revenue streams and overall financial performance.

Knowledge Area: Risk Events (e.g., contributing conditions, loss result) in Risk Management

----

Question Number: 877

Question: Scenario: A manufacturing facility experiences a safety incident resulting in employee injuries. What is the primary contributing condition to this risk event?

Option 1: Inadequate safety protocols and training

Option 2: Equipment malfunction or failure

Option 3: Lack of supervision and oversight

Option 4: Environmental hazards and unsafe working conditions

Correct Response: 1

Explanation: The primary contributing condition to the safety incident risk event is inadequate safety protocols and training. Insufficient safety measures and inadequate training can increase the likelihood of accidents and employee injuries within the manufacturing facility.

Knowledge Area: Risk Events (e.g., contributing conditions, loss result) in Risk Management

----

Question Number: 878

Question: Scenario: An organization faces a significant reputational damage due to a publicized ethical misconduct by a senior executive. What is the primary result of this risk event?

Option 1: Loss of customer trust and loyalty

Option 2: Legal and regulatory consequences

Option 3: Financial losses and decreased revenue

Option 4: Damage to brand reputation and public image

Correct Response: 1

Explanation: The primary result of the risk event, reputational damage, is the loss of customer trust and loyalty. A publicized ethical misconduct by a senior executive can tarnish the organization's reputation, leading to negative perceptions among customers and potential loss of business.

Knowledge Area: Risk Events (e.g., contributing conditions, loss result) in Risk Management

----

Question Number: 879

Question: An organization wants to understand security threats posed by adopting a new cloud platform. What is the BEST approach?

Option 1: Review provider's architecture

Option 2: Conduct penetration test after implementation

Option 3: Perform threat modeling before adoption

Option 4: Wait for audit findings after go-live

Correct Response: 3

Explanation: Threat modeling before adoption identifies risks.

Knowledge Area: Threat Modelling and Threat Landscape in Risk Management

----

Question Number: 880

Question: A bank is concerned about emerging cyber threats to new mobile payment applications. What technique would provide the MOST proactive understanding?

Option 1: Vulnerability testing

Option 2: Threat intelligence monitoring

Option 3: Penetration testing after launch

Option 4: Threat modeling before implementation

Correct Response: 4

Explanation: Threat modeling surfaces risks before launch.

Knowledge Area: Threat Modelling and Threat Landscape in Risk Management

----

Question Number: 881

Question: A healthcare organization is enhancing patient portal security. What is the FIRST step?

Option 1: Implement stronger controls

Option 2: Perform vulnerability scan

Option 3: Engage penetration testers

Option 4: Conduct threat modeling

Correct Response: 4

Explanation: Threat modeling identifies risks to drive control priorities.

Knowledge Area: Threat Modelling and Threat Landscape in Risk Management

----

Question Number: 882

Question: A retailer is piloting new IoT devices with security concerns. What technique would BEST identify risks proactively?

Option 1: Architecture reviews after implementation

Option 2: Threat modeling prior to production

Option 3: Penetration testing before rollout

Option 4: Security scanning after installation

Correct Response: 2

Explanation: Threat modeling finds risks before new devices deploy.

Knowledge Area: Threat Modelling and Threat Landscape in Risk Management

----

Question Number: 883

Question: Scenario: An organization has identified a critical vulnerability in its network infrastructure. What is the primary step in conducting a vulnerability and control deficiency analysis for this vulnerability?

Option 1: Identifying the root causes of the vulnerability and control deficiencies

Option 2: Implementing immediate mitigating controls to address the vulnerability

Option 3: Transferring the risk to an external party through outsourcing or insurance

Option 4: Accepting the vulnerability without taking any action

Correct Response: 1

Explanation: The primary step in conducting a vulnerability and control deficiency analysis for the identified vulnerability is identifying the root causes of the vulnerability and control deficiencies. This analysis helps in understanding the underlying factors contributing to the vulnerability, enabling organizations to develop appropriate corrective measures and strengthen their risk management practices.

Knowledge Area: Vulnerability and Control Deficiency Analysis (e.g., root cause analysis) in Risk Management

----

Question Number: 884

Question: Scenario: An organization experiences a significant control deficiency in its financial reporting process. What is the primary objective of conducting a vulnerability and control deficiency analysis for this deficiency?

Option 1: Identifying the root causes of the control deficiency and developing corrective actions

Option 2: Transferring the control deficiency to an external party through outsourcing

Option 3: Accepting the control deficiency without taking any proactive measures

Option 4: Eliminating all control deficiencies through immediate remediation

Correct Response: 1

Explanation: The primary objective of conducting a vulnerability and control deficiency analysis for the identified control deficiency is identifying the root causes of the control deficiency and developing corrective actions. This analysis helps in understanding the underlying factors contributing to the deficiency, enabling organizations to address the systemic issues, improve their risk management processes, and implement effective controls to mitigate the identified deficiencies.

Knowledge Area: Vulnerability and Control Deficiency Analysis (e.g., root cause analysis) in Risk Management

----

Question Number: 885

Question: Scenario: An organization discovers a critical vulnerability in its web application. What is the primary action to take in response to this vulnerability?

Option 1: Conducting a thorough vulnerability assessment to understand the potential impact

Option 2: Implementing temporary compensating controls until a permanent fix is available

Option 3: Transferring the vulnerability to an external party through outsourcing or insurance

Option 4: Accepting the vulnerability without taking any action

Correct Response: 1

Explanation: The primary action to take in response to the identified vulnerability in the web application is conducting a thorough vulnerability assessment to understand the potential impact. This assessment helps in evaluating the likelihood and severity of the vulnerability, enabling organizations to prioritize their mitigation efforts and implement appropriate measures to address the vulnerability.

Knowledge Area: Vulnerability and Control Deficiency Analysis (e.g., root cause analysis) in Risk Management

----

Question Number: 886

Question: Scenario: An organization experiences a breach in its network security resulting in unauthorized access to sensitive data. What is the primary step in conducting a vulnerability and control deficiency analysis for this breach?

Option 1: Identifying the root causes of the breach and control deficiencies

Option 2: Implementing immediate measures to stop the breach and mitigate the impact

Option 3: Transferring the breach to an external party through legal actions

Option 4: Accepting the breach without taking any action

Correct Response: 1

Explanation: The primary step in conducting a vulnerability and control deficiency analysis for the identified breach is identifying the root causes of the breach and control deficiencies. This analysis helps in understanding how the breach occurred, the weaknesses in the control environment, and developing appropriate measures to prevent future breaches.

Knowledge Area: Vulnerability and Control Deficiency Analysis (e.g., root cause analysis) in Risk Management

----

Question Number: 887

Question: An organization wants to improve its risk assessment by incorporating threat scenarios. What information would be MOST useful in developing scenarios?

Option 1: Recent cyber threats in the news

Option 2: Results of vulnerability scans

Option 3: Outcomes of penetration testing

Option 4: Threat intelligence from CERTs

Correct Response: 4

Explanation: Threat intelligence provides insights into relevant scenarios.

Knowledge Area: Risk Scenario Development in Risk Management

Question Number: 888

Question: A financial firm's risk analysis primarily uses quantitative data. What technique would enhance the risk scenario process?

Option 1: Conduct probabilistic risk modeling

Option 2: Interview business process owners

Option 3: Review threat information from vendors

Option 4: Perform quantitative risk surveys

Correct Response: 2

Explanation: Interviews provide qualitative insights into risk scenarios.

Knowledge Area: Risk Scenario Development in Risk Management

Question Number: 889

Question: An organization performs primarily qualitative risk assessments. What technique would ENHANCE analysis?

Option 1: Brainstorming risk scenarios

Option 2: Incorporating key risk metrics

Option 3: Using Monte Carlo simulations

Option 4: Benchmarking industry loss data

Correct Response: 3

Explanation: Simulations bring quantitative rigor to qualitative assessments.

Knowledge Area: Risk Scenario Development in Risk Management

Question Number: 890

Question: A hospital wants to evaluate emerging risk scenarios. Which data sources would provide the BEST insights?

Option 1: Government healthcare associations

Option 2: Industry loss data consortiums

Option 3: Threat databases and advisories

Option 4: Competing hospital risk registers

Correct Response: 3

Explanation: Threat data provides leading indicators of new scenarios.

Knowledge Area: Risk Scenario Development in Risk Management

Question Number: 891

Question: Which of the following is a commonly used risk assessment framework in risk management?

Option 1: ISO 31000: Risk Management Principles and Guidelines

Option 2: COSO Enterprise Risk Management Framework

Option 3: NIST SP 800-30: Risk Management Guide for Information Technology Systems

Option 4: All of the above

Correct Response: 1

Explanation: ISO 31000: Risk Management Principles and Guidelines, COSO Enterprise Risk Management Framework, and NIST SP 800-30: Risk Management Guide for Information Technology Systems are all commonly used risk assessment frameworks in risk management. These frameworks provide guidance and best practices for conducting risk assessments and managing risks effectively.

Knowledge Area: Risk Assessment Concepts, Standards and Frameworks in Risk Management

----

Question Number: 892

Question: Scenario: An organization is planning to conduct a risk assessment for its information technology systems. Which framework would be most suitable for this purpose?

Option 1: NIST SP 800-30: Risk Management Guide for Information Technology Systems

Option 2: ISO 31000: Risk Management Principles and Guidelines

Option 3: COSO Enterprise Risk Management Framework

Option 4: COBIT (Control Objectives for Information and Related Technologies)

Correct Response: 1

Explanation: For conducting a risk assessment specifically for information technology systems, the NIST SP 800-30: Risk Management Guide for Information Technology Systems would be the most suitable framework. It provides a structured approach and guidance for identifying, assessing, and mitigating risks associated specifically with IT systems.

Knowledge Area: Risk Assessment Concepts, Standards and Frameworks in Risk Management

----

Question Number: 893

Question: Which of the following risk assessment concepts emphasizes the importance of considering the likelihood and impact of risks?

Option 1: Risk likelihood

Option 2: Risk severity

Option 3: Risk appetite

Option 4: Risk tolerance

Correct Response: 1

Explanation: The concept of risk likelihood emphasizes the importance of considering the likelihood or probability of risks occurring. It helps in understanding the chances or frequency of risks happening and allows organizations to prioritize their risk management efforts accordingly.

Knowledge Area: Risk Assessment Concepts, Standards and Frameworks in Risk Management

----

Question Number: 894

Question: Which risk assessment concept refers to the acceptable level of risk that an organization is willing to take?

Option 1: Risk appetite

Option 2: Risk tolerance

Option 3: Risk likelihood

Option 4: Risk severity

Correct Response: 1

Explanation: The risk assessment concept that refers to the acceptable level of risk that an organization is willing to take is called risk appetite. It defines the level of risk that an organization considers acceptable while pursuing its objectives. It helps in guiding risk management decisions and determining the boundaries within which risks can be accepted.

Knowledge Area: Risk Assessment Concepts, Standards and Frameworks in Risk Management

----

Question Number: 895

Question: An organization is creating a risk register. Which components should be included for each risk?

Option 1: Description, rating, response, owner

Option 2: Current status, test results, audit notes

Option 3: Start date, end date, last update, simulator

Option 4: Threat source, annual loss expectancy, control gaps

Correct Response: 1

Explanation: Registers should cover risk description, assessment, response, ownership.

Knowledge Area: Risk Register in Risk Management

Question Number: 896

Question: A company wants to improve its risk register. Which element would enhance visibility into emerging risks?

Option 1: Add threat categories

Option 2: Include risk maps

Option 3: Add leading indicators

Option 4: Expand list of impacts

Correct Response: 3

Explanation: Leading indicators highlight emerging risks.

Knowledge Area: Risk Register in Risk Management

Question Number: 897

Question: An organization is updating its risk register. What new field would BEST strengthen risk response tracking?

Option 1: Expected resolution dates

Option 2: Risk response costs

Option 3: Cross-references to audits

Option 4: Control gaps leading to risk

Correct Response: 1

Explanation: Target remediation dates support risk response tracking.

Knowledge Area: Risk Register in Risk Management

Question Number: 898

Question: What data would BEST profile the organizational relevance of each risk?

Option 1: Likelihood rating

Option 2: Response owners

Option 3: Qualitative business impacts

Option 4: Quantified financial exposure

Correct Response: 4

Explanation: Financial exposure demonstrates business relevance.

Knowledge Area: Risk Register in Risk Management

Question Number: 899

Question: An organization wants to incorporate potential financial losses into its risk analysis. Which methodology would BEST achieve this?

Option 1: PEST analysis

Option 2: Threat modelling

Option 3: Impact assessment

Option 4: Quantitative risk analysis

Correct Response: 4

Explanation: Quantitative risk analysis estimates potential financial losses.

Knowledge Area: Risk Analysis Methodologies in Risk Management

----

Question Number: 900

Question: A company is performing primarily qualitative risk assessments. What technique would ENHANCE analysis by incorporating financial exposures?

Option 1: Decision tree analysis

Option 2: Key risk indicators

Option 3: Risk surveys and workshops

Option 4: Quantitative risk modeling

Correct Response: 4

Explanation: Quantitative modeling provides financial loss insights.

Knowledge Area: Risk Analysis Methodologies in Risk Management

----

Question Number: 901

Question: An organization relies on risk questionnaires for analysis. What technique would provide MORE insights on emerging risks?

Option 1: Teaming workshops

Option 2: Risk indicator monitoring

Option 3: Financial impact analysis

Option 4: Root cause analysis

Correct Response: 2

Explanation: Risk indicators highlight emerging issues not captured in questionnaires.

Knowledge Area: Risk Analysis Methodologies in Risk Management

----

Question Number: 902

Question: A hospital wants to prioritize information security risks. What analysis would provide MOST meaningful rankings?

Option 1: Threat vulnerability analysis

Option 2: Pareto analysis of risk themes

Option 3: Risks mapped on qualitative scales

Option 4: Analysis of potential financial losses

Correct Response: 4

Explanation: Potential losses quantify business impacts for prioritization.

Knowledge Area: Risk Analysis Methodologies in Risk Management

----

Question Number: 903

Question: Scenario: A company is conducting a business impact analysis (BIA) to assess the potential consequences of a major system failure. What is the first step in conducting a BIA?

Option 1: Identifying critical business functions and their dependencies

Option 2: Assessing the financial impact of the system failure

Option 3: Implementing immediate measures to mitigate the system failure

Option 4: Accepting the system failure without taking any action

Correct Response: 1

Explanation: The first step in conducting a business impact analysis (BIA) is identifying critical business functions and their dependencies. This step helps in understanding the interdependencies between different functions and their importance to the organization. It provides a foundation for prioritizing recovery efforts and allocating resources effectively.

Knowledge Area: Business Impact Analysis in Risk Management

Question Number: 904

Question: Scenario: An organization is assessing the potential impacts of a cybersecurity breach. What is the primary objective of conducting a business impact analysis (BIA) in this situation?

Option 1: To evaluate the financial losses from the breach

Option 2: To identify critical data assets and their impact

Option 3: To eliminate all risks associated with the breach

Option 4: To accept the breach without taking any action

Correct Response: 2

Explanation: The primary objective of conducting a business impact analysis (BIA) in this situation is to identify critical data assets and their impact. BIA helps in understanding the potential consequences of a breach, evaluating the impact on data assets, and guiding recovery efforts and resource allocation.

Knowledge Area: Business Impact Analysis in Risk Management

Question Number: 905

Question: Scenario: A company experiences a significant supply chain disruption. What is the main purpose of conducting a business impact analysis (BIA) in this situation?

Option 1: To assess the financial losses from the disruption

Option 2: To identify alternative suppliers and recovery options

Option 3: To eliminate all risks associated with the disruption

Option 4: To accept the disruption without taking any action

Correct Response: 2

Explanation: The main purpose of conducting a business impact analysis (BIA) in this situation is to identify alternative suppliers and recovery options. BIA helps in understanding the potential impacts of the disruption, assessing dependencies, and developing recovery strategies to minimize the impact and ensure continuity.

Knowledge Area: Business Impact Analysis in Risk Management

Question Number: 906

Question: Scenario: An organization wants to assess the potential consequences of a natural disaster. What is the primary step in conducting a business impact analysis (BIA) for this situation?

Option 1: Identifying critical business functions and their dependencies

Option 2: Assessing the probability of the natural disaster

Option 3: Implementing immediate measures to mitigate the natural disaster

Option 4: Accepting the natural disaster without taking any action

Correct Response: 1

Explanation: The primary step in conducting a business impact analysis (BIA) for a natural disaster is identifying critical business functions and their dependencies. This step helps in understanding the interdependencies and impact on the organization, forming the basis for prioritizing recovery efforts and resource allocation.

Knowledge Area: Business Impact Analysis in Risk Management

Question Number: 907

Question: An organization is implementing a new cloud-based CRM system. What should be analyzed FIRST to understand pre-control risks?

Option 1: Total cost of ownership

Option 2: Vendor security architecture

Option 3: Data privacy regulations

Option 4: Inherent risks of the new system

Correct Response: 4

Explanation: Inherent risk assessment considers pre-control risks and vulnerabilities.

Knowledge Area: Inherent and Residual Risk in Risk Management

----

Question Number: 908

Question: A penetration test identified several critical vulnerabilities in an internet-facing ERP application. What type of risk do these findings represent?

Option 1: Residual

Option 2: Compliance

Option 3: Operational

Option 4: Inherent

Correct Response: 1

Explanation: The findings highlight residual risk even after controls were applied.

Knowledge Area: Inherent and Residual Risk in Risk Management

----

Question Number: 909

Question: A risk manager is reviewing open findings from a recent audit of access controls. What type of risk do these findings reflect?

Option 1: Inherent

Option 2: Residual

Option 3: Secondary

Option 4: Patched

Correct Response: 2

Explanation: Open audit findings represent residual risk in access controls.

Knowledge Area: Inherent and Residual Risk in Risk Management

----

Question Number: 910

Question: A company is adopting a new cloud payroll system and wants to perform due diligence. What risk analysis would BEST highlight pre-control risks?

Option 1: Vendor security audit

Option 2: Penetration testing after implementation

Option 3: Review ofInhererent risks prior to adoption

Option 4: Threat modeling after integration

Correct Response: 3

Explanation: Analyzing inherent risks before adoption identifies pre-control issues.

Knowledge Area: Inherent and Residual Risk in Risk Management

----

DOMAIN 1 – GOVERNANCE
Question Number: 911

Question: An organization is defining its risk management program. What should be considered FIRST when setting risk priorities?

Option 1: Industry best practices

Option 2: Regulatory obligations

Option 3: Organization's strategy and objectives

Option 4: Risk appetite

Correct Response: 3

Explanation: Strategy and objectives guide risk priorities.

Knowledge Area: Organizational Strategy, Goals, and Objectives in Risk Management

----

Question Number: 912

Question: A company wants to strengthen risk oversight of strategic objectives. What should the risk team do FIRST?

Option 1: Conduct a RCSA

Option 2: Implement a governance framework

Option 3: Identify critical success factors

Option 4: Define key risk indicators

Correct Response: 3

Explanation: Understand critical success factors to focus risk efforts.

Knowledge Area: Organizational Strategy, Goals, and Objectives in Risk Management

----

Question Number: 913

Question: What should a risk manager do when objectives change significantly?

Option 1: Rely on pre-defined risk priorities

Option 2: Wait for new audit findings

Option 3: Conduct refreshed risk assessment

Option 4: Monitor existing dashboards

Correct Response: 3

Explanation: Refreshed risk assessment ensures alignment with new objectives.

Knowledge Area: Organizational Strategy, Goals, and Objectives in Risk Management

----

Question Number: 914

Question: A merger introduced new business lines and revenues. What is the FIRST priority of risk management?

Option 1: Update policies for new lines

Option 2: Conduct RCSA on merged company

Option 3: Align program to combined strategy

Option 4: Implement combined risk technology

Correct Response: 2

Explanation: Updating risk program for combined strategy drives priorities.

Knowledge Area: Organizational Strategy, Goals, and Objectives in Risk Management

----

Question Number: 915

Question: A growing company wants to establish a formal risk management program. What is the FIRST step?

Option 1: Hire a dedicated risk manager

Option 2: Implement risk management technology

Option 3: Define risk roles and responsibilities

Option 4: Establish a risk management committee

Correct Response: 3

Explanation: Define risk roles and responsibilities first.

Knowledge Area: Organizational Structure, Roles and Responsibilities in Risk Management

----

Question Number: 916

Question: A company's board wants to strengthen risk oversight. What role should be created?

Option 1: Senior risk manager

Option 2: Dedicated risk auditor

Option 3: Chief Risk Officer

Option 4: Risk management committee

Correct Response: 3

Explanation: The Chief Risk Officer leads the risk program at the executive level.

Knowledge Area: Organizational Structure, Roles and Responsibilities in Risk Management

----

Question Number: 917

Question: An organization wants to integrate risk management into operations. Which approach is BEST?

Option 1: Centralized program under CRO

Option 2: Risk responsibilities in job descriptions

Option 3: Decentralized model with shared services

Option 4: Annual risk assessment process

Correct Response: 2

Explanation: Embed risk duties into job descriptions throughout the business.

Knowledge Area: Organizational Structure, Roles and Responsibilities in Risk Management

----

Question Number: 918

Question: What is the MAIN benefit of a "three lines of defense" risk model?

Option 1: Clear separation of duties

Option 2: Centralized expertise

Option 3: Holistic risk coverage

Option 4: Greater operational integration

Correct Response: 1

Explanation: The model provides clear separation between risk functions.

Knowledge Area: Organizational Structure, Roles and Responsibilities in Risk Management

----

Question Number: 919

Question: An organization wants to build a stronger risk culture. What is the FIRST step?

Option 1: Establish zero-tolerance conduct policies

Option 2: Implement mandatory risk training

Option 3: Define desired cultural elements

Option 4: Enforce stringent controls

Correct Response: 3

Explanation: Define desired cultural traits and behaviors first.

Knowledge Area: Organizational Culture in Risk Management

Question Number: 920

Question: Senior management wants to improve risk behaviors. What action would be MOST impactful?

Option 1: Publish a code of conduct

Option 2: Increase accountability for violations

Option 3: Reward positive risk behaviors

Option 4: Enforce mandatory training

Correct Response: 2

Explanation: Increased accountability drives cultural change.

Knowledge Area: Organizational Culture in Risk Management

Question Number: 921

Question: An organization is initiating a risk culture transformation. What is MOST important for the risk team?

Option 1: Assessing risk culture maturity

Option 2: Defining risk appetite

Option 3: Monitoring risk metrics

Option 4: Role modeling desired behaviors

Correct Response: 4

Explanation: The risk team should visibly role model desired cultural traits.

Knowledge Area: Organizational Culture in Risk Management

Question Number: 922

Question: What indicates strong risk culture maturity?

Option 1: Mandatory training completion

Option 2: Level of policy enforcement

Option 3: Employee survey engagement scores

Option 4: Individual accountability for behaviors

Correct Response: 4

Explanation: Accountability for actions demonstrates cultural maturity.

Knowledge Area: Organizational Culture in Risk Management

Question Number: 923

Question: An organization wants to implement new risk management policies. What should be done FIRST?

Option 1: Customize industry standard frameworks

Option 2: Conduct a gap assessment

Option 3: Draft new policy documents

Option 4: Obtain executive approval

Correct Response: 2

Explanation: A gap assessment identifies policy needs and priorities.

Knowledge Area: Policies and Standards in Risk Management

Question Number: 924

Question: A company acquired a business with differing policies. What should occur FIRST?

Option 1: Train employees on new policies

Option 2: Extend parent policies to new business

Option 3: Allow acquired business to maintain status quo

Option 4: Perform policy gap assessment

Correct Response: 4

Explanation: A policy gap assessment determines integration needs.

Knowledge Area: Policies and Standards in Risk Management

Question Number: 925

Question: What is the BEST way to promote policy adherence?

Option 1: Ask employees to acknowledge policies

Option 2: Implement monitoring controls

Option 3: Enforce mandatory training

Option 4: Reward compliance and penalize violations

Correct Response: 4

Explanation: Enforcement incentives drive policy compliance.

Knowledge Area: Policies and Standards in Risk Management

Question Number: 926

Question: How should policy exceptions be managed?

Option 1: Zero tolerance of deviations

Option 2: Recorded and approved through exception workflow

Option 3: Allowed unless explicitly prohibited

Option 4: Not tracked unless required for audit

Correct Response: 2

Explanation: Record and approve exceptions through defined workflow.

Knowledge Area: Policies and Standards in Risk Management

Question Number: 927

Question: An organization wants to identify operational risk exposures. Which approach would provide the BROADEST view?

Option 1: Process audits

Option 2: Risk self-assessments

Option 3: Loss event data analysis

Option 4: Risk workshops

Correct Response: 1

Explanation: Analyzing business processes provides an end-to-end view of risks.

Knowledge Area: Business Processes in Risk Management

Question Number: 928

Question: A company undergoes frequent organizational change. What practice would BEST identify emerging risks?

Option 1: Static risk assessments

Option 2: Key risk indicators

Option 3: Industry benchmarking

Option 4: Regular process analysis

Correct Response: 4

Explanation: Analyze processes regularly for change-driven risks.

Knowledge Area: Business Processes in Risk Management

Question Number: 929

Question: What is an effective way to identify process control gaps?

Option 1: Process walkthroughs

Option 2: Control testing

Option 3: RCSAs

Option 4: Audit findings

Correct Response: 1

Explanation: Process walkthroughs reveal operational vulnerabilities.

Knowledge Area: Business Processes in Risk Management

Question Number: 930

Question: Why should business processes be modeled before automation?

Option 1: To benchmark against competitors

Option 2: To calculate return on investment

Option 3: To inventory systems for replacement

Option 4: To identify risks for controls

Correct Response: 4

Explanation: Modeling first highlights risks to address before automation.

Knowledge Area: Business Processes in Risk Management

Question Number: 931

Question: A company wants to improve information security. What should be done FIRST?

Option 1: Classify data by sensitivity

Option 2: Implement encryption controls

Option 3: Perform risk assessment

Option 4: Prevent use of external drives

Correct Response: 1

Explanation: Classify data to drive appropriate controls.

Knowledge Area: Organizational Assets in Risk Management

Question Number: 932

Question: An organization created a data classification schema. What should be done NEXT?

Option 1: Encrypt based on classifications

Option 2: Assign data owners

Option 3: Perform risk analysis

Option 4: Label datasets by classification

Correct Response: 3

Explanation: Risk analysis on classified data reveals protection priorities.

Knowledge Area: Organizational Assets in Risk Management

Question Number: 933

Question: What practice helps optimize security investment?

Option 1: Annual asset inventory

Option 2: Data lifecycle management

Option 3: 8-year system refresh cycle

Option 4: 3-year quantitative risk analysis

Correct Response: 2

Explanation: Managing data lifecycles aligns protection with value.

Knowledge Area: Organizational Assets in Risk Management

Question Number: 934

Question: How can data warehouses increase compliance risk?

Option 1: Unfiltered extraction from source systems

Option 2: Lack of data classification

Option 3: Not anonymizing sensitive fields

Option 4: Unmonitored access by analysts

Correct Response: 3

Explanation: Sensitive source fields may be exposed improperly.

Knowledge Area: Organizational Assets in Risk Management

Question Number: 935

Question: An organization wants to take an enterprise view of risks. What should be done FIRST?

Option 1: Centralize all risk management functions

Option 2: Implement a common risk technology platform

Option 3: Define the ERM strategy and priorities

Option 4: Conduct an organization-wide risk assessment

Correct Response: 3

Explanation: Define the ERM strategy and priorities first.

Knowledge Area: Enterprise Risk Management and Risk Management Framework in Risk Management

----

Question Number: 936

Question: What is an advantage of implementing an ERM framework?

Option 1: Satisfies industry standards for risk management

Option 2: Provides centralized oversight of all risks

Option 3: Ensures holistic coverage of risk disciplines

Option 4: Enforces top-down consistency across silos

Correct Response: 4

Explanation: ERM provides consistent discipline across decentralized units.

Knowledge Area: Enterprise Risk Management and Risk Management Framework in Risk Management

----

Question Number: 937

Question: An organization performed ERM maturity assessment. What should occur NEXT?

Option 1: Report assessment results to executives

Option 2: Identify industry leading practices

Option 3: Initiate implementation of improvements

Option 4: Define target state maturity objectives

Correct Response: 4

Explanation: Define target state objectives to drive improvement roadmap.

Knowledge Area: Enterprise Risk Management and Risk Management Framework in Risk Management

----

Question Number: 938

Question: How does an ERM framework MOST benefit strategic planning?

Option 1: Catalogs assets requiring protection

Option 2: Highlights critical risk interdependencies

Option 3: Enables quantitative risk modeling

Option 4: Identifies threats tied to objectives

Correct Response: 2

Explanation: ERM highlights cross-risk impacts on objectives.

Knowledge Area: Enterprise Risk Management and Risk Management Framework in Risk Management

----

Question Number: 939

Question: What is the PRIMARY purpose of the three lines of defense model?

Option 1: To integrate risk processes

Option 2: To define risk reporting flows

Option 3: To assign risk roles

Option 4: To segregate risk responsibilities

Correct Response: 4

Explanation: The model separates risk duties across lines.

Knowledge Area: Three Lines of Defense in Risk Management

Question Number: 940

Question: Which role would be part of the SECOND line of defense?

Option 1: Internal auditor

Option 2: Business unit manager

Option 3: Chief Risk Officer

Option 4: Regulator

Correct Response: 3

Explanation: The CRO leads the second line risk management function.

Knowledge Area: Three Lines of Defense in Risk Management

Question Number: 941

Question: A company is implementing a 3LOD model. Where should information security roles MOSTLY reside?

Option 1: 1st line operations

Option 2: 2nd line RM group

Option 3: 3rd line internal audit

Option 4: External consultants

Correct Response: 2

Explanation: Security aligns to second line centralized RM function.

Knowledge Area: Three Lines of Defense in Risk Management

Question Number: 942

Question: What is a common challenge when implementing a 3LOD model?

Option 1: Ambiguity in defining control owners

Option 2: Roles overlapping across lines

Option 3: Too many employees in 1st line

Option 4: Difficulty accessing 3rd line

Correct Response: 1

Explanation: Ownership for controls should be distinct across lines.

Knowledge Area: Three Lines of Defense in Risk Management

Question Number: 943

Question: What should be included in a risk profile?

Option 1: Risk description, impact, causes

Option 2: Audit findings, control gaps, owners

Option 3: Start date, end date, last update

Option 4: Current and target risk ratings

Correct Response: 1

Explanation: Risk profiles cover risk description, assessment, and root causes.

Knowledge Area: Risk Profile in Risk Management

Question Number: 944

Question: A risk manager presents a risk heatmap to the board. What should be included?

Option 1: Residual risk ratings

Option 2: Audit issue tracker

Option 3: Total risk by category

Option 4: Risk profile details

Correct Response: 3

Explanation: The heatmap summaries total risk exposures by type.

Knowledge Area: Risk Profile in Risk Management

Question Number: 945

Question: What metric best indicates the severity of operational risk?

Option 1: Audit deficiencies by location

Option 2: Key risk indicator performance

Option 3: Percentage of blocked threats

Option 4: Value of financial exposure

Correct Response: 4

Explanation: Financial exposure quantifies operational risk impacts.

Knowledge Area: Risk Profile in Risk Management

Question Number: 946

Question: Why are risk interdependency analyses useful?

Option 1: Illustrate cross-functional impacts

Option 2: Satisfy regulatory requirements

Option 3: Enable resource optimization

Option 4: Simplify risk reporting

Correct Response: 1

Explanation: Interdependency mapping shows risk correlations.

Knowledge Area: Risk Profile in Risk Management

Question Number: 947

Question: What guides decisions on risk acceptance and responses?

Option 1: Risk appetite statement

Option 2: Risk register

Option 3: Audit findings

Option 4: Threat intelligence

Correct Response: 1

Explanation: The risk appetite statement guides risk acceptance decisions.

Knowledge Area: Risk Appetite and Risk Tolerance in Risk Management

----

Question Number: 948

Question: How are risk appetite levels set?

Option 1: By external industry benchmarks

Option 2: Based on quantifiable risk metrics

Option 3: Through executive management direction

Option 4: By assessing maturity indicators

Correct Response: 3

Explanation: Executive direction on strategy sets risk appetites.

Knowledge Area: Risk Appetite and Risk Tolerance in Risk Management

----

Question Number: 949

Question: Which metric indicates that risk exceeds defined tolerance?

Option 1: Percentage of blocked threats

Option 2: Volume of audit deficiencies

Option 3: Level of financial exposure

Option 4: Number of data records lost

Correct Response: 3

Explanation: Exceeding the defined financial loss tolerance signals excessive risk.

Knowledge Area: Risk Appetite and Risk Tolerance in Risk Management

----

Question Number: 950

Question: How can overly restrictive risk tolerance impact an organization?

Option 1: Increased staff turnover

Option 2: Lower revenue opportunities

Option 3: Higher cost of risk management

Option 4: Reduced focus on core objectives

Correct Response: 2

Explanation: Excessive restrictions constrain beneficial opportunities.

Knowledge Area: Risk Appetite and Risk Tolerance in Risk Management

----

Question Number: 951

Question: Scenario: An organization operates in a highly regulated industry and is subject to various legal and regulatory requirements. What is the primary purpose of incorporating legal and regulatory requirements in risk management?

Option 1: To ensure compliance with applicable laws and regulations

Option 2: To eliminate all risks associated with legal and regulatory requirements

Option 3: To transfer the responsibility of compliance to external parties

Option 4: To accept non-compliance without taking any action

Correct Response: 1

Explanation: The primary purpose of incorporating legal and regulatory requirements in risk management is to ensure compliance with applicable laws and regulations. By identifying and addressing legal and regulatory requirements, organizations can minimize the legal and financial risks associated with non-compliance. It helps organizations operate within the boundaries of the law, protect their reputation, and avoid potential penalties and legal consequences.

Knowledge Area: Legal, Regulatory and Contractual Requirements in Risk Management

----

Question Number: 952

Question: Scenario: An organization enters into a contract with a third-party vendor to provide services. What is the primary reason for considering contractual requirements in risk management?

Option 1: To ensure that the vendor meets the agreed-upon obligations and standards

Option 2: To eliminate all risks associated with the contract

Option 3: To transfer all risks to the third-party vendor

Option 4: To accept non-compliance with contractual requirements without taking any action

Correct Response: 1

Explanation: The primary reason for considering contractual requirements in risk management is to ensure that the vendor meets the agreed-upon obligations and standards. By incorporating contractual requirements, organizations can mitigate risks associated with non-compliance, ensure the vendor's performance aligns with expectations, and protect their interests. It helps establish clear expectations, responsibilities, and standards to manage risks associated with the contractual relationship.

Knowledge Area: Legal, Regulatory and Contractual Requirements in Risk Management

----

Question Number: 953

Question: Scenario: An organization operates in a highly regulated industry and must adhere to specific legal and regulatory requirements. What is the primary consequence of non-compliance with legal and regulatory requirements?

Option 1: Legal and financial penalties

Option 2: Elimination of all risks

Option 3: Transfer of risks to external parties

Option 4: Acceptance of non-compliance without taking any action

Correct Response: 1

Explanation: The primary consequence of non-compliance with legal and regulatory requirements is the risk of legal and financial penalties. Non-compliance can result in fines, sanctions, legal actions, reputational damage, and loss of business opportunities. Adhering to legal and regulatory requirements is crucial for maintaining compliance, protecting the organization's reputation, and mitigating the potential adverse consequences of non-compliance.

Knowledge Area: Legal, Regulatory and Contractual Requirements in Risk Management

----

Question Number: 954

Question: Scenario: A risk management professional is faced with a situation where they discover unethical behavior within their organization. What is the primary action they should take based on professional ethics?

Option 1: Report the unethical behavior to the appropriate authorities or management

Option 2: Ignore the unethical behavior and continue with their regular duties

Option 3: Confront the individuals involved in the unethical behavior

Option 4: Document the unethical behavior for personal records and take no further action

Correct Response: 1

Explanation: The primary action a risk management professional should take based on professional ethics is to report the unethical behavior to the appropriate authorities or management. Upholding professional ethics involves promoting integrity, transparency, and accountability. Reporting unethical behavior helps in maintaining ethical standards, protecting the organization, and ensuring a healthy work environment.

Knowledge Area: Professional Ethics of Risk Management in Risk Management

----

Question Number: 955

Question: Scenario: A risk management professional is faced with a conflict of interest situation where their personal interests may compromise their professional judgment. What is the best course of action based on professional ethics?

Option 1: Disclose the conflict of interest to relevant stakeholders and recuse oneself from the decision-making process

Option 2: Prioritize personal interests over professional obligations

Option 3: Seek personal gain from the conflict of interest situation

Option 4: Ignore the conflict of interest and proceed with the decision-making process

Correct Response: 1

Explanation: The best course of action based on professional ethics is for the risk management professional to disclose the conflict of interest to relevant stakeholders and recuse themselves from the decision-making process. This ensures transparency, avoids bias, and upholds the integrity of the risk management profession.

Knowledge Area: Professional Ethics of Risk Management in Risk Management

----

Question Number: 956

Question: Scenario: A risk management professional receives confidential information from a colleague that could potentially benefit them financially. What is the appropriate action based on professional ethics?

Option 1: Maintain confidentiality and not use the information for personal gain

Option 2: Share the confidential information with others for personal gain

Option 3: Disclose the confidential information to competitors for personal gain

Option 4: Ignore the confidential information and proceed with regular duties

Correct Response: 1

Explanation: The appropriate action based on professional ethics is for the risk management professional to maintain confidentiality and not use the confidential information for personal gain. Upholding professional ethics involves respecting confidentiality, safeguarding sensitive information, and acting in the best interests of the organization and stakeholders.

Knowledge Area: Professional Ethics of Risk Management in Risk Management

----

Question Number: 957

Question: Scenario: A risk management professional is faced with a situation where they discover a colleague engaging in fraudulent activities. What is the primary action they should take based on professional ethics?

Option 1: Report the fraudulent activities to the appropriate authorities or management

Option 2: Ignore the fraudulent activities and continue with their regular duties

Option 3: Confront the colleague involved in the fraudulent activities

Option 4: Document the fraudulent activities for personal records and take no further action

Correct Response: 1

Explanation: The primary action a risk management professional should take based on professional ethics is to report the fraudulent activities to the appropriate authorities or management. Upholding professional ethics involves promoting integrity, honesty, and accountability. Reporting fraudulent activities helps in protecting the organization, stakeholders, and maintaining ethical standards.

Knowledge Area: Professional Ethics of Risk Management in Risk Management

----

Question Number: 958

Question: What potential challenge or risk can implementing a rigorous governance framework at the enterprise level cause if the increased processes and oversight are not managed carefully?

Option 1: Excessive bureaucracy and processes that impede agility and responsiveness

Option 2: Lack of innovation due to excessive constraints and controls

Option 3: Weakened security through overly complex policies

Option 4: Insufficient funding for critical IT initiatives

Correct Response: 1

Explanation: While governance aims to increase strategic alignment, the increased processes and oversight can also lead to excessive bureaucracy that impedes organizational agility and responsiveness if not implemented in a streamlined, risk-based manner.

Knowledge Area: Bonus Q from Isaca

Question Number: 959

Question: What is a potential negative outcome or risk that can occur from deficiencies and gaps in an organization's corporate and business governance practices and oversight?

Option 1: Increased responsiveness and agility in operations

Option 2: Improved compliance across regulatory requirements

Option 3: Greater overall accountability for meeting goals and objectives

Option 4: Higher strategic risk acceptance at executive levels

Correct Response: 4

Explanation: Poor corporate and business governance practices reduce accountability and oversight, which allows higher risk tolerance that can lead to negative strategic outcomes for the enterprise.

Knowledge Area: Bonus Q from Isaca

Question Number: 960

Question: Why is it essential that an enterprise establish governance practices to oversee arrangements, contracts, and the ongoing performance of third-party IT vendors and service providers?

Option 1: To enforce adherence to internal policies and controls

Option 2: To reduce overall costs associated with external IT services

Option 3: To effectively identify and manage risks associated with relying on external dependencies

Option 4: All of the above are important governance objectives

Correct Response: 4

Explanation: Implementing robust governance over IT arrangements enables enforcement of policies, optimization of costs, and risk management related to third-party relationships.

Knowledge Area: Bonus Q from Isaca

Question Number: 961

Question: What type of risk could arise from deficiencies or gaps in an enterprise's governance practices in overseeing IT arrangements and vendor relationships?

Option 1: IT service delivery failures

Option 2: Project budget and timeline overruns

Option 3: Noncompliance with policies, regulations, and contracts

Option 4: All of these problems may result from poor governance

Correct Response: 4

Explanation: Lack of effective governance over arrangements exposes enterprises to major risks like service failures, budget/timeline issues, and noncompliance.

Knowledge Area: Bonus Q from Isaca

Question Number: 962

Question: How should board directors, executives, and other senior business leaders at the top governance level enact their IT governance responsibilities within the enterprise organizational structure?

Option 1: Make detailed technology architecture and platform decisions

Option 2: Directly oversee and manage mid-level IT operations and delivery

Option 3: Participate in actively managing IT projects

Option 4: Provide broad strategic guidance and oversight

Correct Response: 4

Explanation: Top leadership should focus IT governance activities on setting strategy, priorities, risk tolerance, and oversight rather than making detailed technical decisions.

Knowledge Area: Bonus Q from Isaca

Question Number: 963

Question: What is a common IT governance-related pain point or deficiency that enterprises aim to improve through well-designed governance practices and framework?

Option 1: Ineffective identification and mitigation of IT-related business risks

Option 2: Poor strategic and operational alignment between IT and business goals or needs

Option 3: Lack of innovation within IT to keep pace with a dynamic technology landscape

Option 4: All of the above governance gaps are typical pain points

Correct Response: 4

Explanation: Common IT governance pain points include poor risk management, misalignment between IT and business priorities, and lack of technology innovation.

Knowledge Area: Bonus Q from Isaca

Question Number: 964

Question: How can deficiencies in enterprise IT risk management, a governance responsibility, tangibly manifest resulting in adverse impacts on operations?

Option 1: Regulatory non-compliance due to policies not addressing risk

Option 2: Security breaches enabled by unmanaged vulnerabilities

Option 3: Unexpected IT outages from poor DR practices

Option 4: All of these concrete problems can result from poor risk management

Correct Response: 4

Explanation: Ineffective IT risk management enables compliance failures, outages, breaches that significantly impact operations.

Knowledge Area: Bonus Q from Isaca

Question Number: 965

Question: Scenario: A firm experiences frequent IT system outages that disrupt business operations and cause lost sales. What common IT governance pain point does this situation likely indicate?

Option 1: Inadequate IT staff training on maintaining systems

Option 2: Poor system and infrastructure reliability and disaster recovery practices

Option 3: Lack of a sound methodology for investment prioritization

Option 4: Ineffective identification and mitigation of technology risks

Correct Response: 4

Explanation: The outages likely stem from deficient risk management vs. an IT governance responsibility.

Knowledge Area: Bonus Q from Isaca

Question Number: 966

Question: Scenario: A firm relies heavily on establishing rigid corporate policy structures and directives to govern IT but does not supplement with collaborative processes or engagement. What risk may occur?

Option 1: Discouraging innovation and agility due to excessive constraints

Option 2: Fostering distrust or divisiveness between IT and business leaders

Option 3: Inconsistent compliance and oversight due to lack of buy-in

Option 4: All of the above governance problems may emerge

Correct Response: 4

Explanation: Narrowly focusing governance on structures alone has multilayered risks.

Knowledge Area: Bonus Q from Isaca

Question Number: 967

Question: According to COBIT, failure to achieve strategic fit can lead to which key risks?,

Option 1: Sub-optimal investment decisions,

Option 2: Misallocation of IT resources,

Option 3: Poor business and IT collaboration,

Option 4: All of the above,

Correct Response: 4

Explanation: COBIT identifies that failure to align IT strategy with business strategy and achieve strategic fit can potentially lead to all the risks listed - sub-optimal investment, misallocation of resources, and poor collaboration between business and IT.

Knowledge Area: Bonus Q from Isaca

Question Number: 968

Question: An organization reviewed IT performance metrics monthly but strategic risks emerged. What governance best practice was likely overlooked?

Option 1: Benchmarking

Option 2: Risk modelling

Option 3: Dashboard reporting

Option 4: Performance benchmarking

Correct Response: 2

Explanation: Lack of comprehensive risk modeling allowing proactive mitigation indicates a governance gap.

Knowledge Area: Bonus Q from Isaca

Question Number: 969

Question: Determine the missing key words to complete the sentence: "_____ management is a governance best practice that allows proactively addressing emerging risks through _____ modeling of internal and external factors."

Option 1: Performance, predictive

Option 2: Risk, proactive

Option 3: Benchmarking, retrospective

Option 4: Metrics, holistic

Correct Response: 2

Explanation: Risk management with proactive risk modeling facilitates governing emerging threats in a timely manner through comprehensive situational analysis.

Knowledge Area: Bonus Q from Isaca

Question Number: 970

Question: What are some examples of important governance activities and outcomes that should be communicated frequently to stakeholders in a clear, consistent manner through multiple channels?

Option 1: Ongoing progress on strategic priorities and objective fulfillment

Option 2: Current status and milestones for major projects and programs

Option 3: Assessments of technology and implementation risks requiring awareness

Option 4: Essentially all relevant governance decisions and initiatives

Correct Response: 4

Explanation: Strategic progress, project status, risks require continuous multi-channel communication.

Knowledge Area: Bonus Q from Isaca

Question Number: 971

Question: Why is it important for technology governance leaders to proactively focus on clear explanation of governance activities and provide training opportunities to stakeholders during engagement initiatives?

Option 1: Comprehensive education builds stakeholder knowledge regarding governance priorities, decisions, and their impacts

Option 2: Targeted training drives technology adoption by empowering stakeholders to fully leverage implemented solutions

Option 3: Improved understanding enables more effective organizational risk management surrounding initiatives

Option 4: Accomplishes all of these critical governance communication objectives

Correct Response: 4

Explanation: Explanation and training builds knowledge, drives adoption, and improves risk management across stakeholders.

Knowledge Area: Bonus Q from Isaca

Question Number: 972

Question: Why should technology risk analysis and planning be a high priority for CIOs from a governance perspective during stakeholder engagement?

Option 1: Drives risk-aware decisions calibrated to organizational risk appetites

Option 2: Allows development of risk response plans to treat unacceptable exposures

Option 3: Fosters risk transparency through consistent reporting and communication

Option 4: Enables all of these critical risk management governance outcomes

Correct Response: 4

Explanation: Risk considerations enable risk-aware decisions, response planning, transparency.

Knowledge Area: Bonus Q from Isaca

Question Number: 973

Question: To exercise effective governance, CIOs must clearly and continuously communicate _____ to stakeholders, including risk reporting, assessments, tolerances, and mitigation plans.

Option 1: budget status

Option 2: vendor contracts

Option 3: key risk information

Option 4: resource allocation

Correct Response: 3

Explanation: CIOs should regularly communicate risk appetites, assessments, treatment plans.

Knowledge Area: Bonus Q from Isaca

Question Number: 974

Question: How can technology governance leaders at the CIO level exemplify strong risk management to stakeholders through their actions and initiatives?

Option 1: Implementing a robust risk framework, methodology, and governance model

Option 2: Conducting risk analysis training and building risk management capabilities

Option 3: Instilling an organizational risk-aware culture anchored in transparency

Option 4: Demonstrating leadership across all of these dimensions

Correct Response: 4

Explanation: CIOs can institute risk frameworks, training programs, cultural values.

Knowledge Area: Bonus Q from Isaca

Question Number: 975

Question: Scenario: A CIO leads cyber risk assessment workshops for the board. This exemplifies governance:

Option 1: Enforcing financial controls diligently

Option 2: Overseeing vendor contracts closely

Option 3: Exercising technology risk leadership

Option 4: Monitoring IT resource allocation

Correct Response: 3

Explanation: Leading risk workshops demonstrates CIO risk leadership and engagement.

Knowledge Area: Bonus Q from Isaca

Question Number: 976

Question: Effective governance reporting should encompass timely updates on _____ like KPIs, project milestones, budgets, and risk exposures.

Option 1: financial audits

Option 2: vendor contracts

Option 3: key activities and metrics

Option 4: staffing changes

Correct Response: 3

Explanation: Reporting should cover KPIs, project status, risks, and other key items.

Knowledge Area: Bonus Q from Isaca

Question Number: 977

Question: What is the primary purpose of including the content of governance of enterprise IT communication related to risk in the context of technology governance?

Option 1: To highlight the benefits and opportunities of risk management

Option 2: To communicate the potential risks and their impacts on the organization

Option 3: To promote risk avoidance and mitigation strategies

Option 4: To provide technical details and specifications of risk management processes

Correct Response: 2

Explanation: The primary purpose of including the content of governance of enterprise IT communication related to risk in the context of technology governance is to communicate the potential risks and their impacts on the organization. It aims to educate stakeholders about the risks associated with IT initiatives, create awareness of the potential consequences, and enable informed decision-making. The content may include risk assessments, mitigation strategies, and proactive measures to address risks effectively.

Knowledge Area: Bonus Q from Isaca

Question Number: 978

Question: In governance of enterprise IT communication related to risk, stakeholders need to be aware of the potential risks and _____ associated with IT initiatives.

Option 1: benefits

Option 2: opportunities

Option 3: challenges

Option 4: limitations

Correct Response: 3

Explanation: In governance of enterprise IT communication related to risk, stakeholders need to be aware of the potential risks and challenges associated with IT initiatives. This awareness helps stakeholders understand the potential obstacles, uncertainties, and vulnerabilities that may arise during the implementation of IT initiatives, enabling them to make informed decisions and take appropriate actions.

Knowledge Area: Bonus Q from Isaca

Question Number: 979

Question: Which of the following is NOT a characteristic of governance of enterprise IT communication related to risk?

Option 1: Highlighting the benefits and opportunities of risk management

Option 2: Communicating the potential risks and their impacts on the organization

Option 3: Promoting risk avoidance and mitigation strategies

Option 4: Providing technical details and specifications of risk management processes

Correct Response: 1

Explanation: Highlighting the benefits and opportunities of risk management is not a characteristic of governance of enterprise IT communication related to risk. Instead, the focus is on communicating the potential risks, their impacts on the organization, and promoting risk avoidance and mitigation strategies to ensure effective risk management practices.

Knowledge Area: Bonus Q from Isaca

Question Number: 980

Question: Scenario: A company is implementing a new IT initiative that involves significant risks. The governance team has developed a communication strategy to address these risks. What is the main objective of including risk-related content in the communication strategy?

Option 1: To educate stakeholders about the potential risks and their impacts

Option 2: To emphasize the benefits and opportunities of risk management

Option 3: To provide technical specifications and details of risk management processes

Option 4: To promote risk avoidance and mitigation strategies

Correct Response: 1

Explanation: The main objective of including risk-related content in the communication strategy is to educate stakeholders about the potential risks and their impacts. By providing this information, stakeholders gain a better understanding of the risks associated with the IT initiative, allowing them to make informed decisions and take appropriate actions to manage those risks effectively.

Knowledge Area: Bonus Q from Isaca

Question Number: 981

Question: According to COBIT, what is the view on enterprise architecture in the context of the components of enterprise architecture in technology governance?

Option 1: It provides a framework for strategic planning and implementation of enterprise architecture initiatives

Option 2: It focuses solely on the financial aspects of enterprise architecture initiatives

Option 3: It provides technical specifications and details of enterprise architecture components

Option 4: It evaluates the effectiveness of stakeholder engagement in enterprise architecture initiatives

Correct Response: 1

Explanation: According to COBIT, the view on enterprise architecture in the context of the components of enterprise architecture in technology governance is that it provides a framework for strategic planning and implementation of enterprise architecture initiatives. COBIT emphasizes the alignment of IT and business objectives, governance, and risk management aspects of enterprise architecture to ensure effective and efficient technology governance practices.

Question Number: 982

Question: Which of the following is NOT a characteristic of the COBIT view on enterprise architecture?

Option 1: Focus on financial aspects of enterprise architecture initiatives

Option 2: Emphasis on alignment of IT and business objectives

Option 3: Governance and risk management aspects of enterprise architecture

Option 4: Framework for strategic planning and implementation of enterprise architecture initiatives

Correct Response: 1

Explanation: The focus on financial aspects of enterprise architecture initiatives is NOT a characteristic of the COBIT view on enterprise architecture. COBIT emphasizes the alignment of IT and business objectives, governance, and risk management aspects to ensure effective technology governance practices.

Knowledge Area: Bonus Q from Isaca

Question Number: 983

Question: Scenario: A company is implementing a technology governance framework and wants to define the components of enterprise architecture based on the COBIT view. What is the main benefit of adopting the COBIT view on enterprise architecture in this context?

Option 1: Ensuring alignment of IT and business objectives

Option 2: Focusing solely on the financial aspects of enterprise architecture initiatives

Option 3: Providing technical specifications and details of enterprise architecture components

Option 4: Evaluating the effectiveness of stakeholder engagement in enterprise architecture initiatives

Correct Response: 1

Explanation: The main benefit of adopting the COBIT view on enterprise architecture in the context of implementing a technology governance framework is ensuring alignment of IT and business objectives. The COBIT view provides a comprehensive framework that considers governance, risk management, and alignment with business objectives, enabling organizations to effectively plan, implement, and manage their enterprise architecture initiatives to achieve strategic goals and optimize technology governance practices.

Knowledge Area: Bonus Q from Isaca

Question Number: 984

Question: What is the role of enterprise information security architecture in the context of information governance and information architecture?

Option 1: Ensuring the confidentiality, integrity, and availability of information assets

Option 2: Focusing solely on financial aspects of information governance initiatives

Option 3: Providing technical specifications and documentation for information architecture

Option 4: Replacing the need for other governance frameworks in information management

Correct Response: 1

Explanation: The role of enterprise information security architecture in the context of information governance and information architecture is to ensure the confidentiality, integrity, and availability of information assets. It involves designing and implementing security controls, policies, and procedures to protect sensitive information from unauthorized access, modification, or disclosure. Enterprise information security architecture is essential for effective information governance, safeguarding valuable data and mitigating security risks.

Knowledge Area: Bonus Q from Isaca

Question Number: 985

Question: Which of the following is NOT a characteristic of enterprise information security architecture in the context of information governance and information architecture?

Option 1: Ensuring the confidentiality, integrity, and availability of information assets

Option 2: Focusing solely on financial aspects of information governance initiatives

Option 3: Designing and implementing security controls and policies

Option 4: Mitigating security risks and protecting sensitive information

Correct Response: 2

Explanation: Focusing solely on financial aspects of information governance initiatives is not a characteristic of enterprise information security architecture in the context of information governance and information architecture. Instead, enterprise information security architecture focuses on ensuring the confidentiality, integrity, and availability of information assets, designing and implementing security controls and policies, and mitigating security risks to protect sensitive information.

Knowledge Area: Bonus Q from Isaca

Question Number: 986

Question: Scenario: A company is implementing an information governance framework and wants to ensure the security of its information assets. How does enterprise information security architecture contribute to this goal in this scenario?

Option 1: By ensuring the confidentiality, integrity, and availability of information assets

Option 2: By focusing solely on financial aspects of information governance initiatives

Option 3: By providing technical specifications and documentation for information architecture

Option 4: By replacing the need for other governance frameworks in information management

Correct Response: 1

Explanation: Enterprise information security architecture contributes to the goal of ensuring the security of information assets in this scenario by ensuring the confidentiality, integrity, and availability of information assets. It involves designing and implementing security controls, policies, and procedures to protect sensitive information from unauthorized access, modification, or disclosure. By implementing enterprise information security architecture, the company can effectively safeguard its information assets and mitigate security risks in line with the information governance framework.

Knowledge Area: Bonus Q from Isaca

Question Number: 987

Question: What is one of the primary purposes of conducting a risk assessment in the context of information governance?

Option 1: To identify potential risks and vulnerabilities associated with data

Option 2: To solely focus on financial aspects of information governance initiatives

Option 3: To provide technical specifications and documentation for information architectures

Option 4: To replace the need for other governance frameworks in information management initiatives

Correct Response: 1

Explanation: One of the primary purposes of conducting a risk assessment in the context of information governance is to identify potential risks and vulnerabilities associated with data. By assessing threats and vulnerabilities, organizations can understand the potential impact and likelihood of risks, allowing them to implement appropriate controls and mitigation strategies.

Knowledge Area: Bonus Q from Isaca

Question Number: 988

Question: What is the concept of multisourcing in the context of outsourcing and sourcing strategies of IT resource planning?

Option 1: Engaging multiple vendors to fulfill different aspects of an organization's IT needs

Option 2: Sole focus on financial aspects of IT resource planning initiatives

Option 3: Providing technical specifications and documentation for IT architectures

Option 4: Replacing the need for other sourcing strategies in IT resource planning initiatives

Correct Response: 1

Explanation: The concept of multisourcing in the context of outsourcing and sourcing strategies of IT resource planning involves engaging multiple vendors to fulfill different aspects of an organization's IT needs. It allows organizations to leverage specialized expertise, optimize costs, and mitigate risks by diversifying their vendor portfolio and distributing their IT resources among various providers.

Knowledge Area: Bonus Q from Isaca

Question Number: 989

Question: Scenario: After moving HR systems to a cloud provider, a breach occurs due to a flaw in the provider's infrastructure. This demonstrates:

Option 1: Challenges achieving compliance

Option 2: Cloud security risks realized

Option 3: Need for on-prem backups

Option 4: Resource monitoring gaps

Correct Response: 2

Explanation: A provider flaw causing a breach demonstrates realized cloud security risks.

Knowledge Area: Bonus Q from Isaca

Question Number: 990

Question: What risks or potential downsides should be evaluated when determining if insourcing critical IT activities is the appropriate strategic choice?

Option 1: Insufficient flexibility and agility to scale or adapt the internal IT function

Option 2: Stifling innovation and new thinking by not leveraging external solutions

Option 3: Promoting inefficient IT resource silos and preventing optimization

Option 4: All of these drawbacks that should be mitigated through governance

Correct Response: 4

Explanation: Insourcing risks include inflexibility, lack of innovation, IT silos.

Knowledge Area: Bonus Q from Isaca

Question Number: 991

Question: Why might organizations determine a hybrid strategy is optimal when evaluating different IT sourcing models to meet evolving enterprise technology requirements?

Option 1: To optimize spending across models like cloud, outsourcing, insourcing

Option 2: Retain flexibility to fluidly respond to changes in the business and technology landscapes

Option 3: Mitigate over-reliance risks from depending too much on any singular delivery model

Option 4: To obtain all of these key benefits from taking a hybrid approach

Correct Response: 4

Explanation: Hybrid sourcing enables cost optimization, flexibility, and risk mitigation.

Knowledge Area: Bonus Q from Isaca

Question Number: 992

Question: What key elements of analysis and recommendations should technology leaders present and discuss when seeking formal approval for major IT sourcing strategy decisions from enterprise leadership?

Option 1: Comparative analysis of sourcing options with recommendations based on opportunity assessments

Option 2: Financial justification including total cost of ownership models across multiple scenarios

Option 3: Proposed governance model to manage risks and established controls

Option 4: All of these elements to enable informed decisions on strategy

Correct Response: 4

Explanation: Sourcing approval requires analysis, financials, governance/risks.

Knowledge Area: Bonus Q from Isaca

Question Number: 993

Question: Why is taking a strategic approach to IT capacity planning an important practice for technology leaders seeking to optimize resources required to deliver business capabilities?

Option 1: To develop forecasts of future resource needs based on historical data and pipeline demand

Option 2: To identify potential gaps between projected resource supply and expected demand

Option 3: To mitigate risks of shortages, contention, or service degradation from unexpected capacity limitations

Option 4: For all of these reasons to enable analysis of future needs, supply versus demand, and risk mitigation

Correct Response: 4

Explanation: Capacity planning helps forecast needs, identify gaps, mitigate risks.

Knowledge Area: Bonus Q from Isaca

--- --

Question Number: 994

Question: What elements should guide the structure of an organization's vendor selection process to ensure optimal procurement decisions when seeking an external technology product or service?

Option 1: Conducting cost, risk, and capability fitness analyses to meet needs

Option 2: Checking references and reviewing providers' service track records

Option 3: Benchmarking strengths and weaknesses of leading contenders through scorecards

Option 4: Leveraging all of these financial, competency, reference, and benchmarking factors

Correct Response: 4

Explanation: Vendor selection considers costs, risks, fit; references; benchmarks.

Knowledge Area: Bonus Q from Isaca

Question Number: 995

Question: Complete the statement: Key outsourcing risks include inadequate control over external (1) giving third parties (2) internally sensitive corporate resources and data.

Option 1: access, to

Option 2: processes, of

Option 3: staff, of

Option 4: locations, into

Correct Response: 1

Explanation: Prescriptive literature warns access restrictions avoid privacy/security complications, a core governance parameter. Alternatives do not represent direct risks if appropriately managed through internal guidelines and external contractual obligations.

Knowledge Area: Bonus Q from Isaca

Question Number: 996

Question: What factors should IT leaders when selecting potential outsourcing providers to meet identified business needs to ensure optimal vendor selection and minimal delivery risks?

Option 1: Conducting risk, total cost, and provider capability analyses to evaluate fit

Option 2: Leveraging industry benchmarking data and seeking peer recommendations on providers

Option 3: Assessing internal readiness for change and weighing benefits against transition complexity

Option 4: Factoring in all of these perspectives around risks, costs, capabilities; benchmarks; readiness

Correct Response: 4

Explanation: Outsourcing selection considers risks, costs, capabilities; benchmarks; readiness.

Knowledge Area: Bonus Q from Isaca

Question Number: 997

Question: Why is implementing succession planning and management processes a strategic priority for technology executives managing critical IT workforce capabilities?

Option 1: Mitigates overdependency risks for key roles and single points of failure

Option 2: Provides continuity assurance for business critical technology positions

Option 3: Develops a leadership bench of high potential future managers

Option 4: Achieves all of these succession planning benefits around risk, continuity, development

Correct Response: 4

Explanation: Succession planning reduces risk, ensures continuity, develops leaders.

Knowledge Area: Bonus Q from Isaca

Question Number: 998

Question: Why is vendor management important?

Option 1: Reduces performance risks

Option 2: Optimizes value delivery

Option 3: Cultivates strategic partnerships

Option 4: All of the above

Correct Response: 4

Explanation: Vendor management mitigates risks, optimizes value, enables partnerships.

Knowledge Area: Bonus Q from Isaca

Question Number: 999

Question: An IT organization wants to modify technical architectures and solutions designs within a project being outsourced to a third-party provider. The provider resists changes as being out of scope and threatens increased costs. The IT organization should have originally included provisions and change controls in the contract to enable flexibility while minimizing disputes. This scenario most directly indicates:

Option 1: Ineffective vendor management

Option 2: The risks of uncontrolled change

Option 3: The need for clear contracts

Option 4: Insufficient budget forecasting

Correct Response: 2

Explanation: Inflexible contracts increase risks around required outsourcing changes.

Knowledge Area: Bonus Q from Isaca

Question Number: 1000

Question: What is the purpose of change management in the context of IT performance and oversight?

Option 1: To effectively manage and control changes in IT systems and processes

Option 2: Sole focus on financial aspects of IT performance initiatives

Option 3: To provide technical specifications and documentation for IT architectures

Option 4: To replace the need for other oversight frameworks in IT management initiatives

Correct Response: 1

Explanation: The purpose of change management in the context of IT performance and oversight is to effectively manage and control changes in IT systems and processes. It involves planning, implementing, and monitoring changes to ensure minimal disruption, proper documentation, and alignment with business objectives while mitigating potential risks and maximizing benefits.

Knowledge Area: Bonus Q from Isaca

What do you think about our book?

Don't hesitate to help us improve it!

So-so   Good   Perfect

WalterEducation.com

Amazing!

You have been studying very hard to this stage.

How is your exam preparation so far? Can the practice test meet your needs and expectation? I desperately desire your voice.

Please kindly consider

1. Visiting my exam practice test books and consider purchasing them to assist you to pass your target exam, though the direct links provided at the beginning of this book
2. Visiting my exam practice test courses held at Udemy though the direct links provided at the beginning of this book
3. Leaving a positive review and feedback to me though the direct book review links provided at the next page.

Keep going! See you at the end of the book.

Warm regards,

Walter

Or the **Links at Amazon Book Store:**

CRISC 1200+ Practice Test, 2023 (Exam Simulation and Core & Advanced Knowledge)	
Paperback Review URL:	- https://www.amazon.com/review/create-review?&asin=B0CJ43R78T
Kindle eBook Review URL:	- https://www.amazon.com/review/create-review?&asin=B0CJ72JJLY

Direct URLs to visit all Walter's Practice Tests at Amazon

Visit Walter's author page:
http://WalterEducation.com

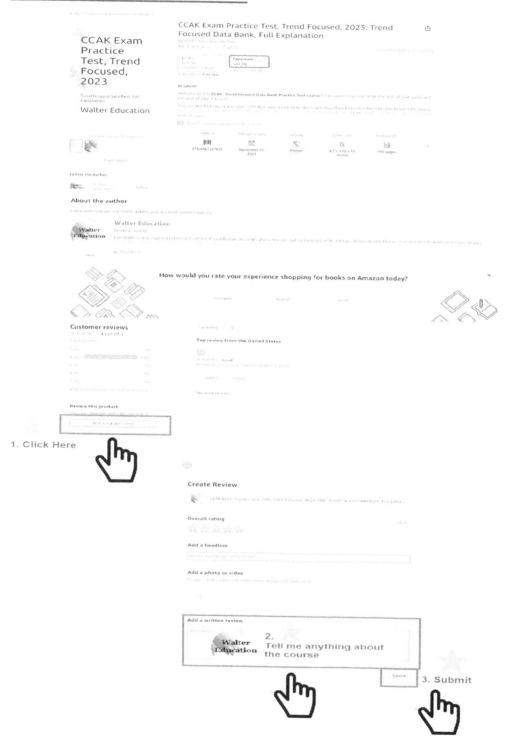

1. Click Here

2. Tell me anything about the course

3. Submit

Question Number: 1001

Question: Scenario: A company is implementing change management practices for IT performance and oversight. How does change management contribute to the success of the company's IT initiatives in this scenario?

Option 1: By effectively managing and controlling changes in IT systems and processes to minimize disruptions and align with business objectives

Option 2: By solely focusing on financial aspects of IT performance initiatives

Option 3: By providing technical specifications and documentation for IT architectures

Option 4: By replacing the need for other oversight frameworks in IT management initiatives

Correct Response: 1

Explanation: Change management contributes to the success of the company's IT initiatives in this scenario by effectively managing and controlling changes in IT systems and processes. It minimizes disruptions, aligns changes with business objectives, and ensures proper documentation, thereby enhancing overall IT performance and oversight while mitigating risks associated with change

Knowledge Area: Bonus Q from Isaca

Question Number: 1002

Question: What is the purpose of business case development and evaluation in the management of IT-enabled investments?

Option 1: To assess the feasibility, benefits, and risks of IT-enabled investments

Option 2: Sole focus on financial aspects of IT-enabled investments

Option 3: To provide technical specifications and documentation for IT architectures

Option 4: To replace the need for other governance frameworks in IT investment management initiatives

Correct Response: 1

Explanation: The purpose of business case development and evaluation in the management of IT-enabled investments is to assess the feasibility, benefits, and risks associated with such investments. It involves conducting a thorough analysis of the potential return on investment, considering financial, strategic, and operational factors, and making informed decisions on whether to proceed with the investment.

Knowledge Area: Bonus Q from Isaca

Question Number: 1003

Question: Fill in the blank: Business case development and evaluation involves assessing the _____ benefits, and risks of IT-enabled investments.

Option 1: feasibility

Option 2: solely focusing on financial aspects of IT-enabled investments

Option 3: technical specifications and documentation for IT architectures

Option 4: replacement of other governance frameworks in IT investment management initiatives

Correct Response: 1

Explanation: Business case development and evaluation involve assessing the feasibility, benefits, and risks of IT-enabled investments. It entails a comprehensive analysis of various factors, including financial viability, strategic alignment, operational impact, and risk assessment, to determine the value and viability of the investment.

Knowledge Area: Bonus Q from Isaca

Question Number: 1004

Question: Which of the following is NOT a characteristic of business case development and evaluation in the management of IT-enabled investments?

Option 1: Assessing the feasibility, benefits, and risks of IT-enabled investments

Option 2: Sole focus on financial aspects of IT-enabled investments

Option 3: Considering strategic alignment and operational impact

Option 4: Providing technical specifications and documentation for IT architectures

Correct Response: 4

Explanation: Providing technical specifications and documentation for IT architectures is not a characteristic of business case development and evaluation in the management of IT-enabled investments. The focus is on assessing feasibility, benefits, and risks, considering strategic alignment, operational impact, and financial viability to make informed investment decisions.

Knowledge Area: Bonus Q from Isaca

Question Number: 1005

Question: Scenario: A company is considering investing in a new IT system to improve operational efficiency. The management team wants to evaluate the feasibility and potential benefits of the proposed investment. How does business case development and evaluation contribute to the decision-making process in this scenario?

Option 1: By assessing the feasibility, benefits, and risks of the IT-enabled investment to make informed decisions

Option 2: By solely focusing on financial aspects of the IT-enabled investment

Option 3: By providing technical specifications and documentation for IT architectures

Option 4: By replacing the need for other governance frameworks in IT investment management initiatives

Correct Response: 1

Explanation: Business case development and evaluation contribute to the decision-making process in this scenario by assessing the feasibility, benefits, and risks of the proposed IT-enabled investment. Through a comprehensive analysis, the company can evaluate the potential returns, operational improvements, and risks associated with the investment, enabling informed decision-making regarding the implementation of the new IT system.

Knowledge Area: Bonus Q from Isaca

Question Number: 1006

Question: What is the concept of portfolio management in the context of IT investment management and reporting of management of IT-enabled investments?

Option 1: The strategic management of a collection of IT investments to achieve business objectives

Option 2: Sole focus on financial aspects of IT investment management initiatives

Option 3: Providing technical specifications and documentation for IT architectures

Option 4: Replacement of other governance frameworks in IT management initiatives

Correct Response: 1

Explanation: The concept of portfolio management in the context of IT investment management and reporting of management of IT-enabled investments is the strategic management of a collection of IT investments to achieve business objectives. It involves the selection, prioritization, and monitoring of IT investments within a portfolio to ensure alignment with business goals, optimize resource allocation, and maximize returns while managing risks and performance.

Knowledge Area: Bonus Q from Isaca

Question Number: 1007

Question: Which of the following is NOT a characteristic of portfolio management in the context of IT investment management and reporting of management of IT-enabled investments?

Option 1: Strategic management of a collection of IT investments to achieve business objectives

Option 2: Sole focus on financial aspects of IT investment management initiatives

Option 3: Optimization of resource allocation and risk management

Option 4: Replacement of other governance frameworks in IT management initiatives

Correct Response: 2

Explanation: Sole focus on financial aspects of IT investment management initiatives is not a characteristic of portfolio management in the context of IT investment management and reporting of management of IT-enabled investments. Portfolio management encompasses a broader range of considerations, including strategic management, resource optimization, risk management, and alignment with business objectives.

Knowledge Area: Bonus Q from Isaca

Question Number: 1008

Question: Scenario: A company has a portfolio of IT investments and wants to ensure effective management and reporting of these investments. How does portfolio management contribute to the success of the company in this scenario?

Option 1: By strategically managing a collection of IT investments to achieve business objectives

Option 2: By solely focusing on financial aspects of IT investment management initiatives

Option 3: By providing technical specifications and documentation for IT architectures

Option 4: By replacing the need for other governance frameworks in IT management initiatives

Correct Response: 1

Explanation: Portfolio management contributes to the success of the company in this scenario by strategically managing a collection of IT investments to achieve business objectives. It involves prioritizing investments, optimizing resource allocation, managing risks, and aligning IT investments with the organization's goals. Effective portfolio management ensures that the company's investments are delivering value, supporting business objectives, and being monitored and reported on to drive informed decision-making.

Knowledge Area: Bonus Q from Isaca

Question Number: 1009

Question: Scenario: A company is undertaking a complex IT project as part of its investment strategy. How does program and project management contribute to the success of the company in this scenario?

Option 1: By providing a systematic approach to planning, executing, and controlling the project to achieve desired outcomes and objectives

Option 2: By solely focusing on financial aspects of IT investment management initiatives

Option 3: By providing technical specifications and documentation for IT architectures

Option 4: By replacing the need for other governance frameworks in IT management initiatives

Correct Response: 1

Explanation: Program and project management contribute to the success of the company in this scenario by providing a systematic approach to planning, executing, and controlling the IT project. It ensures effective management, coordination, and governance of the project, optimizing resources, timelines, and stakeholder engagement to deliver desired outcomes and achieve project objectives. Program and project management help mitigate risks, ensure alignment with business goals, and maximize the success of the IT investment.

Knowledge Area: Bonus Q from Isaca

Question Number: 1010

Question: Which of the following best describes the Risk IT Framework in the context of risk frameworks and standards of risk strategy?

Option 1: A framework developed by ISACA that provides guidance for managing IT-related risks and aligning them with business objectives

Option 2: A framework focused solely on financial aspects of risk strategy

Option 3: Technical specifications and documentation for IT architectures

Option 4: A replacement for other risk frameworks and standards in risk strategy initiatives

Correct Response: 1

Explanation: The Risk IT Framework is a framework developed by ISACA that provides guidance for managing IT-related risks and aligning them with business objectives. It helps organizations identify, assess, and manage IT risks effectively, ensuring they are aligned with the overall risk strategy and business goals.

Knowledge Area: Bonus Q from Isaca

Question Number: 1011

Question: Which of the following is NOT a characteristic of the Risk IT Framework in the context of risk frameworks and standards of risk strategy?

Option 1: solely focused on financial aspects o

Option 2: Provides guidance for managing IT-related risks

Option 3: Developed by ISACA

Option 4: Assists in aligning IT risks with business objectives

Correct Response: 1

Explanation: The Risk IT Framework is not solely focused on financial aspects of risk strategy. Instead, it provides comprehensive guidance for managing IT-related risks and aligning them with business objectives. It assists organizations in understanding and addressing IT risks effectively, ensuring alignment with the overall risk strategy and business goals.

Knowledge Area: Bonus Q from Isaca

Question Number: 1012

Question: Scenario: A multinational company is implementing the Risk IT Framework to manage IT-related risks. The company wants to ensure that its IT risks are effectively identified and aligned with business objectives. Which of the following options best describes the purpose of the Risk IT Framework in this scenario?

Option 1: To provide guidance for managing IT-related risks and aligning them with business objectives

Option 2: A framework focused solely on financial aspects of risk strategy

Option 3: Technical specifications and documentation for IT architectures

Option 4: A replacement for other risk frameworks and standards in risk strategy initiatives

Correct Response: 1

Explanation: The purpose of implementing the Risk IT Framework in this scenario is to provide guidance for managing IT-related risks and aligning them with business objectives. The framework will assist the company in effectively identifying, assessing, and managing IT risks to ensure they are in line with the overall risk strategy and business objectives.

Knowledge Area: Bonus Q from Isaca

Question Number: 1013

Question: What is the role of COBIT for Risk in the context of risk frameworks and standards of risk strategy?

Option 1: Providing a comprehensive framework for managing IT-related risks and aligning them with business objectives

Option 2: Sole focus on financial aspects of risk strategy

Option 3: Technical specifications and documentation for IT architectures

Option 4: Replacement for other risk frameworks and standards in risk strategy initiatives

Correct Response: 1

Explanation: The role of COBIT for Risk in the context of risk frameworks and standards of risk strategy is to provide a comprehensive framework for managing IT-related risks and aligning them with business objectives. COBIT (Control Objectives for Information and Related Technologies) for Risk assists organizations in identifying, assessing, and managing IT risks effectively, ensuring they are in line with the overall risk strategy and business goals.

Knowledge Area: Bonus Q from Isaca

Question Number: 1014

Question: Which of the following best describes the purpose of COBIT for Risk in the context of risk frameworks and standards of risk strategy?

Option 1: Providing a framework for managing IT-related risks and aligning them with business objectives

Option 2: Sole focus on financial aspects of risk strategy

Option 3: Technical specifications and documentation for IT architectures

Option 4: Replacement for other risk frameworks and standards in risk strategy initiatives

Correct Response: 1

Explanation: The purpose of COBIT for Risk is to provide a framework for managing IT-related risks and aligning them with business objectives. It assists organizations in identifying, assessing, and managing IT risks effectively, ensuring alignment with the overall risk strategy and business goals.

Knowledge Area: Bonus Q from Isaca

Question Number: 1015

Question: Which of the following is NOT a characteristic of COBIT for Risk in the context of risk frameworks and standards of risk strategy?

Option 1: Providing a sole focus on financial aspects of risk strategy

Option 2: Providing a comprehensive framework for managing IT-related risks

Option 3: Assisting organizations in aligning IT risks with business objectives

Option 4: Providing guidance for identifying, assessing, and managing IT risks

Correct Response: 1

Explanation: Providing a sole focus on financial aspects of risk strategy is not a characteristic of COBIT for Risk in the context of risk frameworks and standards of risk strategy. Rather, COBIT for Risk provides a comprehensive framework for managing IT-related risks, aligning them with business objectives, and ensuring effective risk management practices.

Knowledge Area: Bonus Q from Isaca

Question Number: 1016

Question: What is the COSO ERM Framework?

Option 1: A widely recognized framework that provides guidance for organizations to design and implement effective risk management processes

Option 2: Sole focus on financial aspects of risk management

Option 3: Technical specifications and documentation for IT architectures

Option 4: A replacement for other risk frameworks and standards in risk management initiatives

Correct Response: 1

Explanation: The COSO ERM Framework is a widely recognized framework that provides guidance for organizations to design and implement effective risk management processes, enabling them to identify, assess, and manage risks in a systematic manner.

Knowledge Area: Bonus Q from Isaca

Question Number: 1017

Question: Which of the following is NOT a characteristic of the COSO ERM Framework?

Option 1: Sole focus on financial aspects of risk management

Option 2: Emphasizes the integration of risk management into an organization's strategic planning and decision-making processes

Option 3: Provides guidance on identifying, assessing, and managing risks

Option 4: Offers a framework for effective risk governance and internal control systems

Correct Response: 2

Explanation: The COSO ERM Framework does not have a sole focus on financial aspects of risk management. It takes a holistic approach, considering various dimensions of risk, including operational, strategic, and compliance risks.

Knowledge Area: Bonus Q from Isaca

Question Number: 1018

Question: Scenario: A multinational corporation is implementing the COSO ERM Framework to enhance its risk management practices. The company wants to ensure that risks are effectively identified, assessed, and managed within the organization. Which option best describes the purpose of implementing the COSO ERM Framework in this scenario?

Option 1: To provide guidance for designing and implementing effective risk management processes

Option 2: Sole focus on financial aspects of risk management

Option 3: Technical specifications and documentation for IT architectures

Option 4: A replacement for other risk frameworks and standards in risk management initiatives

Correct Response: 1

Explanation: The purpose of implementing the COSO ERM Framework in this scenario is to provide guidance for designing and implementing effective risk management processes. The framework helps the multinational corporation enhance its risk management practices, ensuring effective identification, assessment, and management of risks throughout the organization.

Knowledge Area: Bonus Q from Isaca

Question Number: 1019

Question: What principle of ISO 31000 risk management guidelines recommends making decisions based on the potential positive and negative outcomes of uncertainty?

Option 1: Risk management creates and protects value

Option 2: Risk management is an integral part of organizational processes

Option 3: Risk management is systematic, structured and timely

Option 4: Risk management is based on the best available information

Correct Response: 4

Explanation: ISO 31000 principles state to base decisions on the best information about risk.

Knowledge Area: Bonus Q from Isaca

Question Number: 1020

Question: Which practice would be inconsistent with ISO 31000 risk management principles and guidelines?

Option 1: Making risk-aware rather than risk-averse decisions

Option 2: Reviewing risks only annually versus regularly

Option 3: Engaging internal and external stakeholders in risk activities

Option 4: Tailoring the risk framework to the organizational context

Correct Response: 2

Explanation: ISO 31000 promotes regularly reviewing and monitoring risks.

Knowledge Area: Bonus Q from Isaca

Question Number: 1021

Question: An organization implements a risk management framework aligned to ISO 31000 by integrating practices into business activities, leveraging the best available data, and continually monitoring risks and controls. This approach most reflects which underlying ISO 31000 principles?

Option 1: Risk management is systematic and structured

Option 2: Risk management is tailored

Option 3: Risk management is integrated into processes

Option 4: All of the above ISO 31000 principles

Correct Response: 4

Explanation: Integrated, informed, systematic risk management aligns to ISO guidelines.

Knowledge Area: Bonus Q from Isaca

Question Number: 1022

Question: An organization wants to improve its risk management program. It assembles a team with representatives from multiple business units and IT to catalog key assets, system components, threats, and vulnerabilities. The CIO plans to use this risk profile to prioritize remediation. This approach most closely resembles:

Option 1: COSO framework implementation

Option 2: Facilitated risk workshops

Option 3: OCTAVE methodology

Option 4: Third-party risk assessments

Correct Response: 3

Explanation: OCTAVE employs cross-functional teams to build risk profiles of critical assets and threats.

Knowledge Area: Bonus Q from Isaca

Question Number: 1023

Question: What is the risk hierarchy in the context of enterprise risk management?

Option 1: Inherent risk, Residual risk, Control risk, Strategic risk

Option 2: Control risk, Operational risk, Compliance risk, Financial risk

Option 3: Strategic risk, Operational risk, Compliance risk, Financial risk

Option 4: Inherent risk, Residual risk, Operational risk, Compliance risk

Correct Response: 1

Explanation: The risk hierarchy in the context of enterprise risk management consists of inherent risk, residual risk, control risk, and strategic risk. Inherent risk represents the risk level before implementing controls, while residual risk is the risk remaining after controls are in place. Control risk relates to the effectiveness of controls, and strategic risk pertains to risks associated with an organization's strategic objectives.

Knowledge Area: Bonus Q from Isaca

Question Number: 1024

Question: Which of the following is NOT a component of the risk hierarchy in enterprise risk management?

Option 1: Operational risk

Option 2: Financial risk

Option 3: Compliance risk

Option 4: Technology risk

Correct Response: 4

Explanation: The risk hierarchy in enterprise risk management includes operational risk, financial risk, and compliance risk, but not technology risk. Therefore, option "4" is the correct response.

Knowledge Area: Bonus Q from Isaca

Question Number: 1025

Question: Scenario: A company is implementing an enterprise risk management framework to address risks across its operations. The company wants to ensure a systematic approach to risk management. Which option best describes the purpose of the risk hierarchy in this scenario?

Option 1: To provide a structured framework for categorizing and managing risks

Option 2: To solely focus on financial aspects of risk management

Option 3: To provide technical specifications for managing operational risks

Option 4: To replace other risk management frameworks with a standardized approach

Correct Response: 1

Explanation: The purpose of the risk hierarchy in this scenario is to provide a structured framework for categorizing and managing risks. By organizing risks into different levels, such as operational, financial, and compliance risks, the company can systematically identify, assess, and address risks across its operations, enhancing its overall risk management efforts.

Knowledge Area: Bonus Q from Isaca

Question Number: 1026

Question: Which of the following best enables an organization to take a proactive approach for addressing regulatory compliance requirements within its overall risk management processes?

Option 1: Viewing compliance as separate from business risks

Option 2: Having siloed compliance activities across units

Option 3: Focusing solely on financial compliance controls

Option 4: Incorporating compliance as a key risk domain

Correct Response: 4

Explanation: Integrating compliance into risk management makes it proactive.

Knowledge Area: Bonus Q from Isaca

Question Number: 1027

Question: Where does IT risk typically fit in the risk hierarchy within enterprise risk management?

Option 1: Operational risk

Option 2: Financial risk

Option 3: Strategic risk

Option 4: Compliance risk

Correct Response: 1

Explanation: IT risk typically falls under the category of operational risk within the risk hierarchy of enterprise risk management. Operational risk encompasses risks associated with the day-to-day operations and processes of an organization, including those related to IT systems, infrastructure, and cybersecurity.

Knowledge Area: Bonus Q from Isaca

Question Number: 1028

Question: Which of the following is NOT a component of the risk hierarchy in enterprise risk management?

Option 1: Operational risk

Option 2: Financial risk

Option 3: Strategic risk

Option 4: IT risk

Correct Response: 4

Explanation: IT risk is a component of the risk hierarchy in enterprise risk management. Therefore, option "4" (IT risk) is not the correct response.

Knowledge Area: Bonus Q from Isaca

Question Number: 1029

Question: Scenario: A company is implementing an enterprise risk management framework to align IT and enterprise risk management practices. The company wants to identify and manage IT-related risks within the overall risk hierarchy. Which option best describes the purpose of incorporating IT risk in the risk hierarchy in this scenario?

Option 1: To ensure comprehensive identification and management of IT-related risks within the overall risk framework

Option 2: To solely focus on financial aspects of IT risk management

Option 3: To provide technical specifications for IT architectures

Option 4: To replace other risk management frameworks with a standardized approach to IT risk

Correct Response: 1

Explanation: The purpose of incorporating IT risk in the risk hierarchy in this scenario is to ensure comprehensive identification and management of IT-related risks within the overall risk framework. By integrating IT risk alongside other types of risks, the company can effectively address IT-related vulnerabilities and threats, align IT and enterprise risk management practices, and enhance the organization's overall risk management efforts.

Knowledge Area: Bonus Q from Isaca

Question Number: 1030

Question: What is the concept of "Three Lines of Defense" in the context of enterprise risk management?

Option 1: Operational risk, Compliance risk, Financial risk

Option 2: Business units, Risk management function, Internal audit

Option 3: IT risk, Strategic risk, Compliance risk

Option 4: Internal controls, External auditors, Regulatory bodies

Correct Response: 2

Explanation: The concept of "Three Lines of Defense" in enterprise risk management refers to the roles and responsibilities of different functions within an organization to manage risks. The three lines include business units (front-line operations), risk management function (second-line oversight and coordination), and internal audit (third-line independent assurance). This model establishes clear accountabilities and promotes effective risk governance.

Knowledge Area: Bonus Q from Isaca

Question Number: 1031

Question: Which of the following is NOT a component of the "Three Lines of Defense" model in enterprise risk management?

Option 1: Operational risk

Option 2: Business units

Option 3: Internal audit

Option 4: Risk management function

Correct Response: 1

Explanation: Operational risk is not a component of the "Three Lines of Defense" model. The three components are business units (front-line operations), risk management function (second-line oversight and coordination), and internal audit (third-line independent assurance).

Knowledge Area: Bonus Q from Isaca

Question Number: 1032

Question: Scenario: A company is implementing the "Three Lines of Defense" model for enterprise risk management. They want to establish clear roles and responsibilities for managing risks. Which option best describes the purpose of implementing this model in this scenario?

Option 1: To ensure effective risk governance and coordination across the organization

Option 2: To solely focus on operational risk management

Option 3: To provide technical specifications for IT architectures

Option 4: To replace other risk management frameworks with a standardized approach

Correct Response: 1

Explanation: The purpose of implementing the "Three Lines of Defense" model in this scenario is to ensure effective risk governance and coordination across the organization. By clearly defining the roles and responsibilities of business units, risk management function, and internal audit, the model promotes accountability, coordination, and oversight of risk management efforts, enhancing the organization's overall risk management practices.

Knowledge Area: Bonus Q from Isaca

Question Number: 1033

Question: What is the role of the business units in the "Three Lines of Defense" model in enterprise risk management?

Option 1: Front-line operations responsible for identifying and managing risks

Option 2: Internal audit function providing independent assurance on risk management practices

Option 3: Risk management function overseeing and coordinating risk management efforts

Option 4: External auditors performing evaluations of risk management processes

Correct Response: 1

Explanation: The role of the business units in the "Three Lines of Defense" model is to serve as the front-line operations responsible for identifying and managing risks. They are accountable for implementing risk management practices within their respective areas of operation.

Knowledge Area: Bonus Q from Isaca

Question Number: 1034

Question: Which component of the "Three Lines of Defense" model is responsible for providing independent assurance on risk management practices?

Option 1: Business units

Option 2: Internal audit

Option 3: Risk management function

Option 4: External auditors

Correct Response: 2

Explanation: The internal audit function is responsible for providing independent assurance on risk management practices in the "Three Lines of Defense" model. They conduct audits and evaluations to assess the effectiveness of risk management processes and provide objective feedback to enhance risk management practices.

Knowledge Area: Bonus Q from Isaca

Question Number: 1035

Question: What is a key reason organizations define their risk appetite when implementing a risk management program?

Option 1: To completely avoid risks

Option 2: To transfer all risks to third parties

Option 3: To set acceptable levels of risk exposure

Option 4: To insure against any plausible losses

Correct Response: 3

Explanation: Risk appetite guides decisions on acceptable risk levels.

Knowledge Area: Bonus Q from Isaca

Question Number: 1036

Question. Which of the following practices would NOT align with sound risk appetite definition?

Option 1: Linking risk appetite to strategic goals

Option 2: Frequently re-evaluating appetite

Option 3: Setting very high appetite levels

Option 4: Benchmarking against other organizations

Correct Response: 3

Explanation: Very high risk appetite levels often reflect poor alignment.

Knowledge Area: Bonus Q from Isaca

Question Number: 1037

Question: Which of the following is NOT a characteristic of risk appetite in the context of risk appetite and risk tolerance of risk strategy?

Option 1: The maximum amount of financial loss an organization is willing to bear

Option 2: The level of risk an organization is willing to take to achieve its objectives

Option 3: The organization's readiness to embrace risks and pursue opportunities

Option 4: The organization's risk preferences and capacity to handle risks

Correct Response: 1

Explanation: The maximum amount of financial loss an organization is willing to bear is not a characteristic of risk appetite. Risk appetite pertains to the level of risk an organization is willing to take to achieve its objectives, emphasizing the organization's readiness to embrace risks and pursue opportunities.

Knowledge Area: Bonus Q from Isaca

Question Number: 1038

Question: What is risk tolerance in the context of risk appetite and risk tolerance of risk strategy?

Option 1: The level of risk an organization is willing to accept or tolerate in pursuit of its objectives

Option 2: The maximum amount of financial loss an organization is willing to bear

Option 3: The level of risk an organization is willing to transfer to external parties

Option 4: The minimum level of risk an organization is willing to accept to achieve its objectives

Correct Response: 1

Explanation: Risk tolerance refers to the level of risk an organization is willing to accept or tolerate in pursuit of its objectives. It represents the organization's willingness to take on risks and its preparedness to bear the potential consequences associated with those risks.

Knowledge Area: Bonus Q from Isaca

Question Number: 1039

Question: Which of the following is NOT a characteristic of risk tolerance in the context of risk appetite and risk tolerance of risk strategy?

Option 1: The maximum amount of financial loss an organization is willing to bear

Option 2: The level of risk an organization is willing to accept or tolerate

Option 3: The organization's preparedness to bear the potential consequences of risks

Option 4: The minimum level of risk an organization is willing to accept to achieve its objectives

Correct Response: 1

Explanation: The maximum amount of financial loss an organization is willing to bear is not a characteristic of risk tolerance. Risk tolerance relates to the organization's overall willingness to accept or tolerate risk, rather than a specific financial threshold.

Knowledge Area: Bonus Q from Isaca

Question Number: 1040

Question: What is an effective approach for establishing risk appetite that will provide meaningful guidance for enterprise risk management decision making?

Option 1: Basing primarily on prior year losses and risk history

Option 2: Benchmarking against peer organizations and competitors

Option 3: Developing in isolation by the risk management team

Option 4: Aligning appetite to strategic objectives and risk capacity

Correct Response: 4

Explanation: Risk appetite aligned to strategy and capacity gives effective decision guidance.

Knowledge Area: Bonus Q from Isaca

Question Number: 1041

Question: Which of the following practices reflects weaknesses in an organization's process for defining its risk appetite?

Option 1: Seeking board and executive input

Option 2: Linking risk appetite levels across objectives

Option 3: Infrequent re-evaluation of risk appetite

Option 4: Failing to consider risk tolerances

Correct Response: 3

Explanation: Organizations should regularly reassess risk appetite for it to be effective.

Knowledge Area: Bonus Q from Isaca

Question Number: 1042

Question: A manufacturing company is implementing a new risk management program and establishing its overall risk appetite for the first time. What process would provide the most effective way to set risk appetite?

Option 1: Surveying customer preferences

Option 2: Analyzing competitor risk practices

Option 3: Interviewing operational managers

Option 4: Facilitating workshops with executives

Correct Response: 4

Explanation: Executive workshops provide strategic insights to guide risk appetite decision

Knowledge Area: Bonus Q from Isaca

Question Number: 1043

Question: What is resilience in the context of the relationship between risk management approach and business resiliency?

Option 1: The ability of an organization to adapt, recover, and thrive in the face of disruptive events

Option 2: The ability to prevent all risks and disruptions

Option 3: The focus on financial aspects of risk management

Option 4: The replacement of risk management with business continuity planning

Correct Response: 1

Explanation: Resilience refers to the ability of an organization to adapt, recover, and thrive in the face of disruptive events. It involves the capacity to withstand and respond effectively to risks and disruptions, ensuring the continuity of business operations and the organization's ability to achieve its objectives.

Knowledge Area: Bonus Q from Isaca

Question Number: 1044

Question: Which of the following is NOT a characteristic of resilience in the context of the risk management approach and business resiliency?

Option 1: The ability to prevent all risks and disruptions

Option 2: The capacity to adapt and recover from disruptive events

Option 3: The focus on the continuity of business operations

Option 4: The replacement of risk management with business continuity planning

Correct Response: 1

Explanation: The ability to prevent all risks and disruptions is not a characteristic of resilience. Resilience focuses on the organization's capacity to adapt, recover, and thrive in the face of disruptive events, rather than preventing all risks and disruptions.

Knowledge Area: Bonus Q from Isaca

Question Number: 1045

Question: Scenario: An organization is implementing a risk management approach to enhance its business resiliency. The organization aims to develop its capability to adapt and recover from disruptive events. Which option best describes the purpose of implementing this risk management approach in this scenario?

Option 1: To strengthen the organization's ability to adapt, recover, and thrive in the face of disruptive events

Option 2: To solely focus on financial aspects of risk management

Option 3: To provide technical specifications for IT architectures

Option 4: To replace other risk management frameworks with a standardized approach to business resiliency

Correct Response: 1

Explanation: The purpose of implementing the risk management approach in this scenario is to strengthen the organization's ability to adapt, recover, and thrive in the face of disruptive events. By effectively managing risks and developing resilience, the organization can enhance its capacity to withstand challenges, minimize potential disruptions, and maintain continuity in its operations, enabling it to achieve its objectives.

Knowledge Area: Bonus Q from Isaca

Question Number: 1046

Question: Which of the following is NOT a key component of ISO 22301:2019—Societal Security—Business Continuity Management Systems?

Option 1: Risk assessment and management

Option 2: Business impact analysis

Option 3: Crisis management and communication

Option 4: Financial accounting and reporting

Correct Response: 4

Explanation: Financial accounting and reporting is not a key component of ISO 22301:2019. The standard focuses on aspects such as risk assessment and management, business impact analysis, crisis management, and communication to ensure effective business continuity management.

Knowledge Area: Bonus Q from Isaca

Question Number: 1047

Question: What is control risk in the context of risk management and risk categories?

Option 1: The risk associated with the effectiveness of internal controls in mitigating threats

Option 2: The risk of financial loss due to inadequate control measures

Option 3: The risk of compliance failures with regulatory requirements

Option 4: The risk of strategic decisions not aligning with business objectives

Correct Response: 1

Explanation: Control risk refers to the risk associated with the effectiveness of internal controls in mitigating threats. It assesses the probability of control failures or weaknesses that could result in an organization's inability to prevent or detect risks or threats, leading to potential negative impacts on the achievement of objectives.

Knowledge Area: Bonus Q from Isaca

Question Number: 1048

Question: Which of the following is NOT a characteristic of control risk in the context of risk management and risk categories?

Option 1: The risk associated with the effectiveness of internal controls in mitigating threats

Option 2: The risk of financial loss due to inadequate control measures

Option 3: The risk of compliance failures with regulatory requirements

Option 4: The risk of strategic decisions not aligning with business objectives

Correct Response: 4

Explanation: The risk of strategic decisions not aligning with business objectives is not a characteristic of control risk. Control risk specifically focuses on the effectiveness of internal controls in mitigating threats and vulnerabilities, rather than the alignment of strategic decisions with business objectives.

Knowledge Area: Bonus Q from Isaca

Question Number: 1049

Question: What does control risk assess in the context of risk management and risk categories?

Option 1: The effectiveness of internal controls in mitigating threats

Option 2: The financial impact of control failures

Option 3: The compliance status of the organization

Option 4: The alignment of strategic decisions with business objectives

Correct Response: 1

Explanation: Control risk assesses the effectiveness of internal controls in mitigating threats. It evaluates the ability of controls to prevent, detect, and respond to risks, ensuring that the organization's assets, operations, and objectives are adequately protected.

Knowledge Area: Bonus Q from Isaca

Question Number: 1050

Question: What does detection risk refer to in the context of risk management and risk categories?

Option 1: The risk of not detecting errors or misstatements in financial statements

Option 2: The risk of not detecting potential cybersecurity threats

Option 3: The risk of non-compliance with regulatory requirements

Option 4: The risk of strategic decisions not aligning with business objectives

Correct Response: 1

Explanation: Detection risk refers to the risk of not detecting errors or misstatements in financial statements. It is associated with the effectiveness of internal controls and audit procedures in identifying and addressing inaccuracies or omissions in financial reporting.

Knowledge Area: Bonus Q from Isaca

Question Number: 1051

Question: Which of the following is a characteristic of detection risk?

Option 1: The risk of not detecting potential cybersecurity threats

Option 2: The risk of strategic decisions not aligning with business objectives

Option 3: The risk of non-compliance with regulatory requirements

Option 4: The risk of not detecting errors or misstatements in financial statements

Correct Response: 4

Explanation: Detection risk is characterized by the risk of not detecting errors or misstatements in financial statements. It pertains to the effectiveness of internal controls and audit procedures in identifying and addressing inaccuracies or omissions.

Knowledge Area: Bonus Q from Isaca

Question Number: 1052

Question: In the context of risk management, what is the impact of higher detection risk?

Option 1: Increased likelihood of errors or misstatements going unnoticed in financial statements

Option 2: Enhanced ability to detect potential cybersecurity threats

Option 3: Improved compliance with regulatory requirements

Option 4: Better alignment of strategic decisions with business objectives

Correct Response: 1

Explanation: Higher detection risk in risk management increases the likelihood of errors or misstatements going unnoticed in financial statements. It implies a greater chance of inaccuracies or omissions in financial reporting, which can undermine the reliability and accuracy of financial information.

Knowledge Area: Bonus Q from Isaca

Question Number: 1053

Question: What is residual risk in the context of risk management and risk categories?

Option 1: The risk that remains after risk mitigation measures have been applied

Option 2: The risk associated with the likelihood of a threat occurring

Option 3: The risk of non-compliance with regulatory requirements

Option 4: The risk of strategic decisions not aligning with business objectives

Correct Response: 1

Explanation: Residual risk refers to the risk that remains after risk mitigation measures have been applied. It represents the level of risk that persists even after implementing controls or risk mitigation strategies. Residual risk is the risk that an organization is willing to accept or retain, considering the effectiveness of risk management practices.

Knowledge Area: Bonus Q from Isaca

Question Number: 1054

Question: Which of the following is NOT a characteristic of residual risk in the context of risk management and risk categories?

Option 1: The risk that remains after risk mitigation measures have been applied

Option 2: The risk associated with the likelihood of a threat occurring

Option 3: The risk of non-compliance with regulatory requirements

Option 4: The risk of strategic decisions not aligning with business objectives

Correct Response: 4

Explanation: The risk of strategic decisions not aligning with business objectives is not a characteristic of residual risk. Residual risk specifically refers to the risk that remains after implementing risk mitigation measures, while strategic decisions aligning with business objectives are part of the risk management process.

Knowledge Area: Bonus Q from Isaca

Question Number: 1055

Question: What does residual risk represent in the context of risk management and risk categories?

Option 1: The risk that remains after risk mitigation measures have been applied

Option 2: The risk associated with the likelihood of a threat occurring

Option 3: The financial impact of control failures

Option 4: The risk of non-compliance with regulatory requirements

Correct Response: 1

Explanation: Residual risk represents the risk that remains after risk mitigation measures have been applied. It accounts for the risk that cannot be completely eliminated or controlled and helps organizations evaluate the level of risk they are willing to accept or retain.

Knowledge Area: Bonus Q from Isaca

Question Number: 1056

Question: What is design risk in the context of opportunities and risk management?

Option 1: The risk associated with the design and development of products, services, or processes

Option 2: The risk of financial loss due to inadequate design measures

Option 3: The risk of non-compliance with regulatory requirements

Option 4: The risk of strategic decisions not aligning with business objectives

Correct Response: 1

Explanation: Design risk refers to the risk associated with the design and development of products, services, or processes. It encompasses the potential for errors, flaws, or inefficiencies during the design phase, which may impact the quality, functionality, or performance of the final product or service.

Knowledge Area: Bonus Q from Isaca

Question Number: 1057

Question: Which of the following is NOT a characteristic of design risk in the context of opportunities and risk management?

Option 1: The risk associated with the design and development of products, services, or processes

Option 2: The risk of financial loss due to inadequate design measures

Option 3: The risk of non-compliance with regulatory requirements

Option 4: The risk of strategic decisions not aligning with business objectives

Correct Response: 4

Explanation: The risk of strategic decisions not aligning with business objectives is not a characteristic of design risk. Design risk specifically pertains to the potential issues or challenges related to the design and development of products, services, or processes.

Knowledge Area: Bonus Q from Isaca

Question Number: 1058

Question: What does design risk represent in the context of opportunities and risk management?

Option 1: The risk associated with the design and development of products, services, or processes

Option 2: The financial impact of design flaws

Option 3: The compliance status of the organization

Option 4: The alignment of strategic decisions with business objectives

Correct Response: 1

Explanation: Design risk represents the risk associated with the design and development of products, services, or processes. It focuses on the potential challenges, errors, or inefficiencies that may arise during the design phase, which can impact the quality, functionality, or performance of the final outcome.

Knowledge Area: Bonus Q from Isaca

Question Number: 1059

Question: What is operation or rollout risk in the context of opportunities and risk management?

Option 1: The risk associated with the implementation or deployment of new systems, processes, or initiatives

Option 2: The risk of financial loss due to operational inefficiencies

Option 3: The risk of non-compliance with regulatory requirements

Option 4: The risk of strategic decisions not aligning with business objectives

Correct Response: 1

Explanation: Operation or rollout risk refers to the risk associated with the implementation or deployment of new systems, processes, or initiatives. It encompasses the potential challenges, disruptions, or inefficiencies that may arise during the operational phase of new initiatives, including issues related to implementation, training, adoption, and system integration.

Knowledge Area: Bonus Q from Isaca

Question Number: 1060

Question: Which of the following is NOT a characteristic of operation or rollout risk in the context of opportunities and risk management?

Option 1: The risk associated with the implementation or deployment of new systems, processes, or initiatives

Option 2: The risk of financial loss due to operational inefficiencies

Option 3: The risk of non-compliance with regulatory requirements

Option 4: The risk of strategic decisions not aligning with business objectives

Correct Response: 4

Explanation: The risk of strategic decisions not aligning with business objectives is not a characteristic of operation or rollout risk. Operation or rollout risk specifically pertains to the challenges or inefficiencies that may arise during the implementation or deployment of new systems, processes, or initiatives.

Knowledge Area: Bonus Q from Isaca

Question Number: 1061

Question: What does operation or rollout risk represent in the context of opportunities and risk management?

Option 1: The risk associated with the implementation or deployment of new systems, processes, or initiatives

Option 2: The financial impact of operational inefficiencies

Option 3: The compliance status of the organization

Option 4: The alignment of strategic decisions with business objectives

Correct Response: 1

Explanation: Operation or rollout risk represents the risk associated with the implementation or deployment of new systems, processes, or initiatives. It encompasses the potential challenges, disruptions, or inefficiencies that may arise during the operational phase of new initiatives, including issues related to implementation, training, adoption, and system integration.

Knowledge Area: Bonus Q from Isaca

Question Number: 1062

Question: What is cybersecurity in the context of opportunities and risk management?

Option 1: The practice of protecting computer systems and networks from digital attacks

Option 2: The risk of financial loss due to operational inefficiencies

Option 3: The risk of non-compliance with regulatory requirements

Option 4: The risk of strategic decisions not aligning with business objectives

Correct Response: 1

Explanation: Cybersecurity refers to the practice of protecting computer systems and networks from digital attacks, unauthorized access, and data breaches. It involves implementing security measures, protocols, and technologies to safeguard information, systems, and networks from cyber threats and mitigate potential risks.

Knowledge Area: Bonus Q from Isaca

Question Number: 1063

Question: Which of the following is NOT a characteristic of cybersecurity in the context of opportunities and risk management?

Option 1: The practice of protecting computer systems and networks from digital attacks

Option 2: The risk of financial loss due to operational inefficiencies

Option 3: The risk of non-compliance with regulatory requirements

Option 4: The focus on identifying and mitigating cyber threats

Correct Response: 2

Explanation: The risk of financial loss due to operational inefficiencies is not a characteristic of cybersecurity. Cybersecurity primarily focuses on protecting computer systems and networks from digital attacks and mitigating the risks associated with cyber threats.

Knowledge Area: Bonus Q from Isaca

Question Number: 1064

Question: What does cybersecurity aim to achieve in the context of opportunities and risk management?

Option 1: The protection of computer systems and networks from digital attacks

Option 2: The risk of financial loss due to operational inefficiencies

Option 3: The compliance status of the organization

Option 4: The alignment of strategic decisions with business objectives

Correct Response: 1

Explanation: Cybersecurity aims to achieve the protection of computer systems and networks from digital attacks. It involves implementing measures and practices to prevent unauthorized access, data breaches, and other cyber threats. By effectively managing cybersecurity risks, organizations can safeguard their information, systems, and networks, reducing the likelihood of cyber incidents and their potential impact.

Knowledge Area: Bonus Q from Isaca

Question Number: 1065

Question: What is the role of social media in the context of opportunities and risk management?

Option 1: Social media provides opportunities for marketing and customer engagement

Option 2: Social media poses financial risks due to operational inefficiencies

Option 3: Social media ensures compliance with regulatory requirements

Option 4: Social media aligns strategic decisions with business objectives

Correct Response: 1

Explanation: Social media plays a role in providing opportunities for marketing and customer engagement. It allows businesses to reach a wide audience, interact with customers, and promote their products or services. However, it also presents certain risks and challenges that need to be managed effectively.

Knowledge Area: Bonus Q from Isaca

Question Number: 1066

Question: Which of the following is NOT a characteristic of social media in the context of opportunities and risk management?

Option 1: Social media poses financial risks due to operational inefficiencies

Option 2: Social media provides opportunities for marketing and customer engagement

Option 3: Social media can enhance brand reputation and visibility

Option 4: Social media requires active monitoring and management of online presence

Correct Response: 1

Explanation: Social media posing financial risks due to operational inefficiencies is not a characteristic of social media in the context of opportunities and risk management. While social media can present certain operational challenges, it primarily offers opportunities for marketing, customer engagement, and brand visibility.

Knowledge Area: Bonus Q from Isaca

Question Number: 1067

Question: What is one of the risks associated with social media in the context of opportunities and risk management?

Option 1: Potential reputational damage due to negative online interactions

Option 2: Increased financial profits due to operational efficiencies

Option 3: Enhanced compliance with regulatory requirements

Option 4: Strategic decisions not aligning with business objectives

Correct Response: 1

Explanation: One of the risks associated with social media in the context of opportunities and risk management is the potential for reputational damage due to negative online interactions. Social media platforms can amplify negative feedback, criticism, or misinformation, which can adversely affect a company's reputation and brand image. Active monitoring, timely response, and proactive reputation management are necessary to mitigate this risk.

Knowledge Area: Bonus Q from Isaca

Question Number: 1068

Question: What is the concept of consumerization of IT and mobile devices in the context of opportunities and risk management?

Option 1: The trend of personal devices and technologies being used for business purposes

Option 2: The use of mobile devices exclusively for personal communication

Option 3: The risk of financial loss due to the use of mobile devices

Option 4: The risk of non-compliance with regulatory requirements

Correct Response: 1

Explanation: The concept of consumerization of IT and mobile devices refers to the trend of personal devices and technologies being used for business purposes. It involves employees utilizing their personal smartphones, tablets, and other devices in the workplace, blurring the boundaries between personal and professional technology use. This trend presents both opportunities and risks for organizations in terms of increased flexibility, productivity, but also data security and privacy concerns.

Knowledge Area: Bonus Q from Isaca

Question Number: 1069

Question: Which of the following is not a type of business risk that can be addressed using IT resources?

Option 1: Operational risks

Option 2: Financial risks

Option 3: Strategic risks

Option 4: Human resource risks

Correct Response: 4

Explanation: Human resource risks are not typically addressed using IT resources. Operational risks, financial risks, and strategic risks can be mitigated using IT resources.

Knowledge Area: Bonus Q from Isaca

Question Number: 1070

Question: Scenario: A multinational corporation is expanding its e-commerce operations and wants to ensure secure online transactions and protect customer data. Which measure can IT resources provide to address these risks effectively?

Option 1: Implementing robust encryption protocols for data transmission

Option 2: Enhancing physical security measures at the company's brick-and-mortar stores

Option 3: Conducting employee training programs on customer service

Option 4: Developing a new marketing campaign for product promotion

Correct Response: 1

Explanation: IT resources can address the risks by implementing robust encryption protocols for data transmission. This measure ensures secure online transactions and protects customer data from unauthorized access or interception.

Knowledge Area: Bonus Q from Isaca

Question Number: 1071

Question: What is risk reduction/mitigation in the context of risk response strategies related to IT in the enterprise?

Option 1: The process of implementing measures to minimize the likelihood and impact of risks

Option 2: The transfer of risks to external parties through insurance or contracts

Option 3: The acceptance of risks without taking any proactive measures

Option 4: The elimination of risks through the termination of relevant business activities

Correct Response: 1

Explanation: Risk reduction/mitigation involves the process of implementing measures to minimize the likelihood and impact of risks related to IT in the enterprise. It includes the identification and implementation of controls, security measures, and risk management practices to mitigate potential threats and vulnerabilities.

Knowledge Area: Bonus Q from Isaca

Question Number: 1072

Question: Which of the following is an example of risk reduction/mitigation using IT resources?

Option 1: Implementing firewalls and intrusion detection systems to protect against cyber attacks

Option 2: Purchasing insurance to transfer the financial impact of risks

Option 3: Accepting risks without taking any proactive measures

Option 4: Terminating a business activity to eliminate associated risks

Correct Response: 1

Explanation: Implementing firewalls and intrusion detection systems to protect against cyber attacks is an example of risk reduction/mitigation using IT resources. These measures help to minimize the likelihood and impact of cyber risks by enhancing network security and detecting potential threats.

Knowledge Area: Bonus Q from Isaca

Question Number: 1073

Question: What is the primary objective of risk reduction/mitigation in the context of risk response strategies related to IT in the enterprise?

Option 1: To minimize the likelihood and impact of risks through the implementation of controls and security measures

Option 2: To transfer risks to external parties through insurance or contracts

Option 3: To accept risks without taking any proactive measures

Option 4: To eliminate risks through the termination of relevant business activities

Correct Response: 1

Explanation: The primary objective of risk reduction/mitigation in the context of risk response strategies related to IT in the enterprise is to minimize the likelihood and impact of risks through the implementation of controls and security measures. This objective aims to enhance the organization's ability to protect its IT assets, systems, and data from potential threats and vulnerabilities.

Knowledge Area: Bonus Q from Isaca

Question Number: 1074

Question: Which of the following is an example of risk acceptance in the context of IT risk management?

Option 1: Choosing not to invest in additional security measures due to low likelihood and impact of a particular risk

Option 2: Transferring risk to a third-party vendor through a contractual agreement

Option 3: Implementing multi-factor authentication to mitigate the risk of unauthorized access

Option 4: Eliminating a business activity to eliminate the associated risk

Correct Response: 1

Explanation: Risk acceptance in the context of risk response strategies related to IT in the enterprise is the decision to acknowledge and tolerate risks without taking any proactive measures. It involves accepting the potential consequences of risks and their potential impact on the organization, either due to the low likelihood of occurrence, high cost of mitigation, or other strategic considerations.

Knowledge Area: Bonus Q from Isaca

Question Number: 1075

Question: What is the primary objective of risk acceptance in the context of risk response strategies related to IT in the enterprise?

Option 1: To acknowledge and tolerate risks without taking any proactive measures

Option 2: To transfer risks to external parties through insurance or contracts

Option 3: To implement controls and security measures to mitigate risks

Option 4: To eliminate risks through the termination of relevant business activities

Correct Response: 1

Explanation: Choosing not to invest in additional security measures due to the low likelihood and impact of a particular risk is an example of risk acceptance in IT risk management. The organization accepts the risk without taking further action based on the assessment that the risk is adequately managed or the cost of mitigation outweighs the potential impact.

Knowledge Area: Bonus Q from Isaca

Question Number: 1076

Question: What is risk response selection and prioritization in the context of risk response strategies related to IT in the enterprise?

Option 1: The process of identifying and choosing appropriate actions to address identified risks

Option 2: The transfer of risks to external parties through insurance or contracts

Option 3: The decision to accept risks without taking any proactive measures

Option 4: The elimination of risks through the termination of relevant business activities

Correct Response: 1

Explanation: Risk response selection and prioritization involve the process of identifying and choosing appropriate actions to address identified risks related to IT in the enterprise. It includes evaluating various response options, such as risk mitigation, risk transfer, risk acceptance, or risk avoidance, and prioritizing them based on their potential impact, feasibility, cost-effectiveness, and alignment with organizational objectives.

Knowledge Area: Bonus Q from Isaca

Question Number: 1077

Question: Which of the following is an example of risk response selection and prioritization in IT risk management?

Option 1: Implementing a firewall to mitigate the risk of unauthorized access

Option 2: Transferring the risk to a third-party vendor through a contractual agreement

Option 3: Accepting the risk of a low-impact, low-likelihood event without further action

Option 4: Terminating a business activity to eliminate associated risks

Correct Response: 1

Explanation: Implementing a firewall to mitigate the risk of unauthorized access is an example of risk response selection and prioritization in IT risk management. The organization identifies the risk of unauthorized access and selects the appropriate response action of implementing a firewall as a preventive measure.

Knowledge Area: Bonus Q from Isaca

Question Number: 1078

Question: In the context of risk response selection and prioritization, what is the purpose of prioritizing risk responses?

Option 1: To allocate resources effectively and address high-priority risks first

Option 2: To transfer risks to external parties through insurance or contracts

Option 3: To accept risks without taking any proactive measures

Option 4: To eliminate risks through the termination of relevant business activities

Correct Response: 1

Explanation: The purpose of prioritizing risk responses in the context of risk response selection and prioritization is to allocate resources effectively and address high-priority risks first. By prioritizing responses, organizations can focus their efforts and resources on mitigating or managing the most significant risks that pose the highest potential impact or likelihood.

Knowledge Area: Bonus Q from Isaca

Question Number: 1079

Question: What are risk indicators in the context of methods to establish key risk indicators?

Option 1: Quantifiable metrics or factors that provide insights into the presence or level of risk

Option 2: The transfer of risks to external parties through insurance or contracts

Option 3: The acceptance of risks without taking any proactive measures

Option 4: The elimination of risks through the termination of relevant business activities

Correct Response: 1

Explanation: Risk indicators are quantifiable metrics or factors that provide insights into the presence or level of risk. They are used to monitor and assess the likelihood, impact, or severity of risks, allowing organizations to identify potential threats and take appropriate risk mitigation measures.

Knowledge Area: Bonus Q from Isaca

Question Number: 1080

Question: Which of the following is NOT a characteristic of risk indicators in the context of methods to establish key risk indicators?

Option 1: They provide insights into the presence or level of risk

Option 2: They are subjective and based on individual opinions

Option 3: They are quantifiable metrics or factors

Option 4: They help in monitoring and assessing risks

Correct Response: 2

Explanation: Risk indicators are not subjective and based on individual opinions. They are objective and quantifiable metrics or factors that provide insights into the presence or level of risk. They help in monitoring and assessing risks to facilitate effective risk management.

Knowledge Area: Bonus Q from Isaca

Question Number: 1081

Question: What is Six Sigma in the context of methods to monitor the effectiveness of response strategies and/or controls?

Option 1: A data-driven approach for process improvement and quality management

Option 2: The transfer of risks to external parties through insurance or contracts

Option 3: The acceptance of risks without taking any proactive measures

Option 4: The elimination of risks through the termination of relevant business activities

Correct Response: 1

Explanation: Six Sigma is a data-driven approach for process improvement and quality management. It aims to reduce defects and variability in processes to achieve higher levels of efficiency and effectiveness. In the context of monitoring the effectiveness of response strategies and controls, Six Sigma provides a framework for measuring and analyzing performance, identifying areas for improvement, and implementing targeted solutions to mitigate risks and enhance process effectiveness.

Knowledge Area: Bonus Q from Isaca

Question Number: 1082

Question: Which of the following is NOT a characteristic of Six Sigma in the context of monitoring the effectiveness of response strategies and/or controls?

Option 1: A data-driven approach for process improvement and quality management

Option 2: The integration of risk management practices

Option 3: The focus on reducing defects and variability

Option 4: The utilization of statistical tools and techniques

Correct Response: 2

Explanation: The integration of risk management practices is not a characteristic of Six Sigma in the context of monitoring the effectiveness of response strategies and/or controls. While Six Sigma focuses on process improvement and quality management, the integration of risk management practices is not inherent to the Six Sigma methodology.

Knowledge Area: Bonus Q from Isaca

Question Number: 1083

Question: What is segregation of duties in the context of the risk management life cycle?

Option 1: The practice of dividing responsibilities among different individuals to prevent fraud and errors

Option 2: The transfer of risks to external parties through insurance or contracts

Option 3: The acceptance of risks without taking any proactive measures

Option 4: The elimination of risks through the termination of relevant business activities

Correct Response: 1

Explanation: Segregation of duties is the practice of dividing responsibilities among different individuals to prevent fraud and errors. It ensures that no single person has complete control over a critical process or system, reducing the risk of inappropriate actions or intentional misuse. By implementing segregation of duties, organizations establish checks and balances, enhancing control effectiveness and minimizing the potential impact of risks.

Knowledge Area: Bonus Q from Isaca

Question Number: 1084

Question: Which of the following is NOT a characteristic of segregation of duties in the context of the risk management life cycle?

Option 1: The practice of dividing responsibilities among different individuals

Option 2: The prevention of fraud and errors

Option 3: The transfer of risks to external parties

Option 4: The establishment of checks and balances

Correct Response: 3

Explanation: The transfer of risks to external parties is not a characteristic of segregation of duties. Segregation of duties primarily focuses on dividing responsibilities among different individuals within the organization to prevent fraud and errors and establish checks and balances.

Knowledge Area: Bonus Q from Isaca

Question Number: 1085

Question: Who are stakeholders in the context of stakeholder analysis and communication techniques in the risk management life cycle?

Option 1: Individuals or groups who have an interest or are affected by the organization's activities

Option 2: External parties who transfer risks through insurance or contracts

Option 3: Individuals or groups who accept risks without taking proactive measures

Option 4: Individuals or groups who eliminate risks by terminating relevant business activities

Correct Response: 1

Explanation: Stakeholders, in the context of stakeholder analysis and communication techniques in the risk management life cycle, are individuals or groups who have an interest or are affected by the organization's activities. They can include employees, customers, shareholders, suppliers, regulatory bodies, and the local community. Effective stakeholder analysis and communication aim to identify and engage with stakeholders to understand their perspectives, manage expectations, and address their concerns.

Knowledge Area: Bonus Q from Isaca

Question Number: 1086

Question: Which of the following is NOT a characteristic of stakeholders in the context of stakeholder analysis and communication techniques?

Option 1: Individuals or groups who have an interest or are affected by the organization's activities

Option 2: External parties who transfer risks through insurance or contracts

Option 3: Different stakeholders may have different interests, needs, and expectations

Option 4: Effective stakeholder engagement can help manage risks and enhance organizational reputation

Correct Response: 2

Explanation: External parties who transfer risks through insurance or contracts are not characteristics of stakeholders in the context of stakeholder analysis and communication techniques. Stakeholders represent individuals or groups who have an interest in or are affected by the organization's activities, and they play a role in shaping the organization's risk landscape.

Knowledge Area: Bonus Q from Isaca

Question Number: 1087

Question: Who is a risk owner in the context of stakeholder analysis and communication techniques in the risk management life cycle?

Option 1: An individual or entity responsible for managing a specific risk

Option 2: An external party who transfers risks through insurance or contracts

Option 3: An individual or entity who accepts risks without taking any proactive measures

Option 4: An individual or entity who eliminates risks by terminating relevant business activities

Correct Response: 1

Explanation: A risk owner, in the context of stakeholder analysis and communication techniques in the risk management life cycle, is an individual or entity responsible for managing a specific risk. The risk owner takes ownership of the risk, ensures appropriate risk response strategies are in place, and monitors the effectiveness of those strategies. They play a crucial role in identifying, assessing, and mitigating risks within the organization.

Knowledge Area: Bonus Q from Isaca

Question Number: 1088

Question: Which of the following is NOT a characteristic of a risk owner in the context of stakeholder analysis and communication techniques?

Option 1: Responsible for managing a specific risk

Option 2: External party who transfers risks through insurance or contracts

Option 3: Accountable for implementing risk response strategies

Option 4: Monitors the effectiveness of risk management strategies

Correct Response: 2

Explanation: An external party who transfers risks through insurance or contracts is not a characteristic of a risk owner in the context of stakeholder analysis and communication techniques. A risk owner is an internal individual or entity within the organization who takes responsibility for managing a specific risk and is accountable for implementing risk response strategies.

Knowledge Area: Bonus Q from Isaca

Question Number: 1089

Question: What is the primary role of a risk owner in the context of stakeholder analysis and communication techniques?

Option 1: To manage a specific risk and ensure effective risk response strategies

Option 2: To transfer risks to external parties through insurance or contracts

Option 3: To accept risks without taking any proactive measures

Option 4: To eliminate risks by terminating relevant business activities

Correct Response: 1

Explanation: The primary role of a risk owner in the context of stakeholder analysis and communication techniques is to manage a specific risk and ensure effective risk response strategies. They are responsible for identifying and assessing risks, implementing appropriate risk response measures, and monitoring the effectiveness of those strategies. The risk owner plays a crucial role in mitigating risks and ensuring the organization's risk management objectives are achieved.

Knowledge Area: Bonus Q from Isaca

Question Number: 1090

Question: Who is a control owner in the context of stakeholder analysis and communication techniques in the risk management life cycle?

Option 1: An individual or entity responsible for owning and managing specific controls

Option 2: An external party who transfers risks through insurance or contracts

Option 3: An individual or entity who accepts risks without taking any proactive measures

Option 4: An individual or entity who eliminates risks by terminating relevant business activities

Correct Response: 1

Explanation: A control owner, in the context of stakeholder analysis and communication techniques in the risk management life cycle, is an individual or entity responsible for owning and managing specific controls. They are accountable for the design, implementation, and effectiveness of controls to mitigate risks within the organization. The control owner plays a key role in ensuring that controls are in place to manage risks and comply with relevant standards or regulations.

Knowledge Area: Bonus Q from Isaca

Question Number: 1091

Question: Which of the following is NOT a characteristic of a control owner in the context of stakeholder analysis and communication techniques?

Option 1: Responsible for owning and managing specific controls

Option 2: External party who transfers risks through insurance or contracts

Option 3: Accountable for the effectiveness of controls

Option 4: Ensures compliance with relevant standards or regulations

Correct Response: 2

Explanation: An external party who transfers risks through insurance or contracts is not a characteristic of a control owner in the context of stakeholder analysis and communication techniques. A control owner is an internal individual or entity within the organization who takes responsibility for owning and managing specific controls to mitigate risks and ensure compliance.

Knowledge Area: Bonus Q from Isaca

Question Number: 1092

Question: What is a risk register in the context of methods to track, manage, and report the status of identified risks?

Option 1: A document or tool used to capture and track identified risks throughout the risk management process

Option 2: The transfer of risks to external parties through insurance or contracts

Option 3: The acceptance of risks without taking any proactive measures

Option 4: The elimination of risks through the termination of relevant business activities

Correct Response: 1

Explanation: A risk register, in the context of methods to track, manage, and report the status of identified risks, is a document or tool used to capture and track identified risks throughout the risk management process. It serves as a central repository for recording key information about each risk, including its description, likelihood, impact, risk owner, risk response strategies, and current status.

Knowledge Area: Bonus Q from Isaca

Question Number: 1093

Question: Which of the following is NOT a characteristic of a risk register in the context of risk management?

Option 1: It captures and tracks identified risks

Option 2: It serves as a central repository for risk-related information

Option 3: It transfers risks to external parties through insurance or contracts

Option 4: It helps in monitoring and reporting the status of identified risks

Correct Response: 3

Explanation: Transferring risks to external parties through insurance or contracts is not a characteristic of a risk register. Instead, a risk register focuses on capturing, tracking, and managing identified risks within the organization's risk management process.

Knowledge Area: Bonus Q from Isaca

Question Number: 1094

Question: What is a risk audit in the context of methods to track, manage, and report the status of identified risks?

Option 1: A systematic examination and evaluation of risk management processes and controls

Option 2: The transfer of risks to external parties through insurance or contracts

Option 3: The acceptance of risks without taking any proactive measures

Option 4: The elimination of risks through the termination of relevant business activities

Correct Response: 1

Explanation: A risk audit, in the context of methods to track, manage, and report the status of identified risks, is a systematic examination and evaluation of risk management processes and controls. It involves assessing the effectiveness of risk identification, analysis, response strategies, and control implementation. The objective of a risk audit is to identify gaps or weaknesses in risk management practices, enhance risk mitigation measures, and ensure compliance with relevant standards and regulations.

Knowledge Area: Bonus Q from Isaca

Question Number: 1095

Question: Which of the following is NOT a characteristic of risk audits in the context of risk management?

Option 1: Systematic examination and evaluation of risk management processes and controls

Option 2: Transfer of risks to external parties through insurance or contracts

Option 3: Identification of gaps or weaknesses in risk management practices

Option 4: Enhancement of risk mitigation measures and compliance

Correct Response: 2

Explanation: The transfer of risks to external parties through insurance or contracts is not a characteristic of risk audits. Risk audits focus on evaluating and improving internal risk management processes, controls, and practices within the organization.

Knowledge Area: Bonus Q from Isaca

Question Number: 1096

Question: What is a quantitative risk assessment in the context of risk assessment methods of risk management?

Option 1: A method that assigns numerical values to risks based on probability and impact

Option 2: A qualitative analysis that ranks risks based on their severity

Option 3: The transfer of risks to external parties through insurance or contracts

Option 4: The acceptance of risks without taking any proactive measures

Correct Response: 1

Explanation: A quantitative risk assessment, in the context of risk assessment methods of risk management, is a method that assigns numerical values to risks based on their probability and impact. It involves quantifying risks by using statistical data, historical information, and mathematical models to calculate the likelihood and potential consequences of risks. This approach provides a more precise and quantitative understanding of risks, enabling organizations to prioritize and make informed decisions regarding risk mitigation efforts.

Knowledge Area: Bonus Q from Isaca

Question Number: 1097

Question: Which of the following is NOT a characteristic of quantitative risk assessment in the context of risk management?

Option 1: Assigning numerical values to risks based on probability and impact

Option 2: Utilizing statistical data and mathematical models

Option 3: Ranking risks based on their severity

Option 4: Providing a more precise and quantitative understanding of risks

Correct Response: 3

Explanation: Ranking risks based on their severity is not a characteristic of quantitative risk assessment. Quantitative risk assessment involves assigning numerical values to risks based on probability and impact, utilizing statistical data and mathematical models to quantify risks, and providing a more precise and quantitative understanding of risks.

Knowledge Area: Bonus Q from Isaca

Question Number: 1098

Question: When selecting a cloud services provider, what contractual item helps manage privacy risks?

Option 1: Indemnification for regulatory fines

Option 2: Geographic data location requirements

Option 3: Technical security certifications

Option 4: Service uptime SLAs

Correct Response: 2

Explanation: Requiring geographic data controls in contracts manages cloud privacy risks.

Knowledge Area: Bonus Q from Isaca

Question Number: 1099

Question: What aspect of cloud providers increases privacy and security risks?

Option 1: Self-service provisioning

Option 2: Lack of physical access

Option 3: Distributed infrastructure

Option 4: Shared responsibility model

Correct Response: 4

Explanation: The shared responsibility model splits duties between client and provider in ways that can increase risk.

Knowledge Area: Bonus Q from Isaca

Question Number: 1100

Question: What ongoing effort helps manage privacy risks with cloud services?

Option 1: Occasional contract reviews

Option 2: Continuous monitoring of configurations

Option 3: Rarely accessing provider portals

Option 4: Disabling redundant features

Correct Response: 2

Explanation: Continuously monitoring security configurations helps manage cloud privacy risks.

Knowledge Area: Bonus Q from Isaca

Question Number: 1101

Question: When migrating data to a cloud provider, what action manages privacy risks?

Option 1: Accepting default settings

Option 2: Enabling redundant backups

Option 3: Reviewing access logs frequently

Option 4: Configuring security controls carefully

Correct Response: 4

Explanation: Carefully configuring security controls when migrating to the cloud is crucial for risk management.

Knowledge Area: Bonus Q from Isaca

Question Number: 1102

Question: What initial step helps focus risk management activities?

Option 1: Control implementation

Option 2: Risk assessment

Option 3: Training development

Option 4: Policy creation

Correct Response: 2

Explanation: Risk assessment guides focus.

Knowledge Area: Bonus Q from Isaca

Question Number: 1103

Question: Which practice helps prioritize risk treatment activities?

Option 1: Randomized ranking

Option 2: First-in-first-out

Option 3: Cost-benefit analysis

Option 4: Executive selection

Correct Response: 3

Explanation: Cost-benefit analysis enables risk prioritization.

Knowledge Area: Bonus Q from Isaca

Question Number: 1104

Question: What process integrates risk management into decisions?

Option 1: Data classification

Option 2: Vendor management

Option 3: Audit scheduling

Option 4: Risk-informed decision making

Correct Response: 4

Explanation: Risk-informed decision making integrates risk management.

Knowledge Area: Bonus Q from Isaca

Question Number: 1105

Question: What approach frequently uses questionnaires and scoring?

Option 1: Metrics analysis

Option 2: Tabletop exercises

Option 3: Threat modeling

Option 4: Risk matrix

Correct Response: 4

Explanation: Risk matrices incorporate questionnaires and scoring.

Knowledge Area: Bonus Q from Isaca

Question Number: 1106

Question: Why classify tangible assets like devices?

Option 1: To gauge depreciation

Option 2: To enable insurance

Option 3: To highlight security risks

Option 4: To set maintenance cycles

Correct Response: 3

Explanation: Device classification also highlights security risks.

Knowledge Area: Bonus Q from Isaca

Question Number: 1107

Question: Why value intangible assets like reputation?

Option 1: For insurance purposes

Option 2: To enable cost analysis

Option 3: To inform risk analysis

Option 4: To meet accounting standards

Correct Response: 3

Explanation: Valuing reputation informs risk analysis.

Knowledge Area: Bonus Q from Isaca

Question Number: 1108

Question: Why identify threats beyond primary business sectors?

Option 1: For marketing purposes

Option 2: To enable partnerships

Option 3: To reveal overlooked dangers

Option 4: To allow geographic expansion

Correct Response: 3

Explanation: Broad threat scans highlight unseen risks.

Knowledge Area: Bonus Q from Isaca

Question Number: 1109

Question: How are risks tied to assets during identification?

Option 1: By data classification

Option 2: Through vulnerability scans

Option 3: Via market valuations

Option 4: By analyzing threats, vulnerabilities, and impacts

Correct Response: 4

Explanation: Risks arise from threats exploiting vulnerabilities to impact assets.

Knowledge Area: Bonus Q from Isaca

Question Number: 1110

Question: What technique directly reveals risks through practice?

Option 1: Process audits

Option 2: Risk surveys

Option 3: Loss forecasting

Option 4: Threat modeling

Correct Response: 4

Explanation: Threat modeling directly uncovers risks in practice.

Knowledge Area: Bonus Q from Isaca

Question Number: 1111

Question: Which activity highlights potential new privacy risks?

Option 1: Vendor due diligence

Option 2: Incident response

Option 3: Policy approval

Option 4: Emerging technology review

Correct Response: 4

Explanation: Evaluating emerging tech reveals new risks.

Knowledge Area: Bonus Q from Isaca

Question Number: 1112

Question: Why identify risks beyond core business areas?

Option 1: For continuity planning

Option 2: To enable partnerships

Option 3: For insurance purposes

Option 4: To reveal overlooked exposures

Correct Response: 4

Explanation: Looking broadly highlights unseen risks.

Knowledge Area: Bonus Q from Isaca

Question Number: 1113

Question: How does likelihood estimation guide risk analysis?

Option 1: It enables cost-benefit comparisons.

Option 2: It identifies worst-case scenarios.

Option 3: It determines risk tolerance thresholds.

Option 4: It focuses resources on probable events.

Correct Response: 4

Explanation: Likelihood guides focus on probable risks.

Knowledge Area: Bonus Q from Isaca

Question Number: 1114

Question: Why estimate potential impacts from risks?

Option 1: To set insurance coverage

Option 2: To inform risk tolerance

Option 3: To enable prioritization

Option 4: To validate mitigations

Correct Response: 3

Explanation: Impact estimation enables risk prioritization.

Knowledge Area: Bonus Q from Isaca

Question Number: 1115

Question: What analysis technique uses decision tree diagramming?

Option 1: PEST analysis

Option 2: Monte Carlo simulations

Option 3: Fault tree analysis

Option 4: Fishbone diagramming

Correct Response: 3

Explanation: Decision trees diagram risk analysis branching logic.

Knowledge Area: Bonus Q from Isaca

Question Number: 1116

Question: Why is risk correlation analysis crucial?

Option 1: It enables insurance forecasting.

Option 2: It highlights cascading effects.

Option 3: It simplifies data classification.

Option 4: It streamlines vendor oversight.

Correct Response: 2

Explanation: Correlation analysis surfaces cascading risks.

Knowledge Area: Bonus Q from Isaca

Question Number: 1117

Question: Scenario: A company is implementing technical privacy controls to protect sensitive user data. What is a key consideration in establishing control objectives for these controls?

Option 1: Aligning with regulatory requirements and privacy best practices

Option 2: Enforcing penalties for non-compliance

Option 3: Monitoring and evaluating technical controls

Option 4: Providing step-by-step instructions for configuring technical controls

Correct Response: 1

Explanation: A key consideration in establishing control objectives for technical privacy controls is aligning with regulatory requirements and privacy best practices. Control objectives should be designed to address specific privacy risks, meet regulatory requirements, and reflect industry-accepted best practices to ensure the effective implementation of technical privacy controls and protect sensitive user data.

Knowledge Area: Bonus Q from Isaca

Question Number: 1118

Question: Scenario: A company is implementing technical privacy controls to protect user privacy. What is a key consideration in establishing privacy control objectives for these controls?

Option 1: Aligning with legal requirements, industry standards, and privacy best practices

Option 2: Enforcing penalties for non-compliance

Option 3: Monitoring and evaluating technical controls

Option 4: Providing step-by-step instructions for configuring technical controls

Correct Response: 1

Explanation: A key consideration in establishing privacy control objectives for technical privacy controls is aligning with legal requirements, industry standards, and privacy best practices. Privacy control objectives should reflect the specific privacy risks, legal obligations, and industry-accepted best practices to ensure the effective implementation of technical privacy controls and protect user privacy.

Knowledge Area: Bonus Q from Isaca

Question Number: 1119

Question: What are control frameworks in the context of technical privacy controls of privacy architecture?

Option 1: Structured sets of controls and guidelines that help organizations establish and maintain effective privacy controls

Option 2: Frameworks for optimizing technical performance and speed

Option 3: Frameworks for enhancing collaboration and data sharing among stakeholders

Option 4: Frameworks for improving the availability and accessibility of technical resources

Correct Response: 1

Explanation: Control frameworks in the context of technical privacy controls of privacy architecture are structured sets of controls and guidelines that help organizations establish and maintain effective privacy controls. These frameworks provide a systematic approach to managing privacy risks, ensuring compliance with privacy laws and regulations, and implementing best practices in privacy protection.

Knowledge Area: Bonus Q from Isaca

Question Number: 1120

Question: Scenario: A company wants to establish a secure network connection between its offices. What should they consider when selecting network media for this purpose?

Option 1: Dependence on transmission speed, distance, and security requirements

Option 2: Enhancing collaboration and data sharing among employees

Option 3: Optimizing network performance for faster data transfer

Option 4: Increasing the availability and accessibility of network resources

Correct Response: 1

Explanation: When selecting network media for establishing a secure network connection, the company should consider factors such as transmission speed, distance requirements, and security requirements. Different network media have specific characteristics, such as transmission speed limitations, distance limitations, and susceptibility to security risks. Considering these factors helps ensure that the chosen network media aligns with the company's requirements for secure and efficient data transmission.

Knowledge Area: Bonus Q from Isaca

Question Number: 1121

Question: Scenario: An organization wants to ensure that only authorized employees can access personal customer data. What is a recommended privacy control for this purpose?

Option 1: Implement access controls to restrict and manage user access to the data

Option 2: Monitor and analyze network traffic

Option 3: Enhance collaboration and data sharing among stakeholders

Option 4: Optimize network performance and speed

Correct Response: 1

Explanation: A recommended privacy control for ensuring that only authorized employees can access personal customer data is to implement access controls. Access controls restrict and manage user access to resources, ensuring that only authorized individuals can access and handle sensitive data. By enforcing access controls, organizations can limit the risk of unauthorized access and protect the privacy and security of customer data.

Knowledge Area: Bonus Q from Isaca

Question Number: 1122

Question: Which of the following is a key element of the IT risk backgrounder in cloud computing?

Option 1: Identification and assessment of security risks

Option 2: Decreased focus on risk management

Option 3: Limited impact on business operations

Option 4: Higher reliance on cloud service providers

Correct Response: 1

Explanation: The key element of the IT risk backgrounder in cloud computing is the identification and assessment of security risks. This involves understanding the potential risks associated with cloud adoption, evaluating their impact on the organization, and developing risk management strategies to mitigate those risks.

Knowledge Area: Bonus Q from Isaca

Question Number: 1123

Question: Which of the following is NOT a characteristic of the IT risk backgrounder in cloud computing?

Option 1: Comprehensive risk assessment

Option 2: Proactive risk management

Option 3: Limited consideration of security risks

Option 4: Ongoing monitoring and evaluation

Correct Response: 3

Explanation: The IT risk backgrounder in cloud computing involves comprehensive risk assessment, proactive risk management, and ongoing monitoring and evaluation. It does not involve limited consideration of security risks; instead, it focuses on identifying and addressing security risks associated with cloud adoption.

Knowledge Area: Bonus Q from Isaca

Question Number: 1124

Question: Scenario: Company XYZ is planning to migrate its IT infrastructure to the cloud. As part of the risk management process, what does the IT risk backgrounder help Company XYZ with?

Option 1: a. Identification and assessment of security risks.

Option 2: b. Decreased focus on risk management.

Option 3: c. Limited impact on business operations.

Option 4: d. Higher reliance on cloud service providers.

Correct Response: 1

Explanation: The IT risk backgrounder helps Company XYZ with the identification and assessment of security risks related to cloud adoption. It provides a comprehensive understanding of the risks associated with migrating to the cloud and assists in developing appropriate risk management strategies.

Knowledge Area: Bonus Q from Isaca

Question Number: 1125

Question: Scenario: Company ABC is considering adopting cloud services for its IT operations. The management team is concerned about the potential drawbacks of the IT risk backgrounder. What is a potential disadvantage of the IT risk backgrounder for Company ABC?

Option 1: a. Decreased focus on risk management.

Option 2: b. Limited consideration of security risks.

Option 3: c. Enhanced impact on business operations.

Option 4: d. Lower reliance on cloud service providers.

Correct Response: 2

Explanation: A potential disadvantage of the IT risk backgrounder is limited consideration of security risks. If the risk assessment and management processes do not adequately identify and address security risks associated with cloud adoption, it may expose Company ABC to potential security vulnerabilities and threats.

Knowledge Area: Bonus Q from Isaca

Question Number: 1126

Question: What is one of the top security risks associated with the loss of governance in cloud computing?

Option 1: Lack of control over data

Option 2: Enhanced visibility into system activities

Option 3: Improved accountability and transparency

Option 4: Reduced reliance on cloud service providers

Correct Response: 1

Explanation: One of the top security risks associated with the loss of governance in cloud computing is the lack of control over data. When organizations lose governance, they may have limited visibility and control over their data, including data storage, processing, and access, which can lead to potential security breaches and unauthorized data exposure.

Knowledge Area: Bonus Q from Isaca

Question Number: 1127

Question: Which of the following is NOT a consequence of the loss of governance in cloud computing?

Option 1: Decreased accountability

Option 2: Reduced control over data

Option 3: Higher risk of data breaches

Option 4: Enhanced compliance with regulations

Correct Response: 4

Explanation: The loss of governance in cloud computing leads to decreased accountability, reduced control over data, and a higher risk of data breaches. It does not enhance compliance with regulations; in fact, it can introduce compliance challenges due to the lack of visibility and control over data handling and security practices.

Knowledge Area: Bonus Q from Isaca

Question Number: 1128

Question: Scenario: Company XYZ is considering migrating its infrastructure to the cloud. What is a significant security risk associated with the loss of governance for Company XYZ?

Option 1: a. Enhanced visibility into system activities.

Option 2: b. Improved accountability and transparency.

Option 3: c. Reduced control over data.

Option 4: d. Decreased reliance on cloud service providers.

Correct Response: 3

Explanation: A significant security risk associated with the loss of governance for Company XYZ is reduced control over data. When governance is lost, organizations may have limited control over data storage, processing, and access, which can increase the risk of unauthorized access, data breaches, and non-compliance with security and privacy requirements.

Knowledge Area: Bonus Q from Isaca

Question Number: 1129

Question: What is one of the top security risks associated with lock-in in cloud computing?

Option 1: Vendor dependency and limited portability

Option 2: Enhanced flexibility and scalability

Option 3: Reduced cost of migration

Option 4: Improved interoperability with other cloud providers

Correct Response: 1

Explanation: One of the top security risks associated with lock-in in cloud computing is vendor dependency and limited portability. Lock-in occurs when an organization becomes heavily reliant on a particular cloud service provider, making it difficult to transition to another provider or bring services back in-house. This dependency can affect security posture, data accessibility, and business continuity in case of issues with the provider.

Knowledge Area: Bonus Q from Isaca

Question Number: 1130

Question: Scenario: Company XYZ has been using a specific cloud service provider for several years and has become heavily dependent on their services. What is a significant security risk associated with lock-in for Company XYZ?

Option 1: a. Enhanced flexibility and scalability.

Option 2: b. Reduced cost of migration.

Option 3: c. Vendor dependency and limited portability.

Option 4: d. Improved interoperability with other cloud providers.

Correct Response: 3

Explanation: A significant security risk associated with lock-in for Company XYZ is vendor dependency and limited portability. As the organization becomes heavily reliant on a specific cloud service provider, it may face challenges in terms of transitioning to another provider or bringing services back in-house. This dependency can impact security, data accessibility, and the ability to adapt to changing business needs.

Knowledge Area: Bonus Q from Isaca

Question Number: 1131

Question: What is one of the top security risks associated with isolation failure in cloud computing?

Option 1: Data leakage and unauthorized access

Option 2: Enhanced isolation and data segregation

Option 3: Reduced risk of insider threats

Option 4: Improved performance and availability

Correct Response: 1

Explanation: One of the top security risks associated with isolation failure in cloud computing is data leakage and unauthorized access. Isolation failure occurs when the boundaries between different cloud tenants or virtualized environments are compromised, leading to the potential for data breaches, unauthorized access, and exposure of sensitive information to unauthorized parties.

Knowledge Area: Bonus Q from Isaca

Question Number: 1132

Question: Which of the following is NOT a consequence of isolation failure in cloud computing?

Option 1: Data leakage and exposure

Option 2: Increased risk of insider threats

Option 3: Compromised data segregation

Option 4: Enhanced security controls

Correct Response: 4

Explanation: Isolation failure in cloud computing leads to consequences such as data leakage and exposure, increased risk of insider threats, and compromised data segregation. It does not result in enhanced security controls; instead, it undermines the effectiveness of existing security measures and mechanisms.

Knowledge Area: Bonus Q from Isaca

Question Number: 1133

Question: Scenario: Company XYZ is using a cloud service provider for its infrastructure. What is a significant security risk associated with isolation failure for Company XYZ?

Option 1: a. Enhanced isolation and data segregation.

Option 2: b. Reduced risk of insider threats.

Option 3: c. Data leakage and unauthorized access.

Option 4: d. Improved performance and availability.

Correct Response: 3

Explanation: A significant security risk associated with isolation failure for Company XYZ is data leakage and unauthorized access. Isolation failure compromises the boundaries between cloud tenants or virtualized environments, creating the potential for unauthorized parties to gain access to sensitive data, leading to data breaches and privacy violations.

Knowledge Area: Bonus Q from Isaca

Question Number: 1134

Question: What is one of the top security risks associated with compliance risks in cloud computing?

Option 1: Non-compliance with regulations and industry standards

Option 2: Enhanced control over data handling

Option 3: Reduced legal and contractual obligations

Option 4: Improved visibility into security practices

Correct Response: 1

Explanation: One of the top security risks associated with compliance risks in cloud computing is non-compliance with regulations and industry standards. Cloud computing introduces complexities in meeting compliance requirements, such as data privacy, security controls, and auditing, which can lead to legal and regulatory penalties, reputational damage, and loss of customer trust.

Knowledge Area: Bonus Q from Isaca

Question Number: 1135

Question: Which of the following is NOT a consequence of compliance risks in cloud computing?

Option 1: Non-compliance with regulations

Option 2: Increased legal and regulatory obligations

Option 3: Reputational damage

Option 4: Loss of customer trust

Correct Response: 2

Explanation: Compliance risks in cloud computing result in consequences such as non-compliance with regulations, reputational damage, and loss of customer trust. It does not lead to increased legal and regulatory obligations; instead, it may result in penalties or additional obligations due to failure to meet compliance requirements.

Knowledge Area: Bonus Q from Isaca

Question Number: 1136

Question: Scenario: Company XYZ is considering migrating sensitive data to the cloud. What is a significant security risk associated with compliance risks for Company XYZ?

Option 1: a. Enhanced control over data handling.

Option 2: b. Reduced legal and contractual obligations.

Option 3: c. Non-compliance with regulations and industry standards.

Option 4: d. Improved visibility into security practices.

Correct Response: 3

Explanation: A significant security risk associated with compliance risks for Company XYZ is non-compliance with regulations and industry standards. Migrating sensitive data to the cloud brings additional compliance requirements, such as data privacy regulations, security controls, and industry-specific standards, that must be met to avoid legal and regulatory penalties.

Knowledge Area: Bonus Q from Isaca

Question Number: 1137

Question: Scenario: Company ABC is using cloud services for its critical business operations. The management team is concerned about the potential drawbacks of compliance risks. What is a potential disadvantage of compliance risks for Company ABC?

Option 1: a. Enhanced control over data handling.

Option 2: b. Reduced legal and contractual obligations.

Option 3: c. Improved visibility into security practices.

Option 4: d. Non-compliance with regulations and industry standards.

Correct Response: 4

Explanation: A potential disadvantage of compliance risks is non-compliance with regulations and industry standards for Company ABC. Failing to meet compliance requirements in the cloud environment can result in legal and regulatory penalties, reputational damage, and loss of customer trust. It is crucial for organizations to address compliance risks effectively to maintain regulatory compliance and protect sensitive data.

Knowledge Area: Bonus Q from Isaca

Question Number: 1138

Question: What is one of the top security risks associated with management interface compromise in cloud computing?

Option 1: Unauthorized access and control of cloud resources

Option 2: Enhanced security controls and visibility

Option 3: Reduced risk of data breaches

Option 4: Improved availability and performance

Correct Response: 1

Explanation: One of the top security risks associated with management interface compromise in cloud computing is unauthorized access and control of cloud resources. When the management interface is compromised, attackers can gain unauthorized access to sensitive data, manipulate configurations, and potentially disrupt or compromise the entire cloud environment.

Knowledge Area: Bonus Q from Isaca

Question Number: 1139

Question: Scenario: Company XYZ is using a cloud service provider for its infrastructure management. What is a significant security risk associated with management interface compromise for Company XYZ?

Option 1: a. Enhanced security controls and visibility.

Option 2: b. Reduced risk of data breaches.

Option 3: c. Unauthorized access and control of cloud resources.

Option 4: d. Improved availability and performance.

Correct Response: 3

Explanation: A significant security risk associated with management interface compromise for Company XYZ is unauthorized access and control of cloud resources. If the management interface is compromised, attackers can gain unauthorized access to sensitive data, manipulate configurations, and potentially disrupt or compromise the entire cloud environment.

Knowledge Area: Bonus Q from Isaca

Question Number: 1140

Question: What is one of the top security risks associated with data protection in cloud computing?

Option 1: Unauthorized access and disclosure of sensitive data

Option 2: Enhanced data encryption and protection

Option 3: Reduced risk of data breaches

Option 4: Improved data availability and accessibility

Correct Response: 1

Explanation: One of the top security risks associated with data protection in cloud computing is unauthorized access and disclosure of sensitive data. Data stored in the cloud may be at risk of being accessed, disclosed, or manipulated by unauthorized individuals or entities, leading to potential data breaches, privacy violations, and reputational damage.

Knowledge Area: Bonus Q from Isaca

Question Number: 1141

Question: Which of the following is NOT a consequence of data protection risks in cloud computing?

Option 1: Unauthorized access to sensitive data

Option 2: Data breaches and privacy violations

Option 3: Compromised data integrity and confidentiality

Option 4: Enhanced data availability and accessibility

Correct Response: 4

Explanation: Data protection risks in cloud computing lead to consequences such as unauthorized access to sensitive data, data breaches and privacy violations, and compromised data integrity and confidentiality. It does not result in enhanced data availability and accessibility; instead, data protection risks can impact the availability and accessibility of data due to security measures and controls implemented to protect it.

Knowledge Area: Bonus Q from Isaca

Question Number: 1142

Question: Scenario: Company XYZ is considering migrating sensitive data to the cloud. What is a significant security risk associated with data protection for Company XYZ?

Option 1: a. Enhanced data encryption and protection.

Option 2: b. Reduced risk of data breaches.

Option 3: c. Unauthorized access and disclosure of sensitive data.

Option 4: d. Improved data availability and accessibility.

Correct Response: 3

Explanation: A significant security risk associated with data protection for Company XYZ is unauthorized access and disclosure of sensitive data. When sensitive data is stored in the cloud, it becomes critical to ensure that appropriate security controls, encryption, and access management measures are in place to prevent unauthorized access and potential data breaches.

Knowledge Area: Bonus Q from Isaca

Question Number: 1143

Question: Scenario: Company ABC is using cloud services for its critical business operations. The management team is concerned about the potential drawbacks of data protection risks. What is a potential disadvantage of data protection risks for Company ABC?

Option 1: a. Enhanced data encryption and protection.

Option 2: b. Reduced risk of data breaches.

Option 3: c. Improved data availability and accessibility.

Option 4: d. Unauthorized access and disclosure of sensitive data.

Correct Response: 4

Explanation: A potential disadvantage of data protection risks is unauthorized access and disclosure of sensitive data for Company ABC. If proper data protection measures are not in place, the organization may face the risk of unauthorized individuals or entities accessing and disclosing sensitive data, which can lead to data breaches, privacy violations, and reputational damage.

Knowledge Area: Bonus Q from Isaca

Question Number: 1144

Question: What is one of the top security risks associated with insecure or incomplete data deletion in cloud computing?

Option 1: Unauthorized access to residual data

Option 2: Enhanced data encryption and protection

Option 3: Reduced risk of data breaches

Option 4: Improved data availability and accessibility

Correct Response: 1

Explanation: One of the top security risks associated with insecure or incomplete data deletion in cloud computing is unauthorized access to residual data. When data is not properly deleted or erased from cloud storage or systems, remnants of the data may remain accessible, potentially leading to unauthorized access, data breaches, and privacy violations.

Knowledge Area: Bonus Q from Isaca

Question Number: 1145

Question: Scenario: Company XYZ is planning to decommission a cloud-based application. What is a significant security risk associated with insecure or incomplete data deletion for Company XYZ?

Option 1: a. Enhanced data encryption and protection.

Option 2: b. Reduced risk of data breaches.

Option 3: c. Unauthorized access to residual data.

Option 4: d. Improved data availability and accessibility.

Correct Response: 3

Explanation: A significant security risk associated with insecure or incomplete data deletion for Company XYZ is unauthorized access to residual data. During the decommissioning process, if data remnants or residual data are not properly deleted, unauthorized individuals or entities may gain access to sensitive information, leading to potential data breaches and privacy violations.

Knowledge Area: Bonus Q from Isaca

Question Number: 1146

Question: Scenario: Company ABC is using cloud services for its critical business operations. The management team is concerned about the potential drawbacks of insecure or incomplete data deletion. What is a potential disadvantage of insecure or incomplete data deletion for Company ABC?

Option 1: a. Enhanced data encryption and protection.

Option 2: b. Reduced risk of data breaches.

Option 3: c. Improved data availability and accessibility.

Option 4: d. Unauthorized access to residual data.

Correct Response: 4

Explanation: A potential disadvantage of insecure or incomplete data deletion is unauthorized access to residual data for Company ABC. If data is not properly deleted or erased from cloud storage or systems, residual data may remain accessible, posing a risk of unauthorized access, data breaches, and privacy violations. It is crucial for organizations to implement secure data deletion practices to mitigate this risk.

Knowledge Area: Bonus Q from Isaca

Question Number: 1147

Question: What is one of the top security risks associated with malicious insiders in cloud computing?

Option 1: Unauthorized access and misuse of data

Option 2: Enhanced security controls and monitoring

Option 3: Reduced risk of data breaches

Option 4: Improved collaboration and teamwork

Correct Response: 1

Explanation: One of the top security risks associated with malicious insiders in cloud computing is unauthorized access and misuse of data. Malicious insiders, who have legitimate access to cloud resources, can abuse their privileges to gain unauthorized access to sensitive data, manipulate or steal data, and potentially disrupt or compromise the cloud environment and its security.

Knowledge Area: Bonus Q from Isaca

Question Number: 1148

Question: Which of the following is NOT a consequence of malicious insiders in cloud computing?

Option 1: Unauthorized access and misuse of data

Option 2: Compromised data integrity and confidentiality

Option 3: Increased risk of data breaches

Option 4: Enhanced security controls and monitoring

Correct Response: 4

Explanation: Malicious insiders in cloud computing result in consequences such as unauthorized access and misuse of data, compromised data integrity and confidentiality, and increased risk of data breaches. It does not result in enhanced security controls and monitoring; instead, it highlights the need for robust security measures to detect and prevent insider threats.

Knowledge Area: Bonus Q from Isaca

Question Number: 1149

Question: Scenario: Company XYZ is using cloud services for its critical business operations. What is a significant security risk associated with malicious insiders for Company XYZ?

Option 1: a. Enhanced security controls and monitoring.

Option 2: b. Reduced risk of data breaches.

Option 3: c. Unauthorized access and misuse of data.

Option 4: d. Improved collaboration and teamwork.

Correct Response: 3

Explanation: A significant security risk associated with malicious insiders for Company XYZ is unauthorized access and misuse of data. Malicious insiders, who have legitimate access to cloud resources, can abuse their privileges to gain unauthorized access to sensitive data, manipulate or steal data, and potentially disrupt or compromise the cloud environment and its security.

Knowledge Area: Bonus Q from Isaca

Question Number: 1150

Question: Scenario: A healthcare organization is handling sensitive patient data for research purposes. What is a critical security measure to protect the data?

Option 1: Implementing strong access controls.

Option 2: Sharing the data with external parties.

Option 3: Storing the data in an unencrypted format.

Option 4: Allowing unrestricted data access.

Correct Response: 1

Explanation: To protect sensitive patient data, implementing strong access controls is a critical security measure. This ensures that only authorized individuals with the necessary permissions can access the data, reducing the risk of unauthorized access or data breaches.

Knowledge Area: Bonus Q from Isaca

Question Number: 1151

Question: Scenario: A company wants to secure their Big Data environment and protect sensitive data from unauthorized access. Which security capability should they implement?

Option 1: Data masking.

Option 2: Data anonymization.

Option 3: Data replication.

Option 4: Data aggregation.

Correct Response: 2

Explanation: To secure a Big Data environment and protect sensitive data from unauthorized access, the company should implement data anonymization. Data anonymization techniques transform personally identifiable information (PII) into non-identifiable data, allowing for data analysis and processing while preserving privacy. By anonymizing the data, the company can mitigate the risk of unauthorized access to sensitive information.

Knowledge Area: Bonus Q from Isaca

Question Number: 1152

Question: Scenario: An organization is implementing a Big Data solution and wants to ensure data privacy compliance. Which security capability is important to address this concern?

Option 1: Data encryption.

Option 2: Data replication.

Option 3: Data anonymization.

Option 4: Data compression.

Correct Response: 3

Explanation: To address data privacy compliance in a Big Data solution, data anonymization is an important security capability. Data anonymization involves removing or obfuscating personally identifiable information (PII) from the data, protecting privacy and ensuring compliance with data protection regulations. By anonymizing the data, the organization can minimize the risk of unauthorized access to sensitive information.

Knowledge Area: Bonus Q from Isaca

Question Number: 1153

Question: What is the purpose of governance in an organization?

Option 1: To manage financial risks

Option 2: To ensure compliance with legal regulations

Option 3: To provide strategic direction and oversight

Option 4: To improve operational efficiency

Correct Response: 3

Explanation: The purpose of governance in an organization is to provide strategic direction and oversight, ensuring that the organization's objectives are met and risks are managed effectively.

Knowledge Area: Bonus Q from Isaca

Question Number: 1154

Question: Scenario: XYZ Corporation is implementing a governance framework. They are establishing a committee responsible for overseeing risk management, internal controls, and compliance. Which committee is XYZ Corporation most likely setting up?

Option 1: Audit Committee

Option 2: Compensation Committee

Option 3: Nominating and Governance Committee

Option 4: Finance Committee

Correct Response: 1

Explanation: In this scenario, XYZ Corporation is most likely setting up an Audit Committee, as it is responsible for overseeing risk management, internal controls, and compliance.

Knowledge Area: Bonus Q from Isaca

Question Number: 1155

Question: What is the primary goal of cloud governance?

Option 1: Maximizing cost savings

Option 2: Ensuring data security and privacy

Option 3: Accelerating application development

Option 4: Minimizing network latency

Correct Response: 2

Explanation: The primary goal of cloud governance is to ensure data security and privacy, mitigating risks associated with cloud adoption.

Knowledge Area: Bonus Q from Isaca

Question Number: 1156

Question: What is the purpose of risk management in an organization?

Option 1: To eliminate all risks

Option 2: To maximize profits

Option 3: To minimize the impact of uncertainties

Option 4: To achieve operational efficiency

Correct Response: 3

Explanation: The purpose of risk management in an organization is to minimize the impact of uncertainties by identifying, assessing, and managing risks that could affect the achievement of objectives.

Knowledge Area: Bonus Q from Isaca

Question Number: 1157

Question: Which of the following is NOT a step in the risk management process?

Option 1: Risk identification

Option 2: Risk analysis

Option 3: Risk acceptance

Option 4: Risk elimination

Correct Response: 4

Explanation: Risk elimination is not a step in the risk management process. The steps include risk identification, risk analysis, risk evaluation, risk treatment, and risk acceptance.

Knowledge Area: Bonus Q from Isaca

Question Number: 1158

Question: Scenario: XYZ Corporation is implementing a risk management framework. They are conducting a thorough analysis of potential risks and their potential impact on the organization. What is this process called?

Option 1: Risk assessment

Option 2: Risk mitigation

Option 3: Risk avoidance

Option 4: Risk transfer

Correct Response: 1

Explanation: In this scenario, the process of conducting a thorough analysis of potential risks and their potential impact on the organization is called risk assessment.

Knowledge Area: Bonus Q from Isaca

Question Number: 1159

Question: Scenario: ABC Inc. is a multinational company operating in various industries. They want to ensure that risks are managed consistently across all business units. Which of the following approaches should they adopt?

Option 1: Decentralized risk management

Option 2: Independent risk management for each business unit

Option 3: Centralized risk management

Option 4: Outsourcing risk management

Correct Response: 3

Explanation: In this scenario, ABC Inc. should adopt the approach of centralized risk management to ensure that risks are managed consistently across all business units.

Knowledge Area: Bonus Q from Isaca

Question Number: 1160

Question: What is a key risk associated with the use of public cloud services?

Option 1: Limited scalability

Option 2: Reduced data availability

Option 3: Loss of control over data

Option 4: Higher maintenance costs

Correct Response: 3

Explanation: A key risk associated with the use of public cloud services is the potential loss of control over data, as the cloud service provider holds and manages the data on behalf of the customer.

Knowledge Area: Bonus Q from Isaca

Question Number: 1161

Question: Which of the following is a risk trade-off when adopting a cloud service that offers rapid scalability?

Option 1: Increased operational complexity

Option 2: Higher upfront costs

Option 3: Limited data availability

Option 4: Decreased agility

Correct Response: 1

Explanation: A risk trade-off when adopting a cloud service that offers rapid scalability is increased operational complexity, as managing and scaling resources in a dynamic environment requires careful planning and coordination.

Knowledge Area: Bonus Q from Isaca

Question Number: 1162

Question: Scenario: A company is considering cloud adoption and wants to ensure effective BCP/DR. What is a potential risk of not implementing a BCP/DR plan in this scenario?

Option 1: Increased disruption and downtime during a crisis

Option 2: Reduced reliance on data encryption for data protection

Option 3: Limited need for data backups

Option 4: Elimination of the need for a disaster recovery site

Correct Response: 1

Explanation: Not implementing a BCP/DR plan increases the risk of increased disruption and downtime during a crisis. Without a plan in place, the company may struggle to recover critical systems and data, leading to extended downtime and potential losses in revenue, productivity, and customer trust.

Knowledge Area: Bonus Q from Isaca

Question Number: 1163

Question: Scenario: A company is considering cloud adoption and wants to ensure high availability. What is a potential risk of not "Architecting for Failure" in this scenario?

Option 1: Increased downtime and longer recovery times

Option 2: Reduced reliance on cloud services

Option 3: Limited need for data backups and redundancy

Option 4: Elimination of the need for disaster recovery plans

Correct Response: 1

Explanation: Not "Architecting for Failure" in the cloud environment increases the risk of increased downtime and longer recovery times. Without resilient and fault-tolerant architecture, the company may experience extended periods of service disruption and face challenges in recovering from failures or disasters.

Knowledge Area: Bonus Q from Isaca

Question Number: 1164

Question: Which of the following best describes business continuity within the cloud provider in the context of business continuity and disaster recovery in the cloud?

Option 1: The cloud provider's strategy and measures to ensure the availability and continuity of its services

Option 2: The customer's responsibility for business continuity in the cloud

Option 3: The process of migrating business operations to the cloud

Option 4: The cloud provider's approach to data encryption and privacy

Correct Response: 1

Explanation: Business continuity within the cloud provider refers to the cloud provider's strategy and measures to ensure the availability and continuity of its services. It encompasses the provider's efforts to mitigate risks, maintain uptime, and recover from disruptions to ensure uninterrupted service delivery to customers.

Knowledge Area: Bonus Q from Isaca

Question Number: 1165

Question: Scenario: A company is considering cloud adoption and wants to ensure business continuity. What is a potential risk of not evaluating the cloud provider's business continuity capabilities in this scenario?

Option 1: Increased risk of service disruptions and downtime

Option 2: Reduced reliance on the company's own business continuity planning

Option 3: Limited need for data backups

Option 4: Elimination of the need for disaster recovery planning

Correct Response: 1

Explanation: Not evaluating the cloud provider's business continuity capabilities increases the risk of service disruptions and downtime. If the provider lacks robust business continuity measures, the company may experience extended periods of service unavailability during disruptions or disasters, impacting the continuity of its operations.

Knowledge Area: Bonus Q from Isaca

Question Number: 1166

Question: Scenario: A company is considering cloud adoption and wants to ensure business continuity. What is a potential risk of not implementing Chaos Engineering in this scenario?

Option 1: Unidentified vulnerabilities and weaknesses in systems

Option 2: Reduced reliance on business continuity planning

Option 3: Limited risk of disruptions and failures

Option 4: Elimination of the need for disaster recovery testing

Correct Response: 1

Explanation: Not implementing Chaos Engineering increases the risk of unidentified vulnerabilities and weaknesses in systems. Without intentionally creating disruptions and testing the system's resilience, the company may be unaware of potential issues that could lead to disruptions and failures, jeopardizing business continuity.

Knowledge Area: Bonus Q from Isaca

Question Number: 1167

Question: Scenario: A company is considering cloud adoption and wants to ensure business continuity. What is a potential risk of not planning for business continuity in the event of a loss of the cloud provider?

Option 1: Disruption of critical business operations and potential data loss

Option 2: Reduced reliance on cloud services

Option 3: Limited need for data backups and redundancy

Option 4: Elimination of the need for disaster recovery planning

Correct Response: 1

Explanation: Not planning for business continuity in the event of a loss of the cloud provider increases the risk of disruption to critical business operations and potential data loss. Without a contingency plan, the company may face extended periods of service unavailability, loss of data, and potential financial and reputational damage.

Knowledge Area: Bonus Q from Isaca

Question Number: 1168

Question: Which of the following is a typical consideration when planning for continuity in a private cloud environment?

Option 1: Ensuring redundancy and failover capabilities within the private cloud infrastructure

Option 2: Implementing additional security measures for data protection

Option 3: Eliminating the need for data backups and redundancy

Option 4: Reducing reliance on the private cloud infrastructure

Correct Response: 1

Explanation: A typical consideration when planning for continuity in a private cloud environment is ensuring redundancy and failover capabilities within the private cloud infrastructure. This helps ensure high availability and resilience, reducing the risk of service disruptions and enabling quick recovery in the event of failures or disasters.

Knowledge Area: Bonus Q from Isaca

Question Number: 1169

Question: Scenario: A company is considering adopting a private cloud infrastructure and wants to ensure business continuity. What is a potential risk of not planning for continuity in this scenario?

Option 1: Disruption of critical business operations and potential data loss

Option 2: Reduced reliance on the private cloud infrastructure

Option 3: Limited need for data backups and redundancy

Option 4: Elimination of the need for disaster recovery planning

Correct Response: 1

Explanation: Not planning for continuity in a private cloud environment increases the risk of disruption to critical business operations and potential data loss. Without appropriate contingency plans and redundancy measures, failures or disasters may lead to extended periods of service unavailability, loss of data, and potential financial and reputational damage.

Knowledge Area: Bonus Q from Isaca

Question Number: 1170

Question: What is the purpose of assessing a cloud provider's risk management programs?

Option 1: To evaluate the effectiveness of the provider's controls, methodologies, policies, risk profile, and risk appetite.

Option 2: To conduct detailed testing and analysis of financial transactions and records.

Option 3: To review the physical security measures implemented by the cloud provider.

Option 4: To assess the data encryption practices of the cloud provider.

Correct Response: 1

Explanation: The purpose of assessing a cloud provider's risk management programs is to evaluate the effectiveness of their controls, methodologies, policies, risk profile, and risk appetite. This assessment helps organizations understand the provider's approach to managing risks and ensures that the provider has appropriate measures in place to protect data, mitigate risks, and align with the organization's risk management objectives.

Knowledge Area: Bonus Q from Isaca

Question Number: 1171

Question: Which of the following is a key consideration when assessing a cloud provider's risk management programs?

Option 1: Evaluating the provider's controls, methodologies, policies, risk profile, and risk appetite.

Option 2: Conducting detailed testing and analysis of financial transactions and records.

Option 3: Reviewing the physical security measures implemented by the cloud provider.

Option 4: Assessing the data encryption practices of the cloud provider.

Correct Response: 1

Explanation: A key consideration when assessing a cloud provider's risk management programs is evaluating the provider's controls, methodologies, policies, risk profile, and risk appetite. This assessment helps organizations determine the adequacy and effectiveness of the provider's risk management practices and ensures alignment with the organization's risk management objectives and requirements.

Knowledge Area: Bonus Q from Isaca

Question Number: 1172

Question: Scenario: XYZ Corporation is considering engaging a cloud provider for its IT infrastructure. As part of the due diligence process, XYZ Corporation assesses the risk management programs of potential providers. What is the purpose of this assessment?

Option 1: To evaluate the effectiveness of the provider's controls, methodologies, policies, risk profile, and risk appetite.

Option 2: To evaluate the financial performance of the cloud provider.

Option 3: To assess the physical security measures implemented by the cloud provider.

Option 4: To review the data encryption practices of the cloud provider.

Correct Response: 1

Explanation: The purpose of the assessment conducted by XYZ Corporation is to evaluate the effectiveness of the potential cloud provider's controls, methodologies, policies, risk profile, and risk appetite. This assessment helps XYZ Corporation assess the provider's ability to manage risks, protect data, and align with its risk management objectives before making a decision on engaging the provider for its IT infrastructure.

Knowledge Area: Bonus Q from Isaca

Question Number: 1173

Question: Scenario: ABC Company is a technology consulting firm assisting clients in selecting a cloud provider. What is a key consideration for ABC Company when assessing a cloud provider's risk management programs?

Option 1: Considering the adequacy and effectiveness of the provider's controls, methodologies, policies, risk profile, and risk appetite.

Option 2: Conducting detailed testing and analysis of financial transactions and records.

Option 3: Reviewing the physical security measures implemented by the cloud provider.

Option 4: Assessing the data encryption practices of the cloud provider.

Correct Response: 1

Explanation: A key consideration for ABC Company when assessing a cloud provider's risk management programs is considering the adequacy and effectiveness of the provider's controls, methodologies, policies, risk profile, and risk appetite. This consideration ensures that the cloud provider has appropriate measures in place to manage risks and protect client data. By assessing the provider's risk management programs, ABC Company can provide valuable insights to clients regarding the provider's ability to manage risks effectively and align with their risk management objectives.

Knowledge Area: Bonus Q from Isaca

Question Number: 1174

Question: What are regulatory transparency requirements in the context of cloud risk management?

Option 1: Legal obligations that require organizations to provide transparent and timely information to stakeholders, such as breach notification, Sarbanes-Oxley (SOX), and General Data Protection Regulation (GDPR).

Option 2: Conducting detailed testing and analysis of financial transactions and records.

Option 3: Reviewing the physical security measures implemented by an organization.

Option 4: Assessing the data encryption practices in a cloud environment.

Correct Response: 1

Explanation: Regulatory transparency requirements, in the context of cloud risk management, refer to legal obligations that require organizations to provide transparent and timely information to stakeholders. These requirements can include breach notification obligations that mandate organizations to notify individuals and authorities about data breaches, as well as regulations like Sarbanes-Oxley (SOX) and the General Data Protection Regulation (GDPR), which impose transparency and reporting obligations related to financial controls and data protection.

Knowledge Area: Bonus Q from Isaca

Question Number: 1175

Question: Scenario: ABC Company is a technology consulting firm advising clients on cloud risk management. What is a key consideration for ABC Company when explaining regulatory transparency requirements to clients?

Option 1: Ensuring that clients understand their obligations to provide transparent and timely information to stakeholders, such as breach notification requirements and regulatory reporting obligations.

Option 2: Conducting detailed testing and analysis of financial transactions and records.

Option 3: Reviewing the physical security measures implemented by client organizations.

Option 4: Assessing the data encryption practices in client organizations' cloud environments.

Correct Response: 1

Explanation: A key consideration for ABC Company when explaining regulatory transparency requirements to clients is ensuring that clients understand their obligations to provide transparent and timely information to stakeholders. This includes explaining breach notification requirements and other regulatory reporting obligations that clients may be subject to. It is essential for clients to understand their responsibilities regarding transparency and reporting to comply with applicable laws and regulations and to manage their cloud risk effectively.

Knowledge Area: Bonus Q from Isaca

Question Number: 1176

Question: What are the different risk treatment options in the context of enterprise risk management?

Option 1: Avoid, mitigate, transfer, share, and accept.

Option 2: Conduct detailed testing and analysis, review physical security measures, assess data encryption practices, and audit financial transactions and records.

Option 3: Transfer, encrypt, accept, and share.

Option 4: Avoid, accept, transfer, and encrypt.

Correct Response: 1

Explanation: The different risk treatment options in the context of enterprise risk management are avoid, mitigate, transfer, share, and accept. These options allow organizations to address risks based on their risk appetite and the nature of the risk, whether by avoiding the risk altogether, mitigating its impact, transferring the risk to a third party, sharing the risk through insurance or partnerships, or accepting the risk as part of business operations.

Knowledge Area: Bonus Q from Isaca

Question Number: 1177

Question: Which of the following risk treatment options involves shifting the risk to a third party?

Option 1: Transfer

Option 2: Mitigate

Option 3: Avoid

Option 4: Accept

Correct Response: 1

Explanation: The risk treatment option that involves shifting the risk to a third party is transfer. Transferring the risk means transferring the responsibility for managing the risk to another party, typically through the use of insurance or contractual agreements.

Knowledge Area: Bonus Q from Isaca

Question Number: 1178

Question: Scenario: XYZ Corporation has identified a high-risk area in its cloud environment. The management decides to implement additional security controls to reduce the impact of the risk. Which risk treatment option is XYZ Corporation using in this scenario?

Option 1: Mitigate

Option 2: Avoid

Option 3: Transfer

Option 4: Accept

Correct Response: 1

Explanation: In this scenario, XYZ Corporation is using the risk treatment option of mitigate by implementing additional security controls to reduce the impact of the identified high-risk area in its cloud environment. Mitigation aims to reduce the likelihood or severity of a risk through proactive measures.

Knowledge Area: Bonus Q from Isaca

Question Number: 1179

Question: Scenario: ABC Company is a technology consulting firm advising clients on risk management in the cloud environment. What is a key consideration for ABC Company when explaining risk treatment options to clients?

Option 1: Helping clients understand the different options available and selecting the most appropriate ones based on their risk appetite and business objectives.

Option 2: Conducting detailed testing and analysis of financial transactions and records.

Option 3: Reviewing the physical security measures implemented by client organizations.

Option 4: Assessing the data encryption practices in client organizations' cloud environments.

Correct Response: 1

Explanation: A key consideration for ABC Company when explaining risk treatment options to clients is helping clients understand the different options available and selecting the most appropriate ones based on their risk appetite and business objectives. It is crucial to guide clients in making informed decisions about how to address and manage risks in the cloud environment, tailoring the risk treatment options to their specific needs and circumstances.

Knowledge Area: Bonus Q from Isaca

Question Number: 1180

Question: What are different risk frameworks used in enterprise risk management?

Option 1: Examples include COSO ERM, ISO 31000, NIST Cybersecurity Framework, and OCTAVE Allegro.

Option 2: Examples include breach notification requirements, Sarbanes-Oxley (SOX), General Data Protection Regulation (GDPR), and Payment Card Industry Data Security Standard (PCI DSS).

Option 3: Examples include physical security measures, data encryption practices, and access controls.

Option 4: Examples include financial performance analysis, auditing of records, and regulatory compliance.

Correct Response: 1

Explanation: Different risk frameworks used in enterprise risk management include COSO ERM (Committee of Sponsoring Organizations of the Treadway Commission Enterprise Risk Management Framework), ISO 31000 (International Organization for Standardization Risk Management Standard), NIST Cybersecurity Framework (National Institute of Standards and Technology), and OCTAVE Allegro (Operationally Critical Threat, Asset, and Vulnerability Evaluation). These frameworks provide structured approaches to identify, assess, and manage risks within organizations.

Knowledge Area: Bonus Q from Isaca

Question Number: 1181

Question: Which risk framework is widely recognized as a leading framework for enterprise risk management?

Option 1: COSO ERM (Committee of Sponsoring Organizations of the Treadway Commission Enterprise Risk Management Framework)

Option 2: Breach notification requirements

Option 3: Physical security measures

Option 4: Financial performance analysis

Correct Response: 1

Explanation: The risk framework widely recognized as a leading framework for enterprise risk management is COSO ERM (Committee of Sponsoring Organizations of the Treadway Commission Enterprise Risk Management Framework). COSO ERM provides a comprehensive framework for organizations to assess and manage risks, focusing on internal control, risk assessment, and risk response strategies.

Knowledge Area: Bonus Q from Isaca

Question Number: 1182

Question: Scenario: XYZ Corporation is implementing a risk management program and wants to use a well-established risk framework. Which risk framework would be suitable for XYZ Corporation?

Option 1: ISO 31000 (International Organization for Standardization Risk Management Standar

Option 2: Breach notification requirements

Option 3: Physical security measures

Option 4: Financial performance analysis

Correct Response: 1

Explanation: For XYZ Corporation, a well-established risk framework suitable for its risk management program would be ISO 31000 (International Organization for Standardization Risk Management Standard). ISO 31000 provides principles, guidelines, and a framework for managing risks effectively within organizations, helping them identify, assess, and treat risks in a systematic and structured manner.

Knowledge Area: Bonus Q from Isaca

Question Number: 1183

Question: Scenario: ABC Company is a technology consulting firm advising clients on risk management. What is a key consideration for ABC Company when recommending a risk framework to clients?

Option 1: Understanding the client's industry, risk management objectives, and specific needs to select an appropriate risk framework.

Option 2: Conducting detailed testing and analysis of financial transactions and records.

Option 3: Reviewing the physical security measures implemented by client organizations.

Option 4: Assessing the data encryption practices in client organizations' cloud environments.

Correct Response: 1

Explanation: A key consideration for ABC Company when recommending a risk framework to clients is understanding the client's industry, risk management objectives, and specific needs. By having a clear understanding of these factors, ABC Company can recommend an appropriate risk framework that aligns with the client's requirements and helps address the unique risks and challenges they face in their industry. This ensures that the client can effectively implement and manage their risk management program.

Knowledge Area: Bonus Q from Isaca

Question Number: 1184

Question: What are metrics in the context of risk management?

Option 1: Quantitative and qualitative measures used to assess and monitor risks, controls, and the effectiveness of risk management efforts.

Option 2: Conducting detailed testing and analysis of financial transactions and records.

Option 3: Reviewing the physical security measures implemented by an organization.

Option 4: Assessing the data encryption practices in a cloud environment.

Correct Response: 1

Explanation: Metrics, in the context of risk management, are quantitative and qualitative measures used to assess and monitor risks, controls, and the effectiveness of risk management efforts. These metrics provide organizations with objective data and insights to evaluate the current state of risks, the performance of controls, and the progress of risk mitigation activities.

Knowledge Area: Bonus Q from Isaca

Question Number: 1185

Question: Which of the following is a key characteristic of risk management metrics?

Option 1: They provide objective data and insights to evaluate risks, controls, and risk management efforts.

Option 2: Conducting detailed testing and analysis of financial transactions and records.

Option 3: Reviewing the physical security measures implemented by an organization.

Option 4: Assessing the data encryption practices in a cloud environment.

Correct Response: 1

Explanation: A key characteristic of risk management metrics is that they provide objective data and insights to evaluate risks, controls, and risk management efforts. These metrics help organizations assess the effectiveness of their risk management strategies, identify emerging risks, and make informed decisions to mitigate risks and improve their risk management practices.

Knowledge Area: Bonus Q from Isaca

Question Number: 1186

Question: Scenario: XYZ Corporation is implementing a risk management program and wants to establish metrics to monitor the effectiveness of their risk mitigation efforts. What is the purpose of establishing these metrics?

Option 1: To assess and monitor the effectiveness of risk mitigation efforts and make informed decisions for continuous improvement.

Option 2: To evaluate the financial performance of XYZ Corporation.

Option 3: To assess the physical security measures implemented by XYZ Corporation.

Option 4: To review the data encryption practices of XYZ Corporation.

Correct Response: 1

Explanation: The purpose of establishing metrics for monitoring the effectiveness of risk mitigation efforts at XYZ Corporation is to assess and monitor the effectiveness of those efforts and make informed decisions for continuous improvement. These metrics will provide objective data and insights that help XYZ Corporation evaluate the progress of risk mitigation activities, identify areas for improvement, and ensure that risk management efforts are aligned with the organization's objectives.

Knowledge Area: Bonus Q from Isaca

Question Number: 1187

Question: Scenario: ABC Company is a technology consulting firm advising clients on risk management. What is a key consideration for ABC Company when recommending metrics for risk management to clients?

Option 1: Understanding the client's specific risk management objectives, industry, and regulatory requirements to recommend appropriate metrics.

Option 2: Conducting detailed testing and analysis of financial transactions and records.

Option 3: Reviewing the physical security measures implemented by client organizations.

Option 4: Assessing the data encryption practices in client organizations' cloud environments.

Correct Response: 1

Explanation: A key consideration for ABC Company when recommending metrics for risk management to clients is understanding the client's specific risk management objectives, industry, and regulatory requirements. By having a clear understanding of these factors, ABC Company can recommend appropriate metrics that align with the client's risk management goals and help measure the effectiveness of risk mitigation efforts in their specific context. This ensures that the metrics selected are relevant, meaningful, and provide valuable insights for effective risk management.

Knowledge Area: Bonus Q from Isaca

Question Number: 1188

Question: What is the purpose of assessing the risk environment in the context of enterprise risk management?

Option 1: To identify and evaluate risks related to various aspects of the organization, such as service, vendor, infrastructure, and business.

Option 2: Conducting detailed testing and analysis of financial transactions and records.

Option 3: Reviewing the physical security measures implemented by an organization.

Option 4: Assessing the data encryption practices in a cloud environment.

Correct Response: 1

Explanation: The purpose of assessing the risk environment in the context of enterprise risk management is to identify and evaluate risks related to various aspects of the organization. This includes assessing risks associated with service providers, vendor relationships, infrastructure vulnerabilities, and the overall business environment. By understanding the risk landscape, organizations can develop appropriate risk mitigation strategies and make informed decisions to protect their assets and achieve their objectives.

Knowledge Area: Bonus Q from Isaca

Question Number: 1189

Question: Which of the following areas is assessed in the assessment of the risk environment?

Option 1: Service, vendor, infrastructure, and business.

Option 2: Conducting detailed testing and analysis of financial transactions and records.

Option 3: Reviewing the physical security measures implemented by an organization.

Option 4: Assessing the data encryption practices in a cloud environment.

Correct Response: 1

Explanation: The assessment of the risk environment involves assessing risks in various areas, including service, vendor, infrastructure, and business. These areas encompass different aspects of an organization's operations, relationships, and infrastructure that may introduce risks that need to be identified, analyzed, and managed.

Knowledge Area: Bonus Q from Isaca

Question Number: 1190

Question: Scenario: XYZ Corporation is conducting a risk assessment to evaluate the risk environment of its cloud environment. Which areas would be included in this assessment?

Option 1: Service, vendor, infrastructure, and business.

Option 2: Conducting detailed testing and analysis of financial transactions and records.

Option 3: Reviewing the physical security measures implemented by XYZ Corporation.

Option 4: Assessing the data encryption practices in XYZ Corporation's cloud environment.

Correct Response: 1

Explanation: In the risk assessment conducted by XYZ Corporation, the areas included would be service, vendor, infrastructure, and business. This assessment would involve evaluating the risks associated with the cloud services utilized, vendor relationships, the underlying infrastructure, and the overall business environment. By assessing these areas, XYZ Corporation gains a comprehensive understanding of the risk environment in their cloud environment.

Knowledge Area: Bonus Q from Isaca

Question Number: 1191

Question: Scenario: ABC Company is a technology consulting firm advising clients on risk management. What is a key consideration for ABC Company when assessing the risk environment for clients?

Option 1: Understanding the specific risks associated with service, vendor, infrastructure, and business, tailored to each client's unique context.

Option 2: Conducting detailed testing and analysis of financial transactions and records.

Option 3: Reviewing the physical security measures implemented by client organizations.

Option 4: Assessing the data encryption practices in client organizations' cloud environments.

Correct Response: 1

Explanation: A key consideration for ABC Company when assessing the risk environment for clients is understanding the specific risks associated with service, vendor, infrastructure, and business tailored to each client's unique context. This involves identifying and assessing risks that are specific to the client's operations, relationships, and infrastructure, ensuring that the risk assessment is relevant and comprehensive. By considering these specific risks, ABC Company can provide valuable insights and recommendations for effective risk management to their clients.

Knowledge Area: Bonus Q from Isaca

Question Number: 1192

Question: Scenario: ABC Company is a technology consulting firm advising clients on outsourcing and cloud contract design. What is a key consideration for ABC Company when designing business requirements for clients?

Option 1: Understanding the specific needs and objectives of the client to create tailored service-level agreements (SLAs), master service agreements (MSAs), and statements of work (SOWs).

Option 2: Conducting detailed testing and analysis of financial transactions and records.

Option 3: Reviewing the physical security measures implemented by client organizations.

Option 4: Assessing the data encryption practices in client organizations' cloud environments.

Correct Response: 1

Explanation: A key consideration for ABC Company when designing business requirements for clients is understanding the specific needs and objectives of the client. This enables ABC Company to create tailored service-level agreements (SLAs), master service agreements (MSAs), and statements of work (SOWs) that align with the client's unique requirements, objectives, and risk appetite. By considering these specific needs, ABC Company can help clients establish effective outsourcing and cloud contracts that meet their business goals and mitigate risks.

Knowledge Area: Bonus Q from Isaca

Question Number: 1193

Question: What is vendor management in the context of outsourcing and cloud contract design?

Option 1: The process of assessing, selecting, and managing vendors to ensure they meet business requirements and mitigate risks.

Option 2: Conducting detailed testing and analysis of financial transactions and records.

Option 3: Reviewing the physical security measures implemented by an organization.

Option 4: Assessing the data encryption practices in a cloud environment.

Correct Response: 1

Explanation: Vendor management, in the context of outsourcing and cloud contract design, refers to the process of assessing, selecting, and managing vendors to ensure they meet business requirements and mitigate risks. It involves activities such as vendor assessments, due diligence, contract negotiations, and ongoing monitoring to ensure the vendor's performance aligns with the organization's needs and expectations.

Knowledge Area: Bonus Q from Isaca

Question Number: 1194

Question: Which of the following is a key consideration in vendor management?

Option 1: Assessing vendor viability to ensure the vendor is financially stable and capable of fulfilling its obligations.

Option 2: Conducting detailed testing and analysis of financial transactions and records.

Option 3: Reviewing the physical security measures implemented by the vendor.

Option 4: Assessing the data encryption practices in the vendor's cloud environment.

Correct Response: 1

Explanation: A key consideration in vendor management is assessing the vendor's viability. This involves evaluating the vendor's financial stability, track record, market reputation, and ability to fulfill its contractual obligations. Assessing vendor viability helps mitigate the risks associated with relying on a vendor and ensures the business continuity and smooth functioning of outsourced services.

Knowledge Area: Bonus Q from Isaca

Question Number: 1195

Question: Scenario: XYZ Corporation is considering engaging a cloud service provider. As part of the vendor management process, XYZ Corporation conducts a vendor assessment to evaluate the provider's capabilities, reliability, and security practices. What is the purpose of this assessment?

Option 1: To ensure that the cloud service provider meets XYZ Corporation's requirements and mitigates risks.

Option 2: To evaluate the financial performance of the cloud service provider.

Option 3: To assess the physical security measures implemented by the cloud service provider.

Option 4: To review the data encryption practices of the cloud service provider.

Correct Response: 1

Explanation: The purpose of the vendor assessment conducted by XYZ Corporation is to ensure that the cloud service provider meets the organization's requirements and effectively mitigates risks. This assessment evaluates the provider's capabilities, reliability, security practices, and alignment with industry standards to ensure that the provider can deliver the required services and meet XYZ Corporation's expectations.

Knowledge Area: Bonus Q from Isaca

Question Number: 1196

Question: Scenario: ABC Company is a technology consulting firm advising clients on outsourcing and cloud contract design. What is a key consideration for ABC Company when advising clients on vendor management?

Option 1: Helping clients assess vendor lock-in risks and consider contingency plans, such as escrow agreements.

Option 2: Conducting detailed testing and analysis of financial transactions and records.

Option 3: Reviewing the physical security measures implemented by client organizations.

Option 4: Assessing the data encryption practices in client organizations' cloud environments.

Correct Response: 1

Explanation: A key consideration for ABC Company when advising clients on vendor management is helping clients assess vendor lock-in risks and consider contingency plans. This may include advising clients to include escrow agreements in their contracts to protect their interests and ensure access to critical assets or services in the event of vendor failure or disruption. By considering these risks and implementing appropriate measures, clients can mitigate the potential negative impacts of vendor lock-in and maintain business continuity.

Knowledge Area: Bonus Q from Isaca

Question Number: 1197

Question: What is contract management in the context of outsourcing and cloud contract design?

Option 1: The process of overseeing and administering contracts throughout their lifecycle, including activities such as negotiation, implementation, monitoring, and termination.

Option 2: Conducting detailed testing and analysis of financial transactions and records.

Option 3: Reviewing the physical security measures implemented by an organization.

Option 4: Assessing the data encryption practices in a cloud environment.

Correct Response: 1

Explanation: Contract management, in the context of outsourcing and cloud contract design, refers to the process of overseeing and administering contracts throughout their lifecycle. It involves activities such as contract negotiation, implementation, monitoring, and termination. Effective contract management ensures that the parties' rights and obligations are upheld, risks are managed, and the contract's objectives are achieved.

Knowledge Area: Bonus Q from Isaca

Question Number: 1198

Question: Which of the following is a key consideration in contract management?

Option 1: Ensuring compliance with the contract terms, monitoring performance metrics, and managing termination and litigation risks.

Option 2: Conducting detailed testing and analysis of financial transactions and records.

Option 3: Reviewing the physical security measures implemented by an organization.

Option 4: Assessing the data encryption practices in a cloud environment.

Correct Response: 1

Explanation: A key consideration in contract management is ensuring compliance with the contract terms, monitoring performance metrics, and managing termination and litigation risks. This involves tracking and verifying adherence to the contract, managing relationships with the other party, monitoring the achievement of performance metrics, and addressing any issues that arise during the contract's duration.

Knowledge Area: Bonus Q from Isaca

Question Number: 1199

Question: Scenario: ABC Company is a technology consulting firm advising clients on outsourcing and cloud contract design. What is a key consideration for ABC Company when advising clients on contract management?

Option 1: Helping clients establish clear metrics, definitions, termination clauses, and dispute resolution mechanisms to ensure effective contract management.

Option 2: Conducting detailed testing and analysis of financial transactions and records.

Option 3: Reviewing the physical security measures implemented by client organizations.

Option 4: Assessing the data encryption practices in client organizations' cloud environments.

Correct Response: 1

Explanation: A key consideration for ABC Company when advising clients on contract management is helping clients establish clear metrics, definitions, termination clauses, and dispute resolution mechanisms. This ensures effective contract management, enabling clients to measure performance, manage risks, and address any potential conflicts or issues that may arise during the contract's duration. By addressing these considerations upfront, clients can enhance the clarity, enforceability, and effectiveness of their outsourcing and cloud contracts.

Knowledge Area: Bonus Q from Isaca

Question Number: 1200

Question: What is supply-chain management in the context of outsourcing and cloud contract design?

Option 1: The process of managing the flow of goods, services, and information from suppliers to the end customer, including activities such as procurement, logistics, and risk management.

Option 2: Conducting detailed testing and analysis of financial transactions and records.

Option 3: Reviewing the physical security measures implemented by an organization.

Option 4: Assessing the data encryption practices in a cloud environment.

Correct Response: 1

Explanation: Supply-chain management, in the context of outsourcing and cloud contract design, refers to the process of managing the flow of goods, services, and information from suppliers to the end customer. It involves activities such as procurement, logistics, risk management, and coordination with suppliers and intermediaries to ensure the efficient and effective delivery of products or services to the organization and its customers.

Knowledge Area: Bonus Q from Isaca

Question Number: 1201

Question: Which standard provides guidelines for information security in supplier relationships and supply-chain management?

Option 1: ISO/IEC 27036 (International Organization for Standardization/International Electrotechnical Commission)

Option 2: Conducting detailed testing and analysis of financial transactions and records.

Option 3: Reviewing the physical security measures implemented by an organization.

Option 4: Assessing the data encryption practices in a cloud environment.

Correct Response: 1

Explanation: The ISO/IEC 27036 standard provides guidelines for information security in supplier relationships and supply-chain management. It helps organizations establish and maintain secure and trusted relationships with suppliers, manage information security risks, and ensure the confidentiality, integrity, and availability of information exchanged within the supply chain.

Knowledge Area: Bonus Q from Isaca

Question Number: 1202

Question: Scenario: XYZ Corporation wants to ensure the security of its supply chain and manage information security risks. Which standard would be suitable for XYZ Corporation to follow?

Option 1: ISO/IEC 27036 (International Organization for Standardization/International Electrotechnical Commission)

Option 2: Conducting detailed testing and analysis of financial transactions and records.

Option 3: Reviewing the physical security measures implemented by XYZ Corporation.

Option 4: Assessing the data encryption practices in XYZ Corporation's cloud environment.

Correct Response: 1

Explanation: For XYZ Corporation to ensure the security of its supply chain and manage information security risks, the suitable standard to follow would be ISO/IEC 27036 (International Organization for Standardization/International Electrotechnical Commission). This standard provides guidelines for managing information security in supplier relationships and supply-chain management, enabling XYZ Corporation to establish secure relationships, assess and manage risks, and ensure the protection of information within its supply chain.

Knowledge Area: Bonus Q from Isaca

Question Number: 1203

Question: Scenario: ABC Company is a technology consulting firm advising clients on outsourcing and cloud contract design. What is a key consideration for ABC Company when advising clients on supply-chain management?

Option 1: Helping clients establish robust information security practices and guidelines for supplier relationships and supply-chain management, following standards such as ISO/IEC 27036.

Option 2: Conducting detailed testing and analysis of financial transactions and records.

Option 3: Reviewing the physical security measures implemented by client organizations.

Option 4: Assessing the data encryption practices in client organizations' cloud environments.

Correct Response: 1

Explanation: A key consideration for ABC Company when advising clients on supply-chain management is helping clients establish robust information security practices and guidelines for supplier relationships and supply-chain management. This involves following standards such as ISO/IEC 27036 to ensure that information security risks are effectively managed throughout the supply chain. By addressing these considerations, clients can enhance the security and resilience of their supply chain and mitigate potential risks associated with outsourcing and cloud contract design.

Knowledge Area: Bonus Q from Isaca

Review Me

How satisfied are you with our book?

Unsatisfied   Neutral   Satisfied

Thank you for finishing this Book.
Excellent Work!

One Last Thing - Once Again, Walter Need Your Help

You support to Walter and Walter's work is **utmost important**, and it helps the entire profession ecosystem becomes more sustainable, healthier and most importantly more reputable.

Please kindly consider

1. Visiting my exam practice test books and consider purchasing them to assist you to pass your target exam, though the direct links provided at the beginning of this book
2. Visiting my exam practice test courses held at Udemy though the direct links provided at the beginning of this book
3. Leaving a positive review and feedback to me though the direct book review links provided at the next page.

I shall be very grateful if I could have your support to me. Once again, I wish you all the best and good luck in your exam. Thank you.

Warm regards,

Walter

Direct URLs to visit all Walter's Practice Tests at Amazon

Visit Walter's author page:

http://WalterEducation.com

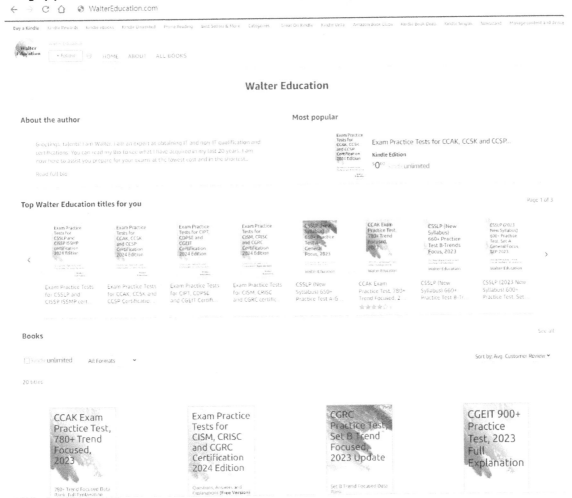

Or the **Links at Amazon Book Store:**

CRISC 1200+ Practice Test, 2023 (Exam Simulation and Core & Advanced Knowledge)	
Paperback Review URL:	- https://www.amazon.com/review/create-review?&asin=B0CJ43R78T
Kindle eBook Review URL:	- https://www.amazon.com/review/create-review?&asin=B0CJ72JJLY

How to give a Review and Rating:

1. Click Here

Create Review

Overall rating
☆☆☆☆☆

Add a headline

Add a photo or video

Add a written review

2. Tell me anything about the course

3. Submit

Made in the USA
Las Vegas, NV
02 November 2023